50 YEARS OF SINGAPORE
AND
THE UNITED NATIONS

World Scientific Series on Singapore's 50 Years of Nation-Building

Published

50 Years of Social Issues in Singapore
  edited by David Chan

Our Lives to Live: Putting a Woman's Face to Change in Singapore
  edited by Kanwaljit Soin and Margaret Thomas

50 Years of Singapore–Europe Relations: Celebrating Singapore's Connections
with Europe
  edited by Yeo Lay Hwee and Barnard Turner

50 Years of Singapore and the United Nations
  edited by Tommy Koh, Li Lin Chang and Joanna Koh

For more information about this series, go to http://www.worldscientific.com/page/sg50

World Scientific Series on
Singapore's 50 Years of Nation-Building

50 YEARS OF SINGAPORE

AND

THE UNITED NATIONS

Editors

Tommy Koh

Li Lin Chang

with

Joanna Koh

World Scientific

NEW JERSEY · LONDON · SINGAPORE · BEIJING · SHANGHAI · HONG KONG · TAIPEI · CHENNAI · TOKYO

Published by

World Scientific Publishing Co. Pte. Ltd.

5 Toh Tuck Link, Singapore 596224

USA office: 27 Warren Street, Suite 401-402, Hackensack, NJ 07601

UK office: 57 Shelton Street, Covent Garden, London WC2H 9HE

Library of Congress Cataloging-in-Publication Data
50 years of Singapore and the United Nations / edited by Tommy Koh, Li Lin Chang ; with Joanna Koh.
    pages cm. -- (World Scientific series on Singapore's 50 years of nation-building)
   Includes bibliographical references and index.
    ISBN 978-9814713030 (alk. paper) -- ISBN 978-9814713047 (pbk. : alk. paper)
   1. United Nations--Singapore. 2. Singapore--Foreign relations--1945–   I. Koh, Tommy T. B.
(Tommy Thong Bee), 1937–   II. Chang, Li Lin. III. Title: Fifty years of Singapore and the United Nations.
   JZ4997.5.S56A2 2015
   341.23'56957--dc23

                                                                    2015021809

British Library Cataloguing-in-Publication Data
A catalogue record for this book is available from the British Library.

First published 2015

Foreword

Singapore became independent on 9 August 1965.

One of the first things which the new republic did was to apply to join the United Nations. As our first Foreign Minister, Mr S. Rajaratnam, explained, we did this to obtain from the UN "an international endorsement of Singapore's sovereignty and integrity".

On 21 September 1965, Singapore was admitted as the UN's 117th member state. This book tells the story of the happy relationship between Singapore and the UN over the past 50 years.

Singapore has benefitted from membership of the UN. At the same time, Singapore and Singaporeans have contributed to the work of the UN and to global governance. For example, Singapore is helping to secure a more stable global financial system through the IMF; promoting peace and the international rule of law, including at sea; championing sustainable development, liveable cities, and water and sanitation; and empowering the small and medium-sized countries of the world through the Forum of Small States and the Global Governance Group.

This year marks the 50th anniversary of Singapore's independence and the 70th anniversary of the UN's founding. I hope that the essays in this book will make Singaporeans more aware of the relevance and usefulness of the UN to Singapore, and highlight some of the significant Singaporean contributions to the work of the UN system.

LEE Hsien Loong
Prime Minister of Singapore

Message

Singapore holds a vital place for many reasons. You are an intellectual centre and a financial crossroads. Your policies, hard work and determination have propelled Singapore to economic growth and prosperity. You have shown the world the dividends that come from investing in education, in healthcare and in people. When you face struggle, as you did during the financial and economic crises, you rise to the challenge. You have confronted threats of terrorism and deadly diseases. But you still remain strong and tolerant. In short, you have much to give and the world has much to gain from the Singapore example.

But no nation, regardless of size or strength, can solve all problems on its own. We need to think and act collectively. Singapore gets it. You are a small country — a "little red dot" as you proudly proclaim. You understand the essential natures of multilateralism in today's world. And you are working to enhance it because all of us have a profound stake in getting it right. You have expanded your voice exponentially through the Forum of Small States. You have built bridges between the UN and the G20 — and between nations large and small — through the Global Governance Group or 3G.

As a densely populated small island, you have shown leadership on issues of climate change and sustainable development. You know well that the global effort to achieve sustainable peace requires sustainable development. This is your history. It is the core of your success. Singapore was once a poor fishing village. Now you are a prosperous global city-state. You are a nation that continues to be at the leading edge of innovation and change. When I visited Singapore in 2012, I visited the NEWater complex to see all that Singapore was doing to improve access to water and sanitation so that people can lead lives of dignity and well-being. You also continue to show the way to building a tolerant society where different races, ethnicities, religions and cultures co-exist in peace and harmony. You may be limited in your geographical borders, but you are showing there is no limit to creativity, possibility and imagination.

Dr BAN Ki-moon
Secretary-General, United Nations

Preface

2015 is an auspicious year for Singapore and for the United Nations. Singapore is celebrating the 50th anniversary of its independence. The UN is celebrating the 70th anniversary of its founding. We have therefore decided to edit a book to tell the story of the mutually beneficial relationship between Singapore and the UN. We thank the 45 essayists for helping us to tell the story. We are grateful to the Prime Minister for his foreword and the UN Secretary-General for his message.

The story begins in 1965 when Singapore was expelled from the Federation of Malaysia and became a sovereign and independent country. At the time of its birth, there were critics, both at home and abroad, who had cast doubts on the legitimacy of Singapore's independence. It was therefore an imperative for Singapore to seek admission to the UN. Singapore was admitted on 21 September 1965 as the 117th member state of the UN.

We have included in the book, the full text of the statement made by then Foreign Minister, Mr S. Rajaratnam, to the UN General Assembly on the occasion of Singapore's admission. It is a seminal speech as it summarises the Singapore worldview and foreign policy. It also explains the importance of the UN to Singapore:

> For us the essentials of the Charter are the preservation of peace through collective security, promotion of economic development through mutual aid and the safeguarding of the inalienable right of every country to establish forms of government in accordance with the wishes of its own people.

It is a great pity that the first Prime Minister of Singapore, Mr Lee Kuan Yew, never spoke to the UN. He did, however, visit the UN on several occasions to call on then Secretary-General U Thant. We have included in the book a photograph taken in 1967. PM Lee Kuan Yew was accompanied by Foreign Minister S. Rajaratnam, Minister of State Rahim Ishak and Ambassador Wong Lin Ken, who served concurrently as the Ambassador to the United States and the UN.

The second Prime Minister of Singapore, Mr Goh Chok Tong, did speak to the UN on several occasions. We have included in the book, a short speech he made on the occasion of the UN's 50th anniversary in 1995. He said:

> Singapore will continue to be deeply committed to the UN. The UN is not perfect, but it is the best institution akin to a world government that we have. Small countries like Singapore need the UN, and must play a constructive role in supporting it. We take the UN seriously, and will actively help build consensus and facilitate agreement.

In the early years of Singapore's independence, the UN system provided Singapore with many benefits, such as, soft loans from the World Bank, technical assistance and expert advice from UNDP, UNICEF, UNIDO, etc. One of the UN experts, Dr Albert Winsemius of the Netherlands, was subsequently appointed by the Singapore Government, as its economic adviser. Another one of them, Dr I. F. Tang, joined the Singapore family and served in many important capacities, including that of the EDB's chairman. There is a Chinese saying that when you drink water, you must remember its source. We will always remember, with gratitude, those who helped us when Singapore was poor, when our prospects were bleak and our future was uncertain.

As Singapore made progress in its developmental journey, we remembered what Mr Rajaratnam had said in 1965, i.e. that, "if we obtain help from others we must be ready to help others as much in return." In that same speech, Mr Rajaratnam also said that we were prepared to share our experience and knowledge with others. Faithful to Mr Rajaratnam's promise, the Singapore Government has implemented a Singapore Cooperation Programme (SCP), to train officials from developing countries. To date, the SCP has trained over 100,000 officials from more than 170 countries.

Singapore and its representatives have played a positive and constructive role in the UN, both in New York and Geneva, as well as in its specialised agencies, programmes, funds and a regional commission. On some occasions, Singapore was given the privilege playing a leadership rule, for example, in presiding over the UN Security Council on two occasions. On other occasions, Singaporeans were chosen to chair major international conferences, such as, the 1980 Diplomatic Conference on the UN Convention on Contracts for the International Sales of Goods; the Third UN Conference on the Law of the Sea; the 1992 Earth Summit; the 1996 WTO Ministerial Conference and the 2006 WIPO Diplomatic Conference. The late Dr Balaji Sadasivan was elected as the Chairman of the WHO's governing board in May 2007. K. Kesavapany was elected as the first chairman of the General Council of the WTO in 1995. Jeffrey Chan, Goh Phai Cheng and Warren Khoo have served as the Chairman of UNCITRAL. A Singaporean, Noeleen Heyzer, is the first woman to have been appointed as head of a UN regional commission (ESCAP). A Singapore soldier, BG Eric Tan Huck Gim, was appointed as Commander of the UN's peacekeeping force in Timor-Leste.

This book contains eight essays by colleagues who have served as our Ambassadors to the UN in New York and six essays by colleagues who have served as our Ambassadors to the UN in Geneva or to the WTO and one by a person who had served as the chairman of a WTO dispute panel. In addition, the book also contains 19 essays by colleagues who have served in the various specialised agencies, programmes and funds. Readers will be amazed that the UN system is so large and diverse and that it affects almost every aspect of our lives.

Readers will also be happily surprised to read the essays of Singaporeans who have made or are making important contributions to the work of the UN system. Noeleen Heyzer had impressed the world with her outstanding work as the Head of the UN Fund for Women, in New York, and as the Executive Secretary of the UN Economic and Social Commission for the Asia Pacific, in Bangkok. Janet Lim has worked tirelessly to help the refugees of the world. Janamitra Devan has served as a Vice-President of the World Bank. Geoffrey Yu was the Deputy Director-General of the World Intellectual Property Organization (WIPO). Paul Cheung has the rare distinction of having served as the Chief Statistician of Singapore and, subsequently, of the UN. Shirin Hamid is the Chief Technology Officer of the UNDP.

One of our favourite essays in the book is that by Andrew Toh. In 1985, there was a famine in Ethiopia. Millions of Ethiopians were in danger of dying from hunger and malnutrition. The World Food Programme dispatched a team of five officials to Ethiopia to establish what was then the largest humanitarian relief operation ever conducted by the UN. Two of the five were Andrew Toh and another Singaporean who was a Chartered Accountant. In 1988, Andrew would be called upon again by WFP to help the starving people of Sudan.

We live in an unequal and unfair world. But, when surrounded by darkness, Singapore believes in lighting a candle instead of cursing the darkness. Thus, in 1992, Singapore took the initiative to form the Forum of Small States in order to unite their strength and amplify their voices. The forum has 105 members. In 2009, Singapore took another initiative to form the Global Governance Group (3G). The group consists of 30 small- and medium-sized countries from all parts of the world. The raison d'être of 3G is to ensure that the interests and views of the vast majority of countries not included in the G20, are taken into account.

We hope that the life stories and experiences shared by our contributors will remind us that however modest our resources or capacity, we can make a difference if we put our hearts and minds to it.

Happy Birthday, Singapore!

Happy Anniversary, UN!

Tommy KOH
Li Lin CHANG
Joanna KOH

Contents

Foreword *by* PM Lee Hsien Loong   v

Message *by* UN Secretary-General Ban Ki-moon   vii

Preface *by* Tommy Koh, Li Lin Chang and Joanna Koh   ix

Statement to the 20th Session of the General Assembly
    by S. Rajaratnam   xix

Address to the UN 50th Anniversary Special Commemorative
    Meeting *by* Goh Chok Tong   xxv

United Nations (New York)

Solving a Messy Business at the UN — A Little Known
Singapore Initiative   3
S. Jayakumar

Singapore and the Security Council   9
Kishore Mahbubani

The UN at the End of the Cold War   15
Chan Heng Chee

This Ain't Kansas, Toto: Some Personal and Eccentric
Reflections on the UN   22
Bilahari Kausikan

A History of the Forum of Small States   35
Chew Tai Soo

Singapore and the Global Governance Group (3G)   39
Vanu Gopala Menon

Small States at the United Nations   45
Albert Chua

World Toilet Day   51
Karen Tan

United Nations (Geneva) · WTO · GATT

Singapore's Role in Multilateral Trade Negotiations   61
See Chak Mun

Singapore and the World Trade Organization (WTO)   66
K. Kesavapany

Who Owns the UN?   72
Tan York Chor

Merits of Multilateralism   78
Burhan Gafoor

WTO: Keep the Faith   85
Kwok Fook Seng

Doing Stuff; Doing Good   89
Foo Kok Jwee

Singapore's Contribution to the WTO Dispute Mechanism:
Reflections of a Singapore Negotiator   95
Margaret Liang

United Nations Specialised Agencies

The Singapore–IAEA Story   107
Chin Siew Fei

Singapore and ICAO   113
Civil Aviation Authority of Singapore

The World's First Independent War Crimes Court —
Reminiscences and Reflections   119
Amarjeet Singh

Singapore and the International Labour Organization (ILO)   125
Halimah Yacob

Singapore and the International Monetary Fund (IMF)   132
Chia Der Jiun

Singapore in the International Maritime Organization (IMO)   138
Mary Seet-Cheng

Singapore and the International Telecommunication
Union: 1965–2015   145
Leong Keng Thai

Singapore and UNCITRAL   152
Jeffrey Chan Wah Teck

Singapore and the United Nations Environment
Programme (UNEP): Working with the Global
Environment Steward   159
Hazri Hassan and Miak Aw Hui Min

More Than a Garden — Singapore's Bid to List the Singapore
Botanic Gardens as a UNESCO World Heritage Site   166
Jean Wee

Helping the Refugees of the World   173
Janet Lim

Singapore's Rise to Prosperity, and Its Evolving Relationship
with the World Bank Group   181
Janamitra Devan

infoDev@World Bank: Alleviating Poverty Through
Sustainable Businesses   190
Valerie D'Costa

Sharing Singapore's Achievements in Education with Africa   195
Tan Jee Peng

Little Red Specks in the United Nations   203
Andrew Toh

Global Health in Action — from Singapore to Indonesia
and Geneva 207
Vernon Lee

A Sojourn in Diplomacy — Working with the WHO
in Geneva 213
David Ho

Intellectual Property and Singapore: A Model of Cooperation
with a United Nations Institution 221
Geoffrey Yu

Monitoring and Predicting Weather and Climate:
The Singapore–WMO Story 229
Meteorological Service Singapore

United Nations Peacekeeping

The SAF and UN Peace Operation 237
Singapore Armed Forces

Policing in a Foreign Land 247
Singapore Police Force

United Nations Secretariat

Advancing Global Statistical and Geospatial Information:
Contributions of the United Nations and Singapore 255
Paul Cheung

"Saving Humanity from Hell": A Personal Perspective
from UNHQ 261
Chew Beng Yong

Financial Administration at the UN: An Insight into the
United Nations Secretariat (1972–2005) 265
Cecil K. Y. Ee

My UNDP Story 271
Shirin Hamid

A United Nations–Singapore Story: The Courage to Transform   277
Noeleen Heyzer

The United Nations and Social Development   285
Thelma Kay

My Experiences with the United Nations Sanctions System   290
Christine Lee

Navigating the (Un)United Nations   296
Dileep Nair

The United Nations — A Personal Experience   302
Yeo Bock Cheng

Index   311

Statement to the 20th Session of the General Assembly*

S. RAJARATNAM

Mr President,

Permit me to add the congratulations of my delegation to those of other distinguished delegates on your election as president of the 20th session of the General Assembly. It is undoubtedly your great experience and wisdom in the ways of men and nations which prompted your colleagues to elect you to this high and responsible office. As a new member my delegation will rely on your wisdom and experience to guide it through this session and my delegation will, for its part, try to lighten your burden by giving you the fullest co-operation throughout the proceedings of this Assembly.

I also take this opportunity to thank all members of the Security Council who scrutinised our application for membership and did not find us wanting. We are particularly grateful to Malaysia, Jordan, the Ivory Coast and the United Kingdom for jointly sponsoring our application for membership. Last but not least I must thank all those member States who co-sponsored the resolution welcoming our admission into the United Nations.

Now that Singapore has been received into the fold of the United Nations, I would like to assure this Assembly that my country will join with other nations in their efforts to realise the aims and objectives of the United Nations charter. For us the essentials of the Charter are the preservation of peace through collective security, promotion of economic development through mutual aid and the safeguarding of the inalienable right of every

---

*This is the statement delivered by S. Rajaratnam, then Foreign Minister of Singapore, to the UN General Assembly on 21 September 1965, on the occasion of Singapore's admission to the UN.

country to establish forms of government in accordance with the wishes of its own people. My country stands by these three essential principles and will give loyal and unflinching support to the United Nations in its efforts to promote these ideals.

We support these ideals because we realise that the well-being, the security and integrity of my country can be assured only on the basis of these principles. It is practical self-interest and not vague idealism which makes it necessary for my country to give loyal support to these essential elements in the UN Charter.

World peace is a necessary condition for the political and economic survival of small countries, like Singapore. For one thing we want peace simply because we have not the capacity to make war on anybody. We are surrounded by bigger and more powerful neighbours with whom we cannot afford to settle issues by force of arms. So it is natural that my country should adhere firmly to the policy of resolving differences between nations through peaceful negotiation; by non-violent means.

At the same time my country is well aware that it is situated in a region of the world which has traditionally been the battleground of big power conflicts. Singapore itself by virtue of its strategic location has attracted the attention of nations who wished to dominate South-East Asia. Under British colonialism Singapore was developed not only as the commercial hub of South-East Asia but also as a military base for consolidating Western imperialism.

Today, with the granting of independence to Singapore, the role of this base is no longer to underwrite British colonialism in South-East Asia. My country has made it clear that it will never allow the base to be used for aggression. The base is there with our consent to ensure our own security in an area of increasing military instability. The moment we can be assured of effective alternative arrangements which will guarantee our security that moment foreign bases would have to go.

My country feels that money spent on weapons of war and armies is money wasted. Furthermore it is obvious to us that, given modern technologies of war, a country of about two million people can never, on its own adequately secure its own defence. Modern defence has to be collective in character especially for small nations and that is why we believe that ultimately our defence and security must be secured through the collective and effective strength of the United Nations. We shall therefore support any and every move to strengthen the peacekeeping effectiveness of the United Nations.

But until such time as the United Nations can really safeguard the security of small nations we shall have to find such temporary solutions as we can so assure our security.

Singapore is essentially a trading community. Almost all our energies, resources and talents are devoted to developing our trade and industries. We have no military aircraft and no tanks. Our army is small. Instead, we have devoted our resources to building homes for the people, schools and hospitals. We seek a welfare state and not a warfare state. If independence and freedom are not to be empty slogans then we must continue to spend as much of our resources as we can on fighting the only war that matters to the people — the war against poverty, ignorance, disease, bad housing, unemployment and against anything and everything which deny dignity and freedom to our fellow men.

To fight this kind of war we need to live in peace with our neighbours. And we want to live in peace with all our neighbours simply because we have a great deal to lose by being at war with them. All we therefore ask is to be left alone to reshape and build our country the way our people want it. We have no wish to interfere in the affairs of other countries or tell them how they should order their life. In return we ask other countries to be friendly with us even if they don't like the way we do things in our own country.

This is why my country has chosen the path of non-alignment. It simply means that we do not wish to be drawn into alliances dedicated to imposing our way of life on other countries. Friendship between two countries should not be conditional on the acceptance of common ideologies, common friends and common foes.

However, Mr President, this does not mean that my country equates non-alignment with indifference to basic issues of right and wrong or that it will evade taking a stand on matters which it considers vital lest it displease some member nations, including those with which it has close ties. Non-alignment is only in regard to narrow power bloc interests and not in regard to the basic principles embodied in the UN Charter. To be non-aligned in regard to the basic tenets of the Charter is to destroy the integrity and effectiveness of the United Nations in which small countries like mine place our hopes.

My country by the very nature of its historic experience is aware that in the contemporary world a developing country must learn to cherish independence without denying the reality of interdependence of nations. Our abhorrence of dependence on others should not drive us into embracing the dangerous myth of absolute sovereignty. In order to learn to live in peace with other countries there must be willing acceptance of the need for interdependence. The cultural and political development of my country has for decades been based on free intercourse and exchange of ideas drawn from many races, from many continents. We are a multiracial society constituted out of the three major racial stocks of Asia — Chinese, Malay and Indian in addition to Arabs, Ceylonese, Eurasians and others.

Four major cultures — Malay, Chinese, Indian and Western — and their representative languages are allowed free and equal development on the basis of cross stimulation. We think of ourselves not as exclusively a Chinese, Indian or a Malay society but as a little united nations in the making. The four cultures which flourish in my country collectively represent the historic achievements of more than half of humanity and we see no reason for suppressing other cultures in order to ensure the supremacy of only one of them. The multiracial and multicultural character of my country has made us somewhat sceptical of those who preach the superiority and exclusiveness of one culture and one race. In a multiracial society one soon learns that no one people has a monopoly of wisdom and that one's own culture is not without flaws. This not only breeds tolerance for different viewpoints but also a readiness to learn and borrow from the accumulated wisdom of other people. These are, we have discovered, attitudes of mind essential for the smooth and constructive development of a multiracial and multicultural society.

The United Nations is also a multinational and multicultural organisation trying with some measure of success to develop a sense of international solidarity and common purpose among the nations of the world. We shall therefore bring to the work of the United Nations the attitude and approaches of a multiracial nation aware that independence and interdependence of peoples and nations are not incompatible goals to pursue.

Finally, Mr President, though we are a small country not endowed with ample natural resources and though we cannot be counted among the highly advanced nations of the world we are nevertheless a highly urbanised community that has acquired experience and knowledge which we are prepared to share with others in the regional cooperation schemes organised by the agencies of the UN. Undoubtedly these offers of assistance can be carried out only on a modest scale but if we obtain help from others we must be ready to help others as much in return.

This is what the United Nations means to us and despite the cynics who focus attention on its many shortcomings my country has faith in the future of the United Nations simply because without it there is no worthwhile future for humanity.

Address to the UN 50th Anniversary Special Commemorative Meeting*

GOH Chok Tong

We congratulate you on your election to preside over this historic 50th session of the General Assembly. I would also like to express our appreciation to the Secretary-General for his leadership of, and dedication to, the Organisation. Let me assure both of you of my delegation's full support.

The UN has been criticised, even maligned. Some of the criticisms are valid, but much of them unfair. Let us not forget that the UN has contributed to a better world, despite its shortcomings and failures in several areas.

Globalisation will be the major driving force in the next 50 years. Advances in telecommunications and technology, new ideas, global concerns over environment and security, multi-national joint ventures in business, the economic reforms and outward-orientation of more and more countries, will push nations to work together rather than against each other.

Regional groupings and multilateral bodies are becoming increasingly important. New institutions and forums like NAFTA, APEC, ASEAN Regional Forum and the proposed Asia-Europe meeting are being created. Existing institutions like NATO, and new ones like the World Trade Organization, are also adapting to the changing environment.

The UN may not necessarily be the primary mover in many world events, given the increasing strength of these regional and multilateral bodies. But it has a very important integrative function, that of maintaining global coherence and ensuring that no country is excluded in the march towards security, peace and prosperity.

---

*Speech by Goh Chok Tong, then Prime Minister of Singapore, at the UN 50th Anniversary Special Commemorative Meeting on 24 October 1995, at the General Assembly Hall, UN.

Globalisation will change the way we look at sovereign authority. Those cities and areas within larger nation-states which can go global and link up with others outside their national boundaries, will flourish as an integral part of a larger region. Those which stay local will lag behind. It is here that the UN can make a big contribution, by helping sovereign states to integrate as parts of a larger economic entity and world community.

To meet these challenges, the UN must streamline and rationalise itself. Financial reform is a critical area. The UN cannot flounder from financial crisis to financial crisis. But no financial reform, however worthy and efficient, will be politically acceptable if the fundamental principle that member states must pay their assessed contributions in full, on time and without conditions is compromised. Assessed contributions are binding legal obligations. They are not to be lightly discarded when inconvenient. To unilaterally flout them goes against the very grain of the UN ideal.

Security council reform is another key area. There is as yet no consensus on which, or how many, or what kind of new members there should be and on what terms. We believe that the most practical means of achieving consensus on the reform of the Security Council is to identify objective general criteria that all permanent members, present or aspiring, must fulfil. This rational approach to set a common standard of responsibilities as well as privileges will better stand the test of time. If we can agree on this, consensus on specific countries will naturally emerge.

Singapore will continue to be deeply committed to the UN. The UN is not perfect, but it is the best institution akin to a world government that we have. Small countries like Singapore need the UN, and must play a constructive role in supporting it. We take the UN seriously, and will actively help build consensus and facilitate agreement.

The UN alone cannot make a better world. It must be backed by the political will and the constructive contribution of its members. The UN will become stronger and more relevant if member states support it with clear, realistic and practical long-term goals. There is no greater hope for a better world than an effective UN whose members are committed to bring this about.

UNITED NATIONS
New York

Solving a Messy Business at the UN —
A Little Known Singapore Initiative

S. JAYAKUMAR

I view the UN through three different lenses. First, the lens of an official at the UN Secretariat. I was appointed Assistant Human Rights Officer in the UN Secretariat from 1966 to 1967. Second, the lens of an Ambassador. I was Singapore's Permanent Representative to the UN from 1971 to 1974. Third, the lens of a Foreign Minister. I was Minister for Foreign Affairs from 1994 to 2004, during which time I had to deal with issues at the UN. Singapore was also a member of the UN Security Council for two years from 2001 to 2002.

I have set out my views about the UN, both in my book *Diplomacy, a Singapore Experience* and my more recent book, *Be at the Table or Be on the Menu: A Singapore Memoir.* I therefore had a dilemma when Professor Tommy Koh asked me to contribute an essay for this book. Any significant comments I had about the UN have already been published and I should not repeat them here. Therefore in this brief contribution, I propose to discuss a little-known initiative of Singapore at the UN. It was not a dramatic headline-grabbing move, but one which was very much appreciated by many other UN member states.

Difference between Bilateral Diplomacy and Multilateral Diplomacy

To put matters in context, one must understand the difference between bilateral diplomacy and multilateral diplomacy, and the role that networking and bilateral meetings play in multilateral diplomacy. Diplomats know the distinction, but many who are not acquainted with foreign affairs may not appreciate the significance. In bilateral diplomacy, the diplomat is focused mainly on enhancing the bilateral relationship with the country to which he is accredited. However, at the UN where there are many agenda items, at any one time a country could have divergent as well as shared interests with different countries depending on the issues.

For example, on any given day there will be meetings of different committees in the UN. In one committee on a particular agenda item, our representative may have to take a position disagreeing with the position of another country. The debate may be quite intense and heated. At the very same time in another committee room, another of our representatives may have to work closely with a delegate of that same country on another issue where our interests coincide.

This has important implications on how our diplomats conduct themselves. They should not get personally exercised and vexed in these proceedings. We need to remember that the representative of the other country is also pursuing his own country's national interests. After the dust has settled on a particular heated issue, our representative needs to keep up cordial relations with his counterpart, perhaps over a coffee session or a meal. You can never tell when both representatives may be on the same side on a totally different matter and have to work closely together. In some of the issues, the other country may not have very strong views, or may be neutral. Our representative will then be able to persuade him to support our position, but that will not be possible if personal relations have become strained.

Networking and Bilateral Meetings Key to Multilateral Diplomacy

In multilateral diplomacy, governments try to find many opportunities to network with as many other countries, for example at the sidelines of international conferences. Of course, heads of government or ministers can also travel to other countries. However, this is time-intensive and there is a limit to how many countries one can visit during a year.

On the other hand, international meetings or conferences provide valuable opportunities for such networking because there are so many other dignitaries gathered there at the same time. Often, delegations would make much preparation in advance to arrange the number of bilateral meetings for their foreign minister or other high dignitaries. Particularly useful are bilateral meetings with other countries where one does not have diplomatic missions. In the case of Singapore for example, because of our limited resources, we do not have embassies in many countries in Europe, Latin America countries, Africa countries or in the Caribbean.

The United Nations General Assembly (UNGA) — Convenient Venue for Intensive Networking

UNGA is a particularly useful platform for networking and bilateral diplomacy. The annual sessions of the General Assembly, commencing in September probably constitute the world's single largest gathering of heads of state, government, and ministers of foreign affairs. For a period of two weeks or so, these high dignitaries descend on the UN headquarters in New York for what is known as the General Debate. The General Debate is actually not a debate at all but a series of speech-making by these leaders. Once these leaders have made their speeches, their Ambassadors and staff try to capitalise on their Ministers' presence in New York to conduct numerous bilateral meetings with their counterpart heads of government or foreign ministers from other countries.

Unsatisfactory and Messy Business at UNGA

Unfortunately, there was no proper system in place for the conduct of such bilateral meetings. There were no special facilities and delegations were left to their own endeavours to find suitable places in UN corridors and to rustle up the odd chairs and tables for their leaders and note takers. There were two lounges known as the Indonesian and Chinese lounges but the facilities there were inadequate. Staffers had to go early to reserve choice locations. As MFA's Peter Tan (now Deputy Secretary) recounted the days when he was a delegate to the General Assembly in 1994:

> I still recall "fondly" the times during the 49th UNGA in 1994 when myself and Razif Aljunied (now our Consul General in Jeddah) — in a typical kiasu Singaporean way — had to go to the UN very early in the morning to "chope" places for the bilateral meetings. Some delegates (not Singapore though) reportedly nearly came to blows with each other over "choping" places.

In 1994 when I was with Ambassador Chew Tai Soo waiting in the UN corridor for my counterpart foreign minister from another country for a scheduled bilateral meeting, I commented that this was a very unsatisfactory and messy arrangement. Such bilateral meetings of course, were not an official part of the UN agenda, but over the years, they had become an indispensable feature of the informal diplomacy at the UN. I wondered if we could request that the UN Secretariat introduce proper booths and facilities and take charge of a proper booking system so that there would not be squabbles over such matters. Tai Soo agreed that the arrangements were most unsatisfactory. However, he told me that it would be almost impossible to get the UN Secretariat to do anything about it. They would be loath to take on this extra burden. The only way they would do it was if they were directed to do so, for example by a UN resolution. So I remarked: In that case, let us do that! I then directed that our delegation work with other interested delegations to draft a resolution on this matter. Tai Soo, a very efficient and competent diplomat, got to work right away.

Our Resolution Adopted at the 49th United Nations General Assembly 1994

Tai Soo obtained tremendous support from other countries and our draft resolution was co-sponsored by some 130 member states (more than two-thirds of the UN membership). It was adopted by consensus.[1]

Chew Tai Soo's speech

In his statement in the Fifth Committee introducing the resolution on behalf of the co-sponsors, Tai Soo made the following points:

- These bilateral meetings have over the years become an integral and very useful part of the annual UNGA.
- The two-week period of the General Debate was a very unique event in the international calendar because a very large number of Foreign Ministers are gathered together in one venue. Over the years, they have evolved the practice whereby they meet informally during the UNGA.

---

[1] UNGA, A/RES/49/221, Pattern of Conferences, Part D.

- The distinct advantage is that they can do so without the glare of publicity.
- The huge increase in the membership of the UN had only made the facilities at the UN woefully inadequate.
- There was no existing system for reservations or bookings of these facilities. It was a free-for-all system. The shortage of facilities in the UN building and the lack of a proper system to allocate the use of these facilities had led delegations resorting to the time honoured system of "first come, first served" and reserving space from the very early hours of the morning.
- This arrangement was clearly unsatisfactory, as member states were unable to be sure at any time they will be able to obtain space for a pre-arranged bilateral meeting between their Foreign Ministers or Heads of State and Government.
- It was also undignified for our leaders and Ministers to be waiting round for seats and be subjected to such ad hoc arrangements.
- Improvements were needed, and the management and allocation of the improved facilities must also be addressed. An equitable and efficient system for the use of these facilities needed to be devised.

Text of the resolution

The resolution which was adopted by consensus, *inter alia*:

- Noted that existing facilities in the Indonesian and Chinese lounges have become inadequate for the holding of bilateral meetings and contacts among member states during the annual sessions of the General Assembly.
- Requested the Secretary-General, as a matter of priority, to improve the arrangements and meeting facilities in the Indonesian and Chinese lounges with a view to enabling more bilateral meetings and contacts among member states to take place.
- Also requested the Secretary-General to make available other venues for such meetings.
- Called upon the Secretariat to examine the possibility of instituting an equitable and efficient system for the use of these facilities and venues.

Today, more than two decades later, when our diplomats go to the UN, they will see an efficient well-run system for bilateral meetings with UN Secretariat officials registering bookings of the facilities such as booths with proper tables and chairs. There are also jugs of drinking water with glasses, which are replenished with every new bilateral meeting.

I wonder, though, how many of them know that all this came about as a result of an initiative by our delegation in 1994! As I said, it is not one of those dramatic diplomatic moves, but the improvements were much appreciated by many countries. As Peter Tan recently told me, Singapore was commended by member states for making this important initiative and he said, *"I recall that many small states that experienced similar problems securing facilities for bilateral meetings were very appreciative of Singapore's initiative."*

This initiative is another illustration of how a small country can play a constructive role, and be regarded by others as a relevant and useful player in international diplomacy.

S. JAYAKUMAR was Singapore's former Deputy Prime Minister and Senior Minister. He has held various portfolios such as Minister for Home Affairs, Minister for Foreign Affairs, Minister for Labour, and was also Minister for Law. Jayakumar served as Singapore's Permanent Representative to the United Nations, and High Commissioner to Canada from 1971 to 1974 and a member of Singapore's delegation to the Third Law of the Sea Convention. In addition he oversaw the Pedra Branca case before the International Court of Justice (ICJ) as well as the Land Reclamation case before the International Tribunal for the Law of the Sea (ITLOS). He is the author of several books, the most recent being *Be at the Table or Be on the Menu: A Singapore Memoir* and *Diplomacy — A Singapore Experience*, and has written many articles on topics of constitutional law, international law and legal education. Jayakumar served as Dean of the National University of Singapore's Faculty of Law. He now serves as the Chairman of the Law Faculty's Advisory Council and also as Chairman of the International Advisory Panel of the Centre for International Law (CIL). He is also consultant at a Singapore law firm, Drew and Napier.

Singapore and the Security Council

Kishore MAHBUBANI

In the first 50 years of its independence, Singapore has served on the UN Security Council (UNSC) only once. By contrast, in the same period our neighbours, Malaysia served four times and Indonesia served three times. It was therefore a real honour and privilege to be called upon to lead Singapore's excellent team of diplomats when Singapore served on the UNSC in 2001–02.

Let me confess, however, that I was not wildly enthusiastic when I was asked to return to New York to serve for a second time as Singapore's Permanent Representative (PR) to the UN. Indeed I felt very bitter about this move. To go from being a Permanent Secretary of a Ministry with a budget of over $100 million to becoming a Permanent Representative of a diplomatic mission with a budget of less than $1 million, felt like a demotion.

This painful demotion turned out to be one of the biggest opportunities of my career. In my two years at the UNSC, I learned more about the hard realities of global geopolitics than I had in the previous 29 years in the Singapore Foreign Service. All the scales fell from my eyes and I began to see and understand the world of international relations as it really was without any illusions. These two years of intense learning have also fuelled the many books and essays about the state of our global order that I have written in the last ten years. My latest book, *The Great Convergence: Asia, the West, and the Logic of One World* is essentially a passionate plea to the world to reform its central institutions of global governance. I could not have written the book if I had not served on the UNSC.

While I have shared the lessons I have learned from the UNSC in my books, I have not yet put in a book the key lessons that my fellow

Singaporeans should bear in mind, now and in the future, in dealing with the UNSC. This is why I commend the editors for bringing out this volume on Singapore and the UN. There are three "hard truths" and three "soft truths" that Singaporeans need to bear in mind about the UNSC.

The first hard truth is that while in theory the UNSC has fifteen members, in practice it has five members (who are the five permanent members, namely China, France, Russia, UK and USA) and ten observers. Even before we joined the UNSC, a shrewd Chilean diplomat told us this hard truth. He was dead right. The five permanent members (commonly referred to in UN parlance as the P5) control the UNSC through their power and their permanence. The P5 often disagree with each other (sometimes violently!) on many substantive issues before the UNSC but they are united in their belief that the P5 should run the Council. A French diplomat captured well the attitudes of the P5 to the ten elected "members": he described them as "tourists".

The P5 Ambassadors were never rude to us. Indeed they treated us with great courtesy, encouraging us to launch peripheral initiatives. Hence, they welcomed Singapore's initiative to improve Peace Keeping Operations (PKOs). However, when we persuaded McKinsey to do a pro bono consultancy to improve the "working methods" of the UNSC, we were firmly rebuffed. The P5 wanted to keep the "rules of procedure" of the UNSC "provisional" so that they could engage in arbitrary behaviour. For example, as I have documented in *The Great Convergence,* the US delegation vetoed an invitation to the President of the World Court to speak to the UNSC. How could the World Court possibly threaten the UNSC? Similarly, some years later, when my successor Ambassador Vanu Gopala Menon, led an initiative by five small states (the S5) to improve the transparency of the UNSC, he too was rebuffed by the P5. As I said in *The Great Convergence,*[1] the P5 serve as the "unelected dictators" of humanity. To make matters worse, the UNSC Secretariat staff often feel compelled to comply with the arbitrary wishes of the P5. They have no choice because if they resisted the diktats of the P5, they would be transferred. Sadly, the Western media has never exposed all this unconscionable behaviour.

---

[1] *The Great Convergence: Asia, the West, and the Logic of One World,* p. 114.

The second hard truth is that while in theory, the UNSC is guided by principles of international law in making its decisions, in practice the interests of the P5 trump all principles. In this area, the academic literature on the UNSC is full of examples. The most horrifying example is that of the Rwandan genocide. Both the Canadian commander of the UN PKO in Rwanda, General Romeo Dallaire and a former Canadian Ambassador to the UN, Stephen Lewis, have documented how the UNSC was provided abundant evidence that genocide was in the making in Rwanda in 1994. However, as the US had just been burned when its intervention in Somalia in 1993 resulted in the killing of US soldiers, the US delegation vetoed intervention in Rwanda. Former President Bill Clinton has since acknowledged that the international community led by him could have done more to prevent the genocide. He said: "The international community, together with nations in Africa, must bear its share of responsibility for this tragedy, as well. We did not act quickly enough after the killing began. We should not have allowed the refugee camps to become safe haven for the killers. We did not immediately call these crimes by their rightful name: genocide."

The US is not the only P5 member to allow its interests to trump its principles. China vetoed the extension of a PKO in Macedonia because Macedonia had maintained diplomatic relations with Taiwan. When the US used the UNSC to block any prosecution of US military personnel by the ICC, the UK allowed its bilateral interests in a close UK-USA relationship to trump its principles in defending the ICC as a signatory of the ICC convention. It was even more horrifying to discover that the P5 would make private commercial deals with each other, as they did with the Iraqi oil contracts. The principle at play among them was "If you scratch my back, I will scratch yours". Many of these backroom deals have not been exposed yet.

The third hard truth is that while in theory, the P5 welcome reforms of the membership of the UNSC to bring in new permanent members, in practice, they oppose it vehemently. The two most hypocritical members in this regard are France and UK. Unlike China, Russia and USA, who are confident that they will retain their permanent seats (and vetoes) in any reformed UNSC, France and UK know that they could well lose their seats. This is also why France and UK have stopped using vetoes. Any French or British veto would lead to a political backlash and jeopardise their permanent seats. This is why the British and French are also the most enthusiastic in supporting India, Japan, Germany and Brazil to come in as new permanent members. However, they happily do so as they know that the conflicting interests between any new aspiring member and its neighbours will block reform. Hence, for example, Pakistan will block India, China and South Korea will block Japan, Italy will block Germany and Argentina will block Brazil.

The UNSC has been discussing reform since 1993 when the Open-Ended Working Group (OEWG) on UNSC Reform was set up. After two decades we have made zero progress. Why? My previous essays explain the complex answers.[2,3] However, one key reason why UNSC reform has not happened is because Washington DC has been adamantly opposed to it. A senior American official confessed this to me privately. The strong American opposition is paradoxically one reason why I am optimistic that UNSC reform will happen.

I begin my book, *The Great Convergence* by quoting from a speech given by Bill Clinton in Yale in 2003. He said there: "If you believe that maintaining power and control and absolute freedom of movement and sovereignty is important to your country's future, there's nothing inconsistent in that [the US continuing to behaving unilaterally]. [The US is] the biggest, most powerful country in the world now. We've got the juice and we're going to use it…. But if you believe that we should be trying to create a world with rules and partnerships and habits of behaviour that we would like to live in when we're no longer the military political economic superpower in the world, then you wouldn't do that. It just depends on what you believe." I agree with Bill Clinton: when America is no longer number one it will then be in America's national interest to support rather than undermine multilateral institutions like the UNSC. Since China's GNP has already become bigger than America's in PPP terms American's national interests are changing.

When America realises that it is in its national interest to see a reformed and strengthened UNSC replace the present UNSC with its declining legitimacy, it will also see that it is in its natural interest to support the 7-7-7 formula I have proposed in *The Great Convergence*. The 7-7-7 formula is the only way to break the current deadlock in UNSC reform as it not only gives a new permanent seat to the most populous states in Asia, Africa and Latin

[2] K. Mahbubani, (2010). "Can Asia re-legitimize global governance?", *Review of International Political Economy*.
[3] K. Mahbubani, (2011). "Dislodging the legitimate dictators", *The Indian Express*.

America (namely India, Nigeria and Brazil) but also gives semi-permanent seats to the middle powers who will as a consequence also benefit from UNSC reform. Singapore should not give up hope that UNSC reforms will take place.

Singapore should also not give up on the UN, even though some of our more cynical minds think we should. There are three equally important soft truths that explain why Singapore should retain its faith in the UN and continue to remain one of its strongest defendants, as advocated by Ambassador Tommy Koh.

The first soft truth is that despite all its imperfections, the UN (including the UNSC) has created a safer world for smaller states like Singapore. It is a fact that before World War II, small states were invaded and occupied regularly. However, after the UN Charter was proclaimed on 24 October 1945, the world has become safer for small states. Though the P5 are hypocritical and often only pay lip service to the principles of the UN Charter, they know that they cannot ignore these principles. Knowing the world is judging them by the standards in the charter does inhibit their activities and, equally importantly, it restrains middle powers from invading small states. The world has become a much safer place for smaller states since the UN Charter was ratified. For empirical evidence of this, please see pages 295 to 377 of Steven Pinker's book *The Better Angels of Our Nature*.

The second soft truth is that the voice of reason does matter. When I spoke to young Singapore diplomats aiming to serve in the New York Mission, I would say to them that the only "weapons" that Singapore diplomats carry as representatives of a small state are reason, logic and charm. This is why Ambassador Tommy Koh was astoundingly successful as Singapore's Ambassador to the UN. No one in the UN could match his repertoire of reason, logic and charm. Only he could persuade the world to accept the UN Convention on the Law of the Sea (UNCLOS). Today, even though the US has not ratified UNCLOS it continues to abide by it. In short, as a result of Ambassador Tommy Koh's reason, logic and charm, a P5 member has agreed to hand-cuff itself with an international convention that effectively restrains its behaviour and that of other great powers too.

The third soft truth is that Singapore is one of the more influential, if not arguably the most influential small state in the UN. Without the UN, Singapore would have zero global influence. With the UN, Singapore has some. It helped that one of my distinguished predecessors, Ambassador Chew Tai Soo, set up the Forum of the Small States (FOSS). Quoting a line from *Star Wars*, a New Zealand Ambassador to the UN would often quip "May the FOSS be with you." Singapore has been the chairman of FOSS since its founding. This has raised Singapore's standing in the UN and enabled us to win a seat in the UNSC.

No one knows when Singapore will run again, if ever, for a seat on the UNSC. I would recommend that Singapore consider doing so in two or three decades. No one knows what the Singapore government will be like then. But whoever is Foreign Minister at that time, once the decision is taken, they should bear in mind the three hard truths and three soft truths I have spelled out in this essay. These truths will not change. Hence, we should understand them deeply.

———•••———

Kishore MAHBUBANI is the Dean of the Lee Kuan Yew School of Public Policy at the National University of Singapore. He is Professor in the Practice of Public Policy. Kishore has had the good fortune of enjoying a career in government and, at the same time, in writing extensively on public issues. He was with the Singapore Foreign Service for 33 years (1971–2004) where he had postings in Cambodia (1973–74), Malaysia, Washington, DC and New York, including two postings as Singapore's Ambassador to the UN and as President of the UN Security Council in January 2001 and May 2002. He was Permanent Secretary at the Foreign Ministry from 1993 to 1998. In the world of ideas he has spoken and published globally. His latest book, *The Great Convergence: Asia, the West, and the Logic of One World*, was selected by the *Financial Times* as one of the best books of 2013. Kishore was conferred the Public Administration Medal (Gold) by the Singapore Government in 1998. The Foreign Policy Association Medal was awarded to him in New York in 2004. He was also listed as one of the top 100 public intellectuals in the world by *Foreign Policy* and *Prospect* magazines in 2005, and included in 2009 *Financial Times'* list of top 50 individuals. He was selected as one of *Foreign Policy's* Top Global Thinkers in 2010 and 2011. In 2011, Kishore was described as "the muse of the Asian century". Most recently, he was selected by *Prospect* magazine as one of the top 50 world thinkers for 2014.

The UN at the End of the Cold War

CHAN Heng Chee

My stint at the United Nations (UN) was brief but took place at a most significant moment of contemporary history. I was privileged to be Singapore's Permanent Representative to the United Nations from February 1989 to February 1991. I arrived a rookie ambassador, coming straight from academia, the first woman to be appointed an ambassador for Singapore, and was launched on a steep learning curve from day one.

From my political science books I had gleaned the formalistic descriptions and analyses of the UN organisational structure. The memoirs of the UN Secretaries-General were illuminating. Nothing prepared me for the heady atmosphere I stepped into. The senior diplomats who had been at the UN much longer than I tried to describe, explain and point out the flesh and spirit of the organisation to me and made me fully aware of the significance of the times. What I was about to witness was a historic moment — the end of the Cold War — which came faster than anyone expected and surprisingly peacefully. This ushered in a new atmosphere and mood at the UN, particularly at the United Nations Security Council (UNSC).

It should be remembered that at the founding of the UN, first at the signing of the agreement in April 1945 in San Francisco, then in October 1945 in New York, the euphoria and bonhomie concealed the big power struggle and tensions that were building up. The UN was founded to deter and defeat aggression. Arising from WWII, the idea of the UN was for the world to deal with another Germany, Japan or Italy. The UNSC was empowered to declare a nation an aggressor and take action on a large military scale. But in 1945 it was politically impossible to do anything with the emergence of the East-West divide and the ideological struggle between the

Soviet Union and the US and its allies. The UN proved to be a disappointment. It was in a state of constant gridlock with little being achieved because any of the Permanent Five (P5) members could cast a veto and it was always along ideological lines.

It has been pointed out that the only reason the UN could take action when North Korea invaded South Korea in 1950 was because the Soviet Union was boycotting the UN at that time. It was protesting against the UN for recognising the Chiang Kai Shek government of Taiwan as the official government for China, ignoring the newly established People's Republic of China. Thus a UN Joint Command was established with 16 states providing troops to fight alongside the South Korean Army. This was the first case of military action taken by the UN at the start of the Cold War. The Soviet Union promptly dropped its boycott and came back to the UN during the Korean War to use the veto to block further initiatives. That was why the United States introduced the resolution "Uniting for Peace" — so that if any of the P5 in the UNSC used the veto to stop initiatives that were important for maintaining peace, the General Assembly could take over the momentum for peace. Trygev Lie, the first UN Secretary-General, supported the US military action and was under so much pressure he resigned. Sir Brian Urquhart called this a depressing start for the UN.

Mikhail Gorbachev became President of the Soviet Union in 1985. Joseph Nye has written that a greater portion of the cause of the end of the Cold War was not Reagan as has often been written up, but Gorbachev. He wanted to reform communism, not end it. Gorbachev introduced "glasnost" and "perestroika" to the Soviet Union. Glasnost meant open discussion and democratisation. Once glasnost took hold, it was hard to hold back the people. They wanted to shake off the system. By the middle of 1989, Eastern Europe was given more freedoms and Gorbachev did not use force to put down the demonstrations. On 9 November 1989, the Berlin Wall was brought down signifying the end of the Cold War. This proved to be a world changing event and it left its mark on the UN as the two superpowers long locked in confrontation seemed more prepared to work together.

When the Cold War came to an end, globally a lot was happening. The UN found many issues on its plate. There was the Soviet withdrawal from Afghanistan, the end of the Iran-Iraq War, the ending of apartheid in South Africa, an issue the UN championed for long looked possible in 1990 when President F.W. de Klerk started negotiations (which eventually led to Nelson Mandela being elected to power in 1994), and Namibia was on the threshold of independence. But the most significant issues for Singapore at that time and which I worked on were two; the ending of the Cambodian conflict, and Iraq's invasion of Kuwait.

The End of the Cambodian Conflict

I had been appointed to the UN at a time when Singapore was campaigning to get Vietnam out of Cambodia together with other ASEAN members, counting among our allies the United States, China and members of the global community. For ten years, ASEAN ran a UNGA Resolution to mobilise the world community to put pressure on Vietnam to withdraw from Cambodia, remove the puppet Hun Sen Government and accept a comprehensive political settlement to the Cambodian conflict. UNSC could not act because of disagreement among its members so it went to the General Assembly. The conflict began in December 1978 when Vietnamese forces invaded Cambodia then under the Khmer Rouge government with Soviet backing. Whatever one might say of the Khmer Rouge government, a sacrosanct principle of international law had been violated. It was open aggression of one country against another. Vietnam at that time was fresh from its victory against the United States forcing a US withdrawal in 1975. In 1978, in another region, the Afghanistan government signed an agreement which allowed them to request for Soviet troops to be sent to the country. The Soviet intervention was in full swing by spring and summer of 1979. The Cambodian conflict was thus also viewed in the light of the Cold War, a proxy war. In 1988, Vietnam unilaterally withdrew from Cambodia but left its puppet Hun Sen government in place.

My job was to ensure that we maintained the support of the international community as this was unfinished business. ASEAN wanted a comprehensive political settlement. Before I left Singapore, Foreign Minister S. Dhanabalan told me that it would be a little more difficult in 1989 to hold the vote given Vietnam's unilateral withdrawal. He told me to try to lose no more than one or two votes. What we did not know at that time was that great change was in the offing. The Soviet Union was pulling back, forcing Vietnam to end its occupation and seek a resolution to the issue. In February 1992, the United Nations Transitional Authority in Cambodia (UNTAC) was emplaced in the country, a peacekeeping operation to take over the administration, monitor the end of the fighting and organise free and fair elections to enable all Cambodians to choose a new government.

After years of obdurate resistance, it was amazing how swiftly the end was negotiated, and relatively smoothly. In 1989, we were still fighting the good fight and mobilising hammer and tongs at the UN for our votes, Vietnam, the Soviet Union, India and its allies on the one side and ASEAN, US, China and other friends and allies on the other. In the end not only did we not lose any vote, the resolution carried by the widest margin since the Cambodian issue came before the Assembly in 1978. 124 countries voted yes, 17 no, and 12 abstained. In 1988 the same resolution won 122 votes, 19 against and 13 abstained. Then Foreign Minister Wong Kan Seng sent the Singapore UN Mission a bottle of champagne after the vote. By 1990 we could produce a consensus resolution and UNSC adopted unanimously Resolution 668. P5 found agreement to facilitate UNTAC.

Iraq's Invasion of Kuwait

The most important issue to come before the UN during my stint was Iraq's invasion of Kuwait. This represented the first case of outright aggression of one country against another in the post-Cold War era and posed a challenge to the post-Cold War world order. It was also an interesting test case of whether the UNSC could take action in the new era. For Singapore, this particular act had a special meaning as it was one of a big state invading a smaller one. The analogue for Singapore was quite clear. We watched how this issue would play out very closely. On 2 August 1990 Iraqi tanks rolled across the border with Kuwait. It should be remembered that a decade earlier Iraq had invaded Iran. There were upheavals in Iran. Ayatollah Khomeini had established a new theocratic regime, there was the Iran hostage taking of Americans. The US, given the loss of its ally the Shah of Iran and humiliated by the hostage taking, closed an eye to Iraq's action. Iran had severely criticised the Soviet Union for Afghanistan and in all, Iraq's action was not seriously censured by UNSC. Action was difficult as no agreement could be got in later years. This may have emboldened Iraq. But when Iraq intervened in Kuwait in 1990, the mood of UNSC was different, the dynamics was different. The UNSC within hours of the invasion condemned the action labelling it a breach of peace and called for the withdrawal of its troops immediately. Within days as nothing happened, it passed Resolution 661 which activated a complete slew of wide ranging sanctions to be imposed on Iraq. It formed a Committee to implement the sanctions. This was swift and effective and many at the UN hailed this as an indication of the new post-Cold War dynamism of the UN. As Poorvi Chitalkar and David Malone pointed out,[1] hitherto the UN had simply been mediator and peacekeeper in its role in dealing with conflict. Now it shifted to set up a legal regulatory mechanism to force compliance. When Saddam Hussein showed no inclination to withdraw, President George H.W. Bush assembled an international coalition of partners to carry out military action against Iraq in 1990 authorised by Resolution 678. Singapore joined the coalition. In fact, Resolution 678 became the template for the UN subsequently to take enforcement actions. It depended on a group of willing states to take action and fund it. In 1990 and 1991, the standing of the UN was very high. The UN was at last functioning as it was supposed to function.

After Operation Desert Storm, a number of humanitarian crises and insurgencies blew up and the P5 had to take decisions on how to deal with them. As the UNSC moved into the area of human rights and humanitarian crises, the consensus in the SC started fraying.

Singapore was in strict and full compliance of the UN sanctions for the Gulf War. As Permanent Representative to the UN, I made many speeches at the UN, in think tanks and forums on why small states view this breach of peace very seriously in the post-Cold War era and why Singapore supported the international coalition for the Gulf War. Many of the US military planes swung from Japan via Singapore for refuelling on route to Saudi Arabia and the war zone. Throughout Operation Desert Storm the SAF sent a 30 member medical team to provide medical support for Allied Forces at the request of the British Government. This team was named Operation Nightingale, the first Peace Support Operation activated by SAF. They were located inside the King Khalid International Airport's uncompleted Terminal 4. It was the 205th General Hospital with 600 beds. All the Gulf States and other Middle East states appreciated our position and contribution and Singapore enjoyed warm relations with them.

---

[1] "The UN Security Council and Iraq", United Nations University, working Papers Series No. 1, Nov. 2013 (http://i.unu.edu/media/unu.edu/publication/40798/WP01-TheUNSCandIraq1.pdf)

But the euphoria and the new found cooperation at the United Nations did not last. Everyone was expecting the world to change after the Berlin Wall fell. That did not happen. Early commentaries argued that traditional power rivalries would now not be as salient. The world could enjoy the peace dividend. Transnational issues would be the new focus. Transnational issues such as human rights, environment, narcotics, refugees, trafficking and migration did come on the global agenda more urgently, but the traditional security issues remained. Iraq's invasion of Kuwait proved it. Other issues had to be settled such as Cambodia, then there was the breakup of Yugoslavia and ethnic cleansing and ethnic wars cropped up in Europe, the Middle East and Africa as well as the threat of chemical weapons and weapons of mass destruction. The UN was called in to solve all categories of problems. The UN became very stretched. Peacekeeping missions were required including humanitarian disaster relief which drew on global assistance. The limit of resources became a reality check for the UN. Old rivalries surfaced again, not as sharply as in the Cold War, but they were certainly there.

I left the UN in February 1991 just after the ground war of Operation Desert Storm started. In that short period, I learned much about the standing of Singapore at the UN. We were seen to be effective and activist, providing leadership in ASEAN to run the Cambodian vote. It was interesting working with the United States and China on the same side for Cambodia. We worked well with both. Ideology and issues aside, I learned that with or without the Cold War, personal relationships helped a great deal in diplomacy, but never more so than at the multilateral forum of the UN. Global issues and conflicts could be the opportunity to develop bilateral relationships to our country's advantage.

CHAN Heng Chee is Ambassador-at-Large with the Singapore Foreign Ministry and concurrently, Singapore's Representative to the ASEAN Intergovernmental Commission on Human Rights (AICHR). She is Chairman of the Lee Kuan Yew Centre for Innovative Cities in the Singapore University of

Technology and Design (SUTD), and Chairman of the National Arts Council (NAC). Heng Chee was appointed Member of the Presidential Council for Minority Rights in July 2012. She is a Trustee of the National University of Singapore and member of the Yale-NUS Governing Board. She sits on the Board of Governors of the S. Rajaratnam School of International Studies, Nanyang Technological University. Heng Chee is a Founding Director on the Board of the S. Rajaratnam Endowment CLG Limited. She is a Trustee of the Asia Society, New York. She is a Member of the Board of Lowy Institute for International Policy, Australia. Heng Chee served as Singapore's Ambassador to the United States from July 1996 to 14 July 2012. She was Singapore's Permanent Representative to the United Nations from 1989 to 1991 and was concurrently High Commissioner to Canada and Ambassador to Mexico.

This Ain't Kansas, Toto: Some Personal and Eccentric Reflections on the UN

Bilahari KAUSIKAN

There is a story about an employee of the United Nations Secretariat out for a walk with his young son on a balmy spring morning along First Avenue in New York. As they passed the United Nations Building, they paused and the man said, "Look, that's where your father works." "Wow" exclaimed the boy, clearly impressed. Oscar Niemeyer's magnificent creation, glistening in the spring sunlight with the East River behind and colourful flags of many nations fluttering in the breeze in front, is a sight to stir even the most jaded heart. "How many people work there, Papa?" asked the boy. The man paused for thought, then replied, "about half".

This is of course a joke. But, alas, one that contains more than a mere kernel of truth. Many talented and dedicated men and women work for the UN. Some have lost their lives in its service. But the UN also attracts perhaps a little more than its fair share of incompetent timeservers and the downright corrupt, protected by powerful networks of vested interests. I learnt this the hard way many years ago when as an impoverished graduate student trying to eke out a meagre stipend, I worked as a stringer for *The Straits Times* at the UN in the late 1970s.

I had chanced upon what I thought was a great story. There was a Singaporean who had acquired Canadian citizenship and in that capacity joined the UN but who subsequently decided that it was to his personal advantage to declare himself a Singapore citizen to the UN. Among other things he was then entitled to take home leave at UN expense in Singapore rather than just across the border. I thought this was wrong on two counts. First, Singapore does not allow dual nationality. So when he acquired Canadian citizenship, the gentleman in question ought to have given up his

Singapore citizenship and if he did not do so, was surely breaking Singapore law. Secondly, by joining the UN under, as it were, a false flag, he was depriving Singapore of one place in the Secretariat as there are national staff quotas.

And so, intrepid reporter as I imagined myself, I made my way to the UN's personnel department and, having inveigled an audience with some high Pooh-Bah, laid out the facts before him. Did he think it proper, I asked with all the self-righteous pomposity of youth, that an organisation dedicated to the ideal of international relations conducted in accordance with law should condone the breach of the domestic law of one of its member states by one of its employees?

His response was to throw me out of his office and try to get my press credentials revoked, clearly at the behest of the gentleman whose case I was pursuing. He failed. Not because my cause was just, but because I had a friend in the UN Department of Public Affairs — or if not a 'friend' in the strict sense of the term, at least someone who disliked the fellow from the personnel department as much as I did — with sufficient juice to ignore him. It was a valuable lesson in how the UN really works.

There is a sequel to this story. Decades later when I was appointed Singapore's Permanent Representative to the UN, I ran into the same Singaporean (or Canadian) still working for the Secretariat. He remembered me and looked distinctly alarmed at meeting the silly young journalist he tried to squash, now improbably transformed into an Envoy Extraordinary and Plenipotentiary. He spent the next three years trying his level best to avoid me. He need not have bothered. I enjoyed his discomfort. But I now had other fish to fry and a better understanding of the ways of the world. There is no perfection to be found this side of heaven. Sometimes toleration for some degree of shenanigans is the necessary price for having any kind of system and sometimes the only sort of system possible is a compromised system.

I had by then learnt that the UN, like all international organisations, has only a very limited autonomous existence apart from the interests of the sovereign states that make up its membership. And since those interests can manifest themselves only through the volitions and actions of all too human individuals, they are not necessarily always the declared purposes of the organisation, and not necessarily always high-minded matters of principle or state. Policy may be made in capital cities, but the mountains are high, and the seas wide and deep, and capitals are far, far away. It is the man on the ground whose finger is on the voting button and what he reports to his capital is known to only himself and whatever God he may believe in.

It is no secret that many Permanent Representatives to the UN (as well as less exalted classes of diplomats), more often than not from the less salubrious parts of the globe, spend much of their time in New York positioning themselves to take up appointments in the Secretariat after their postings or scheming to extend their postings for as long as possible. And since many Secretariat officials are themselves in one way or another dependent on member states for their jobs, there is a strong incentive to scratch each other's backs. It was that network of vested interests that in my youthful folly, I blundered into.

This does not mean that these individuals always ignore or neglect their duty to the interests of their countries or the organisation. Many are, at least by their own lights, honourable men and women, and some are very effective diplomats. There are highly talented and personable individuals among their numbers. And having visited a sampling of their countries, I cannot but sympathise with their desire to entrench themselves in New York. But it certainly colours the way they perceive their national interests and how they pursue them. There is a common interest, or perhaps just a tacit understanding, to regard anything the UN does — or what amounts to the same thing, anything any individual diplomat posted to the UN or any Secretariat official does — as necessarily important. Many a fierce diplomatic battle has been fought over a comma or semi-colon in some resolution whose original purpose has been long forgotten because on that squiggle of ink a career hangs.

There is no better quick introduction to the realities of diplomacy and human nature than to attend a session of the United Nations General Assembly (UNGA). Few UNGA debates are won or lost solely due to the force of logic or the brilliance of arguments or even the merits of the issue. It usually boils down to personal relationships, favours traded or called in, and threats explicit or implied, these ugly realities elegantly and discreetly smothered in high sounding principles. One of the least edifying sights of the UNGA is to watch western, often European, diplomats suavely intimating to the least developed member states that aid may not be forthcoming unless they support one human rights resolution or another. The irony is not apparent to these staunch defenders of human freedom and dignity.

Singapore is fortunate to be dependent on no country for aid. Our diplomats are adequately paid and so a job in the UN Secretariat is not such a glittering prize. Singapore is not perfect, but it is not a city to dread returning to, although the way in which some of our compatriots grumble might make the uninformed believe otherwise. But I think our diplomats know better. So we can calculate our own national interests and speak our mind in the UN relatively free of extraneous constraints. And that is part of the reason why Singapore is respected in the UN.

I could recount more anecdotes about the seamy side of the UN — anyone who has served there has an adequate stock of stories — but I think I have made my point. My point is *not* that the UN is dysfunctional. That is true but trite. The UN is a human institution and so necessarily flawed. But more than just the inevitable flaws of human frailty, the UN is dysfunctional and often internally self-contradictory by design. This is true in different degrees of all international organisations. It is the price we pay to secure the support of sovereign states, in particular the major powers, for them. It is precisely their sub-optimality that makes it impossible for the UN and other international organisations to frustrate the most vital interests of the major powers, while acting as an occasionally useful instrument of their policies.

In the UN, dysfunctionality is exemplified by the veto wielded by the five Permanent Members of the Security Council. The power of the veto directly contradicts the democratic ethos that supposedly infuses the UN Charter or at least is constantly referred to, particularly by the western Permanent Members. The veto often makes it impossible for the UN to act effectively on urgent international issues. But without the assurance that the UN could not act against its vital interests, Stalin's Soviet Union would not have signed on; it is even open to question whether the American Congress would have agreed to join even though the UN was very largely an American creation. Is it better to have no UN if we cannot have a perfect UN? I think not.

Nor is this an attitude peculiar to major powers. If they have a choice, even small countries will not give their vital interests hostage to multilateral institutions. In a 1994 interview with *Malaysian Business*, General Tan Sri Hashim "Freddie" Mohammed Ali, former chief of the Malaysian Armed

Forces, recalled that then Prime Minister Lee Kuan Yew had once told him that "if PAS (Pan-Malaysian Islamic Party) comes to power ... and tries to meddle with the water in Johor Bahru, I'll move my troops in. I will not wait for the Security Council to solve this little problem."[1] Was the good General's recollection accurate? Water is certainly a matter of life and death.

It has become axiomatic — or at least the constant refrain of our senior diplomats and policy-makers, myself included — that a world governed by international law and multilateral organisations like the UN is in the fundamental interests of small countries like Singapore. As with all axioms, this seems self-evidently true. Unfortunately this one is at best only partially true. Axioms are general statements of principle. Like all general statements — indeed like all principles — they must in practice be constantly bent to fit into a messy reality. Law and international organisations can be great equalisers and therefore undoubtedly in the interests of small states. But we should not make the mistake of confusing our hopes and wishes, or even our interests, with reality.

This is not an equal world and the UN is not an egalitarian organisation. The General Assembly, which is the only UN organ where the vast majority of member states can regularly participate in UN affairs, is meant to give most members only the *sensation* of involvement in issues that the Permanent Five intended to settle themselves. There is no justice in the world except what we seize ourselves, and what we consider "just" may well be injustice to someone else. This harsh fact is inherent in the structure of an international system based on sovereign states. By definition a Sovereign acknowledges no limit on its Will except what it accepts by exercise of its own Will. When sovereignties clash there is no objective criteria to determine right, only power. Therefore the very notion of "sovereign equality" on which organisations like the UN are in theory premised is something of an oxymoron. Notions of "Right" or "Justice" or for that matter "Law" are not autonomous realities, only civilising myths that we choose to believe in so that we may, at least occasionally, live in a civilised manner. So too the UN, which as much reflects the inequalities and injustices of the world as it sometimes mitigates them.

---

[1] Shukri Rahman, "An Officer and a Gentleman", *Malaysian Business*, Kuala Lumpur, 16 February 1994, pp. 22–24.

Multilateralism is not a sacred creed and the UN is, in Mark Mazower's memorable phrase, "no enchanted palace".[2] Recourse to the UN is one instrument among others of foreign policy, to be deployed or not according to circumstances. The UN is not always the appropriate means to advance or protect our interests. Singapore is fortunate to be an economically successful country. We thus have the wherewithal to create other options and an international identity that is something more than just a flag, a seat and a vote at the UN. Economic success makes us internationally relevant and so gives us choices that are not always available to the majority of UN members.

These qualifications to our statements about international law and international organisation are well known to, if not often explicitly stated by, our senior diplomats and policy-makers. But I do not think they are well enough known to the majority of Singaporeans whose interest in and knowledge of international relations is generally cursory. I fear that they may well assess the UN at more than its due weight. As our domestic politics evolves, it is probably inevitable that foreign policy will be subject to domestic debates. Small countries have narrow margins for error. It is thus essential that debate be informed by a realistic understanding of the world and bounded by a common understanding of the possible. Naiveté about the UN is as misleading as unthinking cynicism and can be perilous.

When I was Permanent Representative to the UN, I was approached by one of the Under-Secretaries-General responsible for management to second a Singapore civil servant to the UN Secretariat for a few months to advise it on some financial and administrative issues. This was testimonial to the high regard with which the Singapore public service was held internationally. A senior civil servant was identified as suitable. He was initially reluctant. But I, among others, persuaded him to accept in the national interest. He did very well; so well that after he had retired from our civil service a few years later, the UN offered him a contract at a very senior level. I, among others, again encouraged him to accept. The new job, shorn of bureaucratic euphemism, was to investigate maleficence in the Secretariat. Again he did his job very well. Too well.

---

[2] Mark Mazower, *No Enchanted Palace: The End of Empire and the Ideological Origins of the United Nations.* Princeton: Princeton University Press, 2009.

There is a vast difference between working in the Secretariat for only a few months — one is then just a passing inconvenience — and being a long-term, embedded challenge to vested interests. He was subjected to vicious personal attacks tacitly encouraged by some major powers whose nationals in the Secretariat felt threatened. He was lucky, with the support of our government, to emerge with his reputation intact. No one has ever been penalised for doing a job without fear or favour in the Singapore civil service. Not so in the UN where a feel for and accommodation to the realities of power is essential. I still feel somewhat guilty for my role in thrusting him into a nest of vipers without having made that sufficiently clear.

This is just a minor example — a microcosm of sorts involving only one individual — of what misunderstanding, or worse still idealising, the UN can lead to. Still, nothing I have written is meant to suggest that the UN is without utility. When we speak of the UN what instinctively comes to mind are the main New York organs — the Security Council and the General Assembly — and this is the sense in which I have been using the term. But there are many other parts of the UN system that generally work quite well, usually the Specialized Agencies, Funds and Programmes that deal with technical matters such as the WHO, the FAO, the IMO, the ICAO, the UPU, UNICEF, UNRWA and UNHCR, among others, without which many of the conveniences of modern life to which we have become accustomed would not be possible and life for the wretched of the earth even more nasty, brutish and short.

To the extent Singapore's UN diplomacy has been successful, it is because we regard the beast with clinical eyes and understand what tricks we can or cannot make it perform. The beast can be savage. We should not court trouble unless our interests are clear. In the early 2000s, towards the end of Kofi Annan's term as Secretary-General, rumours began to circulate in the UN that a Singaporean should be the next Secretary-General. It was indeed Asia's turn to hold the post. Specific names began to be mentioned, including former Prime Minister Goh Chok Tong and former Foreign Minister Professor S. Jayakumar. It soon became clear that if either had run for the post, Singapore would have been practically a shoo-in. But I thought it was an extremely bad idea.

The UN Secretary-General is a post of great prestige but almost no power. Although the UN Charter explicitly says that no member should seek to influence him, this is a counsel of perfection that to my knowledge has never been honoured. In practice, the Secretary-General is not expected to display independence of thought or action but to do the bidding of the Permanent Five, while at the same time doing what he can to appease the very diverse views coming out of the General Assembly. And since the interests of the Permanent Five are often at odds with each other or with those of the membership at large, the Secretary-General — and his country of origin — is invariably harried hither and thither and almost always ends up pleasing nobody. It is an impossible job. I saw no real political advantage for Singapore, only downsides and potentially disastrous damage to our credibility.

Few Secretary-Generals emerge with their reputations intact. Those who have escaped criticism either studiously did nothing or became poodles of the Permanent Five. One early Secretary-General may well have been murdered, who by is now under official investigation by the Swedish government. Another was in all probability blackmailed by the Permanent Five to do their bidding. A Singaporean is incapable of doing nothing and would never become anyone's pet. If a Singaporean had been elected, our country would have experienced an ephemeral glow of pride but the end was unlikely to be pleasant. Boutros Ghali was unceremoniously removed when he displeased the Americans. Even his replacement, Kofi Annan, a UN insider who knew the score and played the game more skilfully than most, came under severe attack when he dared utter a few critical words about US actions in Iraq.

I was then back in MFA headquarters. I did not at first take the rumours too seriously. But I grew greatly alarmed when it became apparent that at least some of my colleagues were in fact tempted to have a Singaporean run for the post. I mustered all the skills of advocacy at my command to repeatedly argue against it. But our political masters kept their own counsels and the matter was left open. It did my nerves no good. Eventually the matter was clarified when, on the way out from a meeting in Washington DC, former President George W. Bush, in an almost casual manner, directly asked Mr Goh whether Singapore wanted the position and told him that the US would support him if we did. After a dramatic pause that almost stopped my heart, Mr Goh answered "No". I breathed again. Later, back at our hotel, I quaffed a few celebratory and restorative bourbons.

But to those who know the game, the General Assembly and the Security Council can be very useful, although not necessarily in the way they were intended to function by the framers of the UN Charter. Those intentions were wrecked on the shoals of the Cold War. But even during that period the UN served as a neutral ladder for the US and the Soviet Union to climb down without loss of face when their conflicts of interests grew too directly dangerous. The UN played an important role in decolonisation when, for entirely different reasons, the conveniences of the US and the Soviet Union often coincided.

And it was during the Cold War that Singapore's UN diplomacy reached its apotheosis when during the decade of the 1980s, we and our ASEAN partners prevented the acceptance of a fait accompli at the UN after the Vietnamese invasion of Cambodia. This eventually made it possible for the major powers to broker a UN-supervised compromise that restored a measure of autonomy to that unfortunate country. Foreign Service Officers of my generation learnt our trade during that decade. For that reason I will admit to a tad of sentimentality about the UN; but only a tad and, I trust, not an uncritical sentimentality.

The Cambodian issue also illustrates what is perhaps the UN's most important currency: international legitimacy. Even if debased by the inevitable hypocrisies of diplomacy — and we should not forget as someone once said, that hypocrisy is the tribute that vice pays to virtue — it a coin only the UN can mint. General Assembly resolutions are non-binding and can be ignored with impunity. But they do represent at least a tentative consensus on what *ought* to be right. Security Council resolutions are legally binding but are oftentimes — too often — presented in the full expectation of attracting a veto by one Permanent Member or another. Still they delegitimise the other side's position and so impose costs that occasionally forces some sort of compromise even when vetoed. This may not seem like very much, and indeed it is not very much. But it is better than nothing and taken together with the work of the specialised agencies and programmes, represents a modicum of order in what would otherwise be an entirely anarchic international system.

But international legitimacy is a coin that must be spent sparingly and wisely if is to retain its value. The end of the Cold War raised unrealistic expectations, or at least evoked overly ambitious rhetoric, about what the

UN could now achieve. This did the UN no favours even when motivated by the best of intentions and this was not always the case. The structural constraints imposed by an international system of sovereign states did not disappear just because the Soviet Union imploded and set limits to what any international organisation could achieve even if the major powers had the stomach (and the money) for it. Double standards and selective implementation, always a feature of international relations in general and the UN diplomacy in particular, became even more pronounced. Unrealistically ambitious goals for the UN's socio-economic agenda were set. Their implementation would have required enormous sums that everybody knew were not really going to be forthcoming. But never mind. Forward! Setting the goal became the goal.

I served as Permanent Representative to the UN from 1995 to 1998. It seemed to me then that the West no less than the former Soviet Union was enervated by the exertions of the Cold War and for the most part wanted little more than to strut and swagger and *appear* to act in the UN, while scheming how best to exploit their triumph to their own advantage. All this of course dressed up in high sounding talk about democracy and human rights and other noble ideals. This was a time when some in the West even dared to presume that history had ended. It made me sick. All things considered I thought that the Cold War conflicts that I witnessed, and in a minor way participated in, at the UN during the 1980s was far more honest than the post-Cold War UN.

After the Berlin Wall came down, effective action with the use of force authorised by the Security Council was taken when Saddam Hussein was foolish enough to invade Kuwait and thus threatened Saudi Arabia's oil fields. A "new world order" was proclaimed. But not too long afterwards genocide in Rwanda was greeted only with pious exclamations of dismay and the token force of UN peacekeepers that was despatched was explicitly forbidden by the major powers to do anything really useful. Compelled to witness horrors that he was powerless to stop, the commander of the UN forces had a nervous breakdown and later reportedly attempted suicide. In response to massacres of civilians in Bosnia and Kosovo, the Security Council passed fiercely worded resolutions, including some threatening "all necessary measures" — UN-speak for military action — even as representatives of the Permanent Three, the US, the UK and France, were almost simultaneously creeping up to the 38th floor of UN Secretariat building to quietly warn the Secretary-General that they didn't really mean it and he should do nothing.

All countries always act only in their own interests, but this was more than the usual level of hypocrisy. It was only when Serbia went too far by publically threatening and humiliating Dutch peacekeepers that the West decided to do more than talk. Holland is a member of NATO and it was not just the lives of a few Slavs that was at stake. It was not an accident that when the western Permanent Members led by the US finally bestirred themselves to action in the Balkans, NATO not the UN was their preferred instrument. Earlier Security Council resolutions may have legitimised the operation, but I suspect that the proximate catalyst for action was not so much Bosnian lives as NATO credibility. Current western support for Kosovo reflects a belated sense of guilt.

Can the UN do substantially better? It certainly ought to and most members of the UN would readily agree. Do they all mean it? I doubt it and even if they did, recognition of a problem does not necessarily mean that political will for a solution follows. So at least in its core function of maintaining international peace and security, what we now see in the UN is pretty much what we are going to get. NATO's role in the Balkans underscores a central point about the UN: all international organisations work best when they accurately reflect the global configuration of power. In this respect the Security Council is clearly archaic and Security Council reform must be at the centre of meaningful change in the UN. The Five Permanent Members were the victors of the Second World War, the great powers of the day, and even then there were originally only three until Franklin Roosevelt insisted on including China and Winston Churchill on France.

But it has been a very long time since the Permanent Five represented the real global configuration of power. If the Permanent Members of the Security Council are really the major powers best placed to maintain international peace and security, then there should logically be only one Permanent Member because the US is currently the only truly global power; or perhaps one and a half since China clearly has global potential but is still inching its way towards taking up global responsibilities. Russia's capacity to act is now and for the foreseeable future mainly in its 'near abroad'. And are the UK and France Permanent Members because they are really major powers, or do we out of diplomatic politesse still accord them the title because they cling to Permanent Membership? Both are broke and if the EU really takes its "common foreign and security policy" seriously there should be only one European seat. In any case, Japan and India have as good if not better claims to Permanent Membership as the UK and France.

But of course Security Council reform is not going to happen. Any change in the composition of Permanent Membership will constitute an intolerable loss of status for one or another of the current Permanent Members and will attract a veto. The current phase of discussions on Security Council reform has lasted more than two decades without any meaningful result. I expect none. Any prospect of real change will be resisted. A few years ago even a non-binding UNGA resolution that suggested a few changes of working methods to make Security Council proceedings a little more transparent to the general membership was scuttled by pressures from the Permanent Five. And it is not just the Security Council. Three entire chapters of the UN Charter are clearly obsolete since they essentially concern decolonisation which is now substantially complete. They serve no useful purpose and need at least to be revised if not entirely scrapped. But Charter revision even in such a clear case is impossible because any change will in all likelihood lead to demands for other changes and any change will be regarded by one member or another as not in its interest.

The UN system and their sister Bretton Woods institutions will not disappear even if their increasing disjuncture from reality and the resistance to change is beginning to spawn alternatives such as the G-20, the BRICS Bank and the AIIB. There will no doubt in time be others. They will coexist with the UN system; for now uneasily, but hopefully in the future in a complementary manner. If it is in the interest of none of the Permanent Five to see the UN system work too effectively, it is equally not in the interests of any of them to destroy it. After all they occupy the core of the UN system and that position is at least partially why they are great powers. No ordinary member state has the power to do so even if it wanted to. And so the Security Council and the General Assembly will limp along much as they now do: their occasional successes taken for granted or ignored, their more frequent failures trumpeted. But I am realistic not cynical about the UN.

Even when the dreary, interminable and too often futile and absurd debates of the UN tempt one to hear in them the melancholy, long, withdrawing roar of the tide of internationalism, we should not forget that it is a tide that may constantly withdraw but never runs entirely dry. And that is just as well. Because if the tide should recede entirely, it may portend a tsunami to follow.

———•◦•———

Bilahari KAUSIKAN retired in June 2013 and is currently Ambassador-at-Large and Policy Adviser in the Ministry of Foreign Affairs (MFA). From 2001 to May 2013, he was first the Second Permanent Secretary and then Permanent Secretary of MFA. He had previously served in a variety of appointments, such as Director for Southeast Asia, Director for East Asia and the Pacific and as Deputy Secretary for Southeast Asia. Bilahari had also served as the Permanent Representative to the United Nations in New York and as Ambassador to the Russian Federation. He has been awarded the Public Administration Medal (Gold) and the Pingat Jasa Gemilang (Meritorious Service Medal) by the government of Singapore. Bilahari has also been awarded the Order of Bernardo O'Higgins with the rank of Gran Cruz by the President of the Republic of Chile and the Oman Civil Merit Order by the Sultan of Oman. Raffles Institution, the University of Singapore and Columbia University in New York all attempted to educate him.

A History of the Forum of Small States[1]

CHEW Tai Soo

The Forum of Small States (FOSS) celebrated its 20th anniversary with a Conference on 1 October 2012, during the 67th UN General Assembly. Held in the UN, it was chaired by Singapore's Minister of Foreign Affairs Mr K. Shanmugam. It was a recognition that FOSS was born of an idea by Singapore diplomats twenty years earlier, to promote the potential of Small States in the UN, and had been chaired since then by the succeeding Singapore Permanent Representatives. Secretary-General of the UN Mr Ban Ki-moon opened the Conference, which was attended by Member States of the UN, both FOSS and non-FOSS. This was followed by keynote speeches by the President of the UNGA Mr Vuk Jeremic and the US Secretary of State Mrs Hillary Clinton. The events of the Conference included two panel discussions and a luncheon address by the former President of Finland, Mr Martti Ahtisaari. The Conference was a testimony to the important role and influence played by small states in the UN.

FOSS came about from a simple observation that small states, which formed the majority of the membership in the UN, tended to be disadvantaged because they lack "strategic weight". I arrived in New York in the spring of 1991 to take up post as Singapore's Permanent Representative to the United Nations. In the course of the year and throughout the 46th Session of the UNGA, I was struck by three shortcomings which small member states of the UN faced.

First, small states particularly those which do not belong to a recognised grouping were often excluded from the inner sanctums of negotiations. This was very clearly illustrated during the negotiations at the UNCED

---

[1] A version of the essay was first published in the commemorative book for the 20th Anniversary of FOSS (2012).

PrepComm IV meetings. Austria and Switzerland, among others, were excluded from the meetings called by the Chairman to negotiate the Earth Charter. They were either not big enough in themselves, unlike the US or Japan, or did not belong to a group, such as the EU. Second, and related to the first, small countries often lacked in-depth information on what went on in the UN; unless they had a team of very active diplomats. Third, and most critically small states had by tradition been proportionally under-represented in the principal organs of the UN and boards of the UN specialised agencies. This came about because it was difficult for small states to be elected to these organs and agencies. I had observed at the 1991 Economic and Social Council (ECOSOC) elections that the big regional countries were easily elected at the first round of voting. The smaller countries were then left to fight over the remaining seats.

These disadvantages led me to question what small states could do to overcome them. During the year, I had intensive discussions with two important Permanent Representatives (PRs) of small states. They were Ambassador Jose Luis Jesus of the Cape Verde, a member of the UNSC, and Ambassador Besley Maycock of Barbados, a longtime member of the Advisory Committee on Adminstrative and Budgetary Questions (ACABQ). Both were supportive of my idea of starting a forum of small states. They also provided excellent comments and feedback to a non-paper on the Forum of Small States (FOSS) which I had prepared.

The non-paper proposed several objectives for FOSS:

(a) that small states seek to redress the problem of under-representation in the principal organs of the UN and in UN specialised agencies.
(b) that the Forum serves as a platform in the UN:-
(i)   to support each other's candidature in the various UN elections;
(ii) for views of small states to be heard;
(iii) to pressure the international community to adhere to Charter principles; and
(c) that the Forum serves as a consultative vehicle on issues of mutual interest.

The non-paper also defined small states not by physical size but by population. I suggested that a population of 10 million should be the criterion as it would include at that time just over 100 countries. This would give FOSS the necessary numbers to wield political clout. Membership would include both "developed", as well as "developing" small states. Hence "small" would not be based on a country's economic status.

Following the initial discussions by the three of us, an invitation to participate in further discussions was extended to 13 other small countries. They were Honduras, Jamaica, Suriname, Uruguay, Botswana, Djibouti, Gabon, Tunisia, Bahrain, Mongolia, PNG, Vanuatu and Malta. Together these 16 countries were to form the "Core Group" for the setting up of a forum of small states.

The Core Group held meetings monthly to concretise the proposals in the non-paper. In June 1992 it endorsed the idea of FOSS and agreed on its basic objectives, rationale and structure. The Core Group also decided to formally put the establishment of FOSS in motion on 16 July 1992. There was agreement that for a start, some 40-odd countries, which were not in conflict situations either internally or with others, would be invited to the first meeting. Other small states could apply to join subsequently. As I had initiated the idea, there was agreement among the Core Group that I would chair FOSS in the first instance.

FOSS got off to a good start at the UN. Ambassador Maycock was able to get agreement for us to use the UN premises for our meetings and for interpretation to be provided. This was extremely important for a new informal grouping as it provided legitimacy and recognition. As the UN financial crisis developed in 1993 and 1994, interpretation services were withdrawn from FOSS meetings. However, we were still able to use the UN meeting rooms.

At the meetings, we discussed forthcoming elections in the UN and the candidatures of FOSS members to these elections. They also allowed for information on the developments in the UN to be shared. A short summary note by the Chairman was circulated after each meeting on the understanding that such notes were drawn up entirely at the responsibility of the Chairman. Member countries also briefed FOSS on various issues such as the negotiations to draft a resolution on the reform of the Security Council and progress in the Working Group set up to consider this question. Other issues discussed at FOSS meetings in 1994 included administrative and financial matters and Liechtenstein's initiative on its resolution, in the 3rd Committee, on the right of self-determination through autonomy.

I left New York in mid 1995 and my successor, Ambassador Bilahari Kausikan (later the Permanent Secretary of the Ministry of Foreign Affairs) took over its chairmanship by consensus of FOSS members. He strengthened the non-election objective of FOSS by bringing in prominent personalities and experts to brief the members on issues of interest to FOSS. This was highly successful and appreciated by members. During his term in New York, the financial situation of the UN had worsened. The use by FOSS of UN meeting rooms was terminated in 1995. Since that time, all FOSS meetings have been held in the Singapore Mission. At the request of its members, the Chairmanship of FOSS has remained with Singapore for the last twenty years.

The 20th Anniversary celebration of FOSS was organised by then Chairman and PR Ambassador Albert Chua. Its success underlines the importance and influence of Small States in the UN, and of the longevity of FOSS.

————•◦•————

CHEW Tai Soo is currently Ambassador-at-Large and concurrently Non-Resident Ambassador to Iran. He is also a Senior Adviser in the Ministry of Foreign Affairs. Tai Soo was Singapore's Ambassador to France from 2004 to 2007. Before that, he was Ambassador to Japan from 1998 to 2004. He was the Deputy Secretary in the Ministry of Foreign Affairs and Ambassador-at-Large from 1995 until March 1998. From 1991 to 1995, he served as Singapore's Permanent Representative to the United Nations in New York. He served as Singapore's Permanent Representative to the United Nations and GATT in Geneva from 1982 to 1986. Tai Soo was the Chairman of the GATT Committee on Trade and Development in 1984 and the Chairman of three GATT Dispute Settlement Panels in 1988. In 1992, he initiated the founding of the Forum of Small States for countries with population of less than 10 million in the United Nations and was its Chairman until 1995. In 1993, he was elected as Co-Vice Chairman of the Working Group on the Reform of the Security Council. Tai Soo was awarded the Public Administration Medal (Gold) in 2000 and the Meritorious Service Medal in 2010.

Singapore and the Global Governance Group (3G)

Vanu Gopala MENON

At the height of the 2008 financial crisis, United States' President George W. Bush decided that there was an urgent need for the major economies to come together and play an active role in tackling some of the immediate problems afflicting the world economy. In this context, the Bush Administration revived the moribund G20, which had been created by former Canadian Finance Minister Paul Martin to tackle the financial crisis of 1997/98. However, instead of keeping the process at the Finance Ministers' level, the November 2008 G20 meeting was elevated to a meeting of Heads of State and Government. Overall, it was a timely initiative. By taking some decisive steps to stimulate the global economy, the G20, under American leadership, helped to avert a possible global economic depression in 2009.

Rise of the G20

The 2008 financial crisis also underscored the need for more effective global governance mechanisms for policy coordination and international cooperation. It highlighted the reality that key decisions on global economic issues could no longer be the preserve of a small elite group of developed economies. Any such mechanism must now include key emerging economies, such as China, India and Brazil, and other important stakeholders. The designation of the G20 process as the "premier forum for international economic cooperation" at the G20 Summit in Pittsburgh in September 2009 thus represented a major step towards developing such a framework for economic issues.

Genesis of the Global Governance Group (3G)

These developments involving the G20, while generally positive for the global economy, nevertheless raised a number of questions in the area of global governance. These included how decisions were going to be made in the future on global issues, what the G20 process might mean for the United Nations (UN), and how the decisions taken by the G20 might affect the rest of the world. Smaller but fairly robust economies (like Singapore) were also concerned with the rather unilateral manner in which the G20 was acting. While the G20 was taking decisions supposedly on behalf of the rest of the world, some of its decisions were clearly self-serving and made without any consultation with the countries affected by the G20's decisions. This was the backdrop against which the Global Governance Group (more popularly called the 3G) came into existence.

The specific genesis for the 3G was the April 2009 G20 Summit meeting in London where the G20 Leaders adopted "A Progress Report on the Jurisdictions Surveyed by the OECD Global Forum in Implementing the Internationally Agreed Tax Standard". Singapore, along with several other medium-sized and small-sized economies, was listed on the OECD's so-called grey list of countries which had not substantially implemented the OECD's tax standard, and threatened with sanctions.

What was even more galling was that all the key G20 countries were listed as "jurisdictions that have substantially implemented the internationally agreed tax standard", when it was well-known that a number of them had territories which, for all intents and purposes, were tax havens. *The Economist*, in an article dated 26 March 2009 entitled "Haven Hypocrisy", pointed out that "*The most egregious examples of banking secrecy, money laundering and tax fraud are found not in remote alpine valleys or on sunny tropical isles but in the backyards of the world's biggest economies*". It cited Nevada, Delaware and Wyoming as being amongst the worst culprits. In fact, at the London Summit, then Chinese President Hu Jintao made it clear that China would not accept the listing of Hong Kong and Macau as jurisdictions which had not substantially implemented the OECD's tax standard. As a result, a footnote was added to make it clear that these Special Administrative Regions had committed to implement the OECD's standard, without them being named in the document!

In view of the London Summit decision, Singapore's initial sense was that we should not let such clearly unfair treatment pass quietly. I was then serving as Singapore's Permanent Representative to the UN in New York and was tasked to bring together a group of small and medium-sized countries similarly affected by the G20's decision in London. It was in this context that an informal grouping of 21–23 countries came together to discuss how best to respond to the G20. We only decided much later to call ourselves the Global Governance Group or 3G, as suggested by Liechtenstein Foreign Minister Aurelia Frick.

It was apparent from our initial meetings at the Singapore Mission that many countries in the group agreed on the importance of the major economies taking the lead to address global challenges. In this regard, the G20 process could play a useful role in tackling some of the big issues of the day. That said, it was equally important that the G20 process developed legitimacy even as it evolved. If it remained an exclusive club, the G20 would not be effective. As a result, the 3G decided that since the G20's decisions and actions had implications beyond its membership, we should aim to influence the G20 by developing a constructive dialogue on coordination and cooperation between G20 and non-G20 members. This would in turn hopefully encourage the G20's decision-making process to take into account the interests of the wider UN membership, the vast majority of whom had no say in the G20 process. A more inclusive and transparent G20 process would also allow for the G20's decisions to be more representative and fully benefit all countries.

Creating Synergy between the G20 and the UN

Arising from this, the 3G continued to hold meetings with the objective of identifying ways in which we could reach out to the G20 and the wider UN membership. As a start, we invited the UN Secretary-General's (UNSG) office as well as Canada and the Republic of Korea, who were both hosting G20 Summits in 2010, to meet with us. I must say that there were others in the G20 who were initially quite reluctant to engage the 3G. They probably did not think much of our group. However, when the G20 faced difficulties in persuading the rest of the UN membership to even simply take note of some of its discussions and decisions made at G20 Summits, the G20 countries quickly realised the value of engaging the 3G, which served as a "bridge" between the G20 and the wider UN membership. That said, even our interactions with the wider UN membership proved to be challenging at times during those early days as some countries that were stridently against the G20 process were cautious about engaging with the 3G given their concerns that our efforts would lend legitimacy to the G20.

At our meetings with representatives from the UNSG's office (and on occasion with the UNSG himself) and the G20 Chairs, the 3G made it clear that while we were generally supportive of the G20 process, we also firmly believed that the process should enhance and not undermine the UN, an organisation with universal membership. The G20 process would need to be transparent, inclusive and consultative if its deliberations and decisions were to gain buy-in and translate into effective actions on a truly global scale. In this regard, the 3G raised several ideas on how to improve the engagement between the G20 and the UN.

First, the G20 should, before its Summits, undertake regular consultations as widely as possible with non-G20 countries. It was important for all countries, especially smaller ones that comprise the majority of the UN membership, to have the opportunity to raise issues of concern with the G20. The G20 should also provide the rest of the UN membership with updates and take feedback after its meetings.

Second, the UNSG and his Sherpa should be able to participate in all aspects of the G20 process in a meaningful and substantive manner. While the UNSG could not be expected to represent the national positions of every UN Member State, he would be able to convey the broad sense of the house. We also pointed out that it would not satisfy the wider membership of the UN if the UNSG was only given a token role in the G20 process.

Third, the G20 should continue to invite established regional groupings, like the African Union (AU) and ASEAN, to participate in its meetings. We also felt that the participation of these regional groupings should be formalized. The G20 now regularly invites the Chairs of ASEAN, the AU and the New Partnership for Africa's Development (NEPAD) to its Summits.

Fourth, in order to adequately represent the interests of small and medium-sized states, the G20 decision-making process should allow non-G20 countries to participate in G20 meetings on specialized issues, so as to benefit from their relevant contributions. Such a configuration of "variable geometry" would not only render the G20's initiatives more transparent but also ensure that its deliberations on key issues of global concern involved all the relevant parties. We argued that such engagement would enhance the effectiveness of the G20.

Most of these ideas were subsequently encapsulated in the 3G paper entitled "Strengthening the Framework for G20 Engagement of Non-members" and circulated as a UN document. This was at the suggestion of then Swiss Foreign Minister, Micheline Calmy-Rey, who felt, quite correctly, that there should be some guiding principles for the 3G.

The 3G Today

Today, the 3G comprises 30 countries from various geographical regions: Southeast Asia, the South Pacific, the Middle East, Africa, Europe, Latin America and the Caribbean.[1] The 3G meets at the Ministerial and Ambassadorial levels in New York and Geneva. It actively engages with key stakeholders, such as the UNSG, the President of the UN General Assembly and the hosts of G20 Summits. The 3G also prepares common positions on some G20 agenda items. For example, we have submitted inputs to the G20 Working Group on Development. Some of these suggestions were incorporated by the G20 into the Seoul Action Plan on Development. The 3G has also conveyed papers to the G20 on a variety of other topics, such as global governance, liveable cities, labour issues, food security and encouraging transparency in the G20's interactions with international organisations. During the Australian G20 Presidency in 2014, the 3G contributed two papers to the G20 process, on employment as well as on development and governance.

Since the G20 Summit in Seoul in 2010, one or more members of the 3G have always been represented at G20 Summits. As the convenor of the 3G, Singapore attended the G20 Summits in Seoul (2010), Cannes (2011), St. Petersburg (2013) and Brisbane (2014). 3G members Chile and New Zealand also attended the G20 Summits in Los Cabos (2012) and Brisbane (2014) respectively.

In the process, the 3G has established itself as a serious grouping with an abiding interest in global governance issues. This has allowed us to not only serve as a "check" on the G20 by "keeping it honest", but also made it

---

[1] The members of the 3G are Bahamas, Bahrain, Barbados, Botswana, Brunei Darussalam, Chile, Costa Rica, Finland, Guatemala, Jamaica, Kuwait, Liechtenstein, Luxembourg, Malaysia, Monaco, Montenegro, New Zealand, Panama, Peru, Philippines, Qatar, Rwanda, San Marino, Senegal, Singapore, Slovenia, Switzerland, United Arab Emirates, Uruguay, and Vietnam.

possible for us to contribute to the G20 process meaningfully, including by giving small and medium-sized economies the opportunity to convey their views and concerns to the G20. The fact that the 3G has grown from 23 members to its current size of 30 is testimony to its utility and growing impact on G20 discussions. The 3G has helped display Singapore's role as a constructive player and moderate voice in the multilateral arena. I would also say that as Singapore can still bring value-add to the 3G, it is worth our while to continue playing a leadership role in the group.

——•—•—

Vanu Gopala MENON is currently Singapore's High Commissioner to Malaysia. He is a career Foreign Service Officer who has been with the Ministry of Foreign Affairs (MFA) since June 1985. He last served in MFA HQ as Deputy Secretary from August 2011 to October 2014. Prior to that, he was Singapore's Permanent Representative to the United Nations in New York from August 2004 until August 2011, where he was actively involved in the establishment of the Global Governance Group (3G). He has also been posted to Geneva as Permanent Representative to the UN and other international organisations, including the World Trade Organization, from December 2001 to August 2004.

Small States at the United Nations

Albert CHUA

Small states make up the majority of the world's nations today. At the United Nations, out of 193 members, at least 105 are considered small, being members of the Forum of Small States or FOSS. We have populations under 10 million. Small states encompass a broad range of countries with different geopolitical circumstances and varying levels of development, from Luxembourg to landlocked Lao People's Democratic Republic to the island state of Tonga.

Small states are vulnerable to the external environment. History is littered with examples of many small states which did not survive for long. Even Venice, which existed for over a millennium, was eventually swallowed up by larger neighbours. Small states also face many challenges and constraints. First, we have limited resources and coverage. Many small missions in New York might have a team of no more than three officers (including the Permanent Representative or PR) to cover the six Main Committees of the General Assembly, Security Council, Economic and Social Council (ECOSOC) and its subsidiary bodies, and other UN-related issues. Some have even fewer. Second, small states lack access and heft. It is a constant challenge for small countries to be heard, let alone have our interests taken into account. Third, small states are price-takers, rather than price-setters, in global politics. We do not determine the global order or international regimes. But because we are small, a favourable global order is critical for our survival. Fourth, small states are often vulnerable to external pressure. Taking principled positions on issues at the UN, without due concern for the reactions of major powers is a luxury not everyone can afford. Just examine the voting records at the UN.

At the UN, all states are equal and have one vote each but some states, particularly those with vetoes, are more equal than others. It is not easy for small states to get a seat at the table; sometimes, even getting into the room is a challenge. And if you do not have a seat at the table, you may well end up on the menu. Unless small states make our views heard, decisions are taken or norms developed which may be inimical to our national interests.

To ensure our success, and indeed survival, small states have to create our political and diplomatic relevance. Some like Switzerland have opted for a strict policy of neutrality. Others have done the opposite, latching on to a great power patron. Those who have read *The Origin of Species* will know that the race is not to the swift, nor the battle to the strong. The Darwinian theory of evolution prescribes that those who can best adapt and make themselves relevant to the changing environment — the "fittest" — will survive and thrive. Small states need to find our ecological niche; we will not be relevant to the international agenda and major powers will not naturally engage us, unless we make ourselves relevant and worth engaging.

Small states survive better in a world governed by the rule of law rather than might alone, and where there are international norms that respect the sovereignty of states. This is why small states are passionate advocates for the UN and its central role in international affairs. The UN, for all its flaws, is the embodiment of such a global order. The principles of the UN Charter on non-resort to force; peaceful settlement of disputes; non-interference in a country's internal affairs; all these provide the international framework for small states to coexist alongside larger and more powerful states. This is why Singapore played an active role in the evolution of the UN Convention on the Law of the Sea (UNCLOS) and continues to take an active interest.

Singapore occupies an unusual niche at the UN. We are not beholden to any country for aid and because we campaign for very few candidatures, we are free to speak our minds and take positions on principle. There is admiration for Singapore, our leaders and our achievements. Many developing countries want to study our development experience. But we should not assume that this state will persist indefinitely. Our reputation is built on our success. For small states, things can change quickly; if we are no longer economically successful and domestically united, our international standing will be quickly eroded.

Let me give a few examples of how, during my tenure as Singapore's PR to the UN, we tried to make change in small ways, and contribute to the international agenda.

In November 2011, in the run-up to the UN Conference on Sustainable Development or Rio+20 Conference, Sweden and Singapore formed a Group of Friends (GoF) to push the agenda on Sustainable Cities. Sweden and Singapore have experience in urbanisation and both delegations felt strongly that this was a critical issue for the sustainable development agenda. According to UN Habitat, the world's urban population today already exceeds the rural population and by 2050, 70% of the world's population will be urbanised. If we get our cities wrong, we will add greatly to the world's ongoing list of problems. But if we get our cities right, they can become an important development solution — environmentally sustainable, socially responsible and economically productive. Comprising 29 Member States and spanning all the major regions, the GoF reached out to national authorities, local and regional governments and Non-Government Organisations. Because of the political constituency we were able to create, negotiations on the section on sustainable cities were the least controversial of the entire Rio+20 Outcome Document.[1] In fact, the Leaders agreed that sustainable cities and human settlements are critical components in the sustainable development agenda. If *"they are well planned and developed, including through integrated planning and management approaches, cities can promote economically, socially and environmentally sustainable societies"* (paragraph 134 of the Outcome Document). Building on the outcome of Rio+20, the GoF has continued to raise awareness at the UN on the importance of sustainable urbanisation in the Post-2015 Development Agenda, and provide inputs into the formulation of practical and action-oriented Sustainable Development Goals.

Another initiative spearheaded by Singapore was to get the UN to focus on sanitation through the designation of 19 November as World Toilet Day. Amongst the various Millennium Development Goals, the target for sanitation is significantly under-achieved. Today, 2.5 billion people still do not have proper sanitation and 1.1 billion defecate in the open. A UN study concluded that more people have access to mobile phones than toilets!

---

[1] For the full document, visit http://www.un.org/ga/search/view_doc.asp?symbol=A/RES/66/288&Lang=E

Young girls avoid school because of the absence of safe and proper toilets. Ending open defecation will lead to a 35% reduction of diarrhoea, which results in 760,000 deaths of children under five years of age every year. Although there was the danger of becoming the butt of many toilet jokes, Singapore chose to champion this small but pivotal issue of sanitation as it can help to achieve disproportionate and positive outcomes in terms of health, gender equality, economic prosperity and personal dignity of millions of the poorest people. The resolution was passed by consensus, with more than a hundred co-sponsors, showing the wide-spread support achieved.

Small states have a strong stake in the effective functioning of the UN and its extended family of institutions that together form the bedrock of the rules-based international system. Security Council reform is clearly one area of interest. After more than 20 years, negotiations on expansion of the Security Council have not progressed beyond the ritualistic delivery of formal statements and are likely to remain intractable. During one session of the Intergovernmental Negotiations, the PR of a Permanent Five (P5) member made it very clear that his country had a seat on the Security Council not because it had won it through a lottery but because it had won the last World War; in effect, he was saying that the composition of the Council could not be altered unless or until there was another World War!

For those of us who do not harbour illusions of grandeur, reform of the working methods of the Council to make it more transparent, inclusive and accountable to the wider UN membership would have a far greater and more positive impact than the expansion of the Council. In 2005, the "Small Five" (S5) comprising Costa Rica, Jordan, Liechtenstein, Singapore and Switzerland came together to advocate reform of the working methods of the Security Council. One would assume that an initiative which would benefit the majority of UN Member States would receive universal support. But the reality was that the P5 did everything they could to block attempts to reform the working methods, which they regard as their own prerogative, even as they continued to protest their support for efforts to make the Council more transparent, open and effective.

The S5's efforts exemplified the constraints faced by small states in influencing the global order. In May 2012, the S5 presented a draft resolution

A/66/L.42. The aims of the resolution were modest and the impact of the recommendations would have been limited but the P5 resorted to strong-arm tactics. P5 members were particularly unhappy about proposals that they consider refraining from using the veto to block Council action aimed at preventing or ending genocide, war crimes and crimes against humanity. Even those P5 members who are ardent supporters of Responsibility to Protect (R2P), i.e. the principle that states must protect or be made to protect their populations from mass atrocities, adamantly rejected any limitations on their use of the veto. In response to a query from the 66th President of the General Assembly, the Office of Legal Affairs (OLA) gave an interpretation stating that an absolute two-thirds majority (not just those present and voting) would be required for the S5's draft resolution to pass. This clearly contradicted the OLA's earlier advice, which showed that the P5 had exerted its influence behind the scenes. Worse, Member States first learnt of this when a P5 member circulated the OLA's legal opinion to all Member States on the morning of the formal consideration of the draft resolution, with an admonition that they support a no-action motion on L.42. Ultimately, the resolution was withdrawn because of the lack of willingness of some of our partners to stand against the strong and unified opposition from the P5.[2]

In conclusion, despite our inherent vulnerability, constraints and limitations, small states are not entirely powerless. If we play our hand well, we can seize the opportunities to influence international events. The UN remains an important arena for small states. The multilateral setting provides small states with the space to manoeuvre and create relevance. In Chinese martial arts, the *tai chi* master executes a classic move which uses a small force to counteract a much larger force — "using four ounces of strength to counteract a force of a thousand pounds" (四两拨千斤). If small states are skilful, we avoid placing ourselves on the menu, and may even occupy a temporary seat at the high table every now and then.

---

[2] For the full discussion on this resolution, please see http://www.securitycouncilreport.org/atf/cf/%7B65BFCF9B-6D27-4E9C-8CD3-CF6E4FF96FF9%7D/a%2066%20pv%20108.pdf

Albert CHUA is Second Permanent Secretary in the Ministry of Foreign Affairs. He served as Deputy Trade Representative at the Singapore Trade Office in Taipei from March 1994 to February 1997 and Singapore's High Commissioner to Australia from March 2008 to June 2011. He was Singapore's Permanent Representative to the United Nations in New York from August 2011 to June 2013.

World Toilet Day

Karen TAN

Since 2013, 19 November has been designated World Toilet Day (WTD)[1] at the United Nations (UN). While this piece of information may not seem particularly important or interesting, it has significance for the 2.5 billion people who still do not have access to a toilet. It is also the result of a Singapore-initiated resolution entitled "Sanitation for All", co-sponsored by more than 120 UN members.

In 2015, when we commemorate World Toilet Day for the third time, I will have completed, almost to the day, 30 years as a diplomat. When I completed all the necessary paperwork to join the Ministry of Foreign Affairs (MFA) as a Foreign Service Officer (FSO) on 18 November 1985, little did I know that I was beginning a career that would take me to live and work all over the world, much less that I would eventually end up in New York, as Singapore's Permanent Representative to the UN.

When I was asked to write this essay, it took some time to finally settle on a theme. After all, there have been many milestones in Singapore's "UN Story" over the past five decades, many of which have been well documented. Also, at this time when we get ready to celebrate 50 years of our membership in the UN, it would be timely not only to take stock and reflect on how our UN membership has been beneficial to Singapore, but also the ways we have contributed to the organisation and its membership. By talking about toilets, I am writing about an initiative that I have been directly involved in while at the same time highlighting Singapore's involvement in the development pillar of the UN's work.

---

[1] http://www.unwater.org/worldtoiletday

Some might find toilets a surprising and rather unsavoury topic to talk about, or for Singapore to champion. We Singaporeans take access to a clean toilet for granted. And, because we are living in Singapore, we have forgotten the downsides of not having one. But not having access to a sanitary toilet is a real and prevalent problem in many parts of the developing world. I saw this first-hand when I was High Commissioner in India, and I can attest to the importance of sanitation in creating economic development and in preserving human dignity. More about this later.

As we draw attention the importance of "Sanitation for All", we should not forget our own journey from independence to where we are today as a nation. It was not that long ago that Singapore was described as a "poor little market in a dark corner of Asia" by Dutch economist Dr Albert Winsemius. He was referring to the Singapore of the 1960s when he was head of a UN Development Programme (UNDP) Survey Mission advising our government economic development. Today, that "poor little market" has a per capita GDP of US$55,000! I mention Dr Winsemius not to take issue with his description of Singapore, but rather as an important reminder of the key role that the UN played in Singapore's development.

As a small country without natural resources, our vulnerabilities as a new-born country on 9 August 1965 were stark. Our admission, to the United Nations, less than two weeks after we gained independence, helped us secure recognition and underpinned our sovereignty and territorial integrity. In his statement to the UN General Assembly on 21 September, on the occasion of our admission to the UN, Foreign Minister S. Rajaratnam assured the Assembly that:

> Singapore will join with other nations in their efforts to realise the aims and objects of the United Nations Charter …. the preservation of peace through collective security, promotion of economic development through mutual aid and the safeguarding of the inalienable right of every country to establish forms of government in accordance with the wishes of its own people. Singapore stands by these three essential principles and will give loyal and unflinching support to the United Nations in its efforts to promote these ideals… It is practical self-interest and not vague idealism which makes it necessary for Singapore to give loyal support to these essential elements in the UN Charter.

Over the past 50 years, we have sought to live by these ideals, while at the same time not losing sight of our national interests, to never allow tests to our sovereignty and independence to go unchallenged. From our early years until today, the fundamentals of our foreign policy have not changed. However, as we have matured and recorded successes as a nation state, and our expertise increased, Singapore has gained a reputation as a country that "punches above its weight" on the global stage.

This has not come about by chance, but rather, by careful planning and first class execution by our leaders and FSOs who have, year-in and year-out, created strategic alliances and built up constituencies of support through a combination of networking and diplomacy. In 1992, Singapore established the Forum of Small States (FOSS). This informal group which we chair provides a useful platform for more than 100 small states at the UN to share their views and experiences and to support each other's candidatures. Singapore has also had the honour to Chair norm-setting Conferences such as the Earth Summit and the Conference on the Law of the Sea. Besides our active participation in the UN General Assembly and its Committees, we have also contributed to the discussions on the reform of the Security Council, especially its working methods. In areas where we have core interests such as the maintenance of peace and security, the rule of law, the environment and oceans, Singapore has played a constructive role, all the while defending our interests on matters as diverse as the Cambodian issue, the use of the death penalty and our contributions to the UN regular and peacekeeping budgets. To ensure that the UN remains at the core of multilateralism, Singapore formed the Global Governance Group or 3G in 2009, to act as a bridge between the UN and the G20.

My career in the Foreign Service has afforded me a front row seat to many of the key milestones in Singapore's "UN Story". From the lobbying on the Cambodian issue when I was Desk Officer for Vietnam, Laos and Cambodia; to our decision to run for a seat in the UN Security Council (2001–2002) and the lobbying campaign that followed and the fight over the death penalty, in my capacity as Director for International Organisations and then Deputy Permanent Representative; to collaboration with the UNDP when I was Ambassador to the Lao PDR; to the setting up of the 3G, when I was Permanent Representative in Geneva and finally; to our active role in the elaboration of the Sustainable Development Goals or SDGs since my arrival in New York. We were also asked to take on the Co-Chairmanship of the Preparatory Committee for the 3rd Small Island Developing States (SIDS) Conference, which took place in Apia, Samoa in September 2014.

With a small team here at the Permanent Mission in New York, we cannot cover every issue that arises in the UN with the same consistency, depth and involvement. However, over the years, with more resources and manpower, we have been able to adopt a broader agenda at the UN allowing us to support processes which contribute to the work of the UN and its membership, such as the 3G and our role in Groups of Friends covering areas such as Sustainable Cities (which we co-Chair), the Rule of Law, Climate Change and Responsibility to Protect. At the same time, we have been able to increase our involvement in the mainstream work of the UN, taking up causes of key constituencies such as the SIDs as well as initiatives such as World Toilet Day.

Sanitation for All

On 24 July 2013, a month before I arrived to take up post in New York as Permanent Representative, the Singapore-sponsored resolution A/67/291, "Sanitation for All", designating 19 November as World Toilet Day (WTD) was adopted by consensus and co-sponsored by 121 other countries. It was the successful culmination of several rounds of negotiations with UN member states from April to June 2013 chaired by the Singapore delegation to the UN, and spearheaded by Deputy Permanent Representative Mark Neo. It was also the first UN General Assembly resolution we sponsored after a long hiatus.

At the time, many asked why Singapore, well known for its modern, litter-free cityscape, was tabling such a "trite" if not (toilet) humorous resolution at the UN. It was after substantive lobbying that we agreed to support the Singapore-based NGO World Toilet Organization (WTO)'s initiative to have the UN recognise 19 November as WTD. The idea was to champion a major global development issue at the UN, and by doing so, we would profile Singapore's positive contributions to the UN and the international community. It would also showcase Singapore's expertise in waste water and water supply management.

More importantly, toilets and sanitation are an issue that greatly impacts the quality of life, if not life itself, for billions of people in mostly developing countries. Some facts are worth highlighting. 2.5 billion people do not have access to improved sanitation and 1 billion still defecate in the open. This means that despite our best efforts, it is unlikely that the Millennium Development Goal (MDG) target of 75 percent coverage for sanitation will be met by 2015. This has economic, social and environmental consequences. For instance, open defecation is linked to diarrhoeal diseases and about 760,000 preventable child deaths. The lack of access to proper sanitation leads to an estimated US$260 billion in economic losses annually. For women and girls in particular, the consequences of the lack of toilets undermines efforts to educate girls, reduce maternal deaths, infant mortality, increases stunting for children and increases negative effects on gender equality. Women and girls are also constantly at risk of sexual violence because of the absence of proper sanitation facilities. Clearly more needs to be done to raise awareness of the importance of toilets and sanitation. While they do not seize headlines like wars and natural disasters, the impact of the lack of toilets and poor sanitation is no less severe.

Our decision to support this cause has provided us with a platform for us to work with member states, the UN Secretariat and its agencies such as UN-Water, UNICEF, UN-Women and the UNDP. We have also appeared on the radar screens of CSOs and NGOs as well as private sector companies such as Unilever, keen to partner with member states to take up this cause. In the 2014 WTD event, UN Deputy Secretary-General Jan Eliasson, a passionate advocate of "Sanitation for All", delivered the keynote address. Among member states, UN delegations like Fiji, India, Hungary and South Africa have taken part as panellists. In 2013, to promote WTD, someone dressed up as a toilet and we handed out bottles of NeWater and rolls of specially printed toilet rolls. The following year, a 15-foot inflatable toilet was erected outside the UN Headquarters. Leveraging on social media, UN-Water coordinated a campaign centred on the WTD 2014 webpage under the hashtag #wecan'twait, with the potential impact on 375 million people. Also in support of WTD, Samoa commissioned a special "Toilet" postage stamp while Global Poverty Project (GPP) issued a mock newspaper entitled "The Toilet Paper". Prior to the WTD, at its annual Global Citizen Festival, the GPP invited newly-elected Indian Prime Minister Narendra Modi as well as Raya, a new Sesame Street muppet, to shine a spotlight on toilets and the need to end the practice of open defecation. Two years into our "Toilet" advocacy, more and more is being done to champion toilets in developing countries. All this cooperation and collaboration has underscored the value of partnerships at the UN.

Overall, sanitation, water and hygiene as well as toilets have become an important plank in Singapore's positive agenda at the UN. It ranks with our advocacy of SIDS, the FOSS, the 3G and sustainable cities. In the ongoing negotiations at the UN, we took an active role in ensuring that water and sanitation became a Sustainable Development Goal by, inter alia, leveraging on the WTD panel discussions and we are working to position it prominently in the Post-2015 Development Agenda. Slowly and steadily, through substantive initiatives like the WTD campaign, we are broadening the institutionalisation of Singapore's engagement with the UN. This has not gone unnoticed among UN member states and has earned us goodwill and recognition especially from other developing countries, our key constituency of support in the international community.

This year, as the UN celebrates its 70th anniversary, world leaders will gather in New York in September to adopt the Post-2015 Development Agenda which will address poverty eradication and sustainable development. This offers us an opportunity to shape the agenda to ensure that targets are realistic and implementable. We can also share our development experiences through south-south and triangular partnerships under the Singapore Cooperation Programme. At the SIDS Conference in Samoa, we announced a special technical assistance package for SIDs which focussed on sustainable development and climate change, disaster management and public health and Non-Traditional Security issues such as food, energy and water. At this important juncture of our nation building and our own development journey, there are plans for Singapore to announce a substantial technical assistance package, aimed at advancing the elements of the Post-2015 Development Agenda.

50 years after Foreign Minister S. Rajaratnam's inaugural speech at the UN, we can vouch for the fact that Singapore has kept to its commitment to "*stand by the 3 essential principles and give loyal and unflinching support to the United Nations in its efforts to promote these ideals.*" What the next 50 years will bring is anyone's guess, but even as new global powers jostle for a permanent seat at the horseshoe table in the Security Council, the United Nations, its members and agencies, will continue to work to maintain international peace and security, to address ongoing development challenges and

to promote a world of dignity for all. To quote Mr Rajaratnam again, *"Singapore has faith in the future of the United Nations simply because without it there is no worthwhile future for humanity."*

——•◦•——

Karen TAN is currently the Permanent Representative of Singapore to the United Nations. Prior to this, Karen served as High Commissioner to India from 2011 to 2013, with concurrent accreditation as Singapore's Ambassador to Bhutan and Nepal. Before taking up her post in New Delhi, Karen served as Permanent Representative to the World Trade Organization and the World Intellectual Property Organization (WIPO) in Geneva from 2007 to 2010. She was Ambassador to the Lao People's Democratic Republic between 2004 and 2007. She also served as First Secretary in Paris, from 1989 to 1992, and as Counsellor and subsequently Deputy Permanent Representative at the United Nations in New York from 1997 to 1999. She has held various positions at the Foreign Ministry's headquarters, including Director of Human Resources and Director of Policy, Planning and Analysis Directorate II, having joined the Foreign Service in 1985. Karen holds a Bachelor of Arts degree in History from the University of London, and a Master of Science in European Studies from the London School of Economics and Political Science.

UNITED NATIONS
Geneva · WTO · GATT

Singapore's Role in Multilateral Trade Negotiations

SEE Chak Mun

I have had the privilege of being posted as Singapore's Permanent Representative to the United Nations in Geneva and as Ambassador to the GATT/WTO (World Trade Organization) twice, in 1986–1991 and 1997–2001. As Ambassador to the GATT/WTO, my priorities were on multilateral trade negotiations: firstly in the substantive negotiations resulting in the draft Final Act of the Uruguay Round in 1991; and secondly in launching the Doha Development Agenda (DDA) Round at the Doha WTO ministerial meeting in 2001.

Despite Singapore's small physical size and limited domestic market, Singapore actually ranks fairly high as a trading nation. In 2012, Singapore was among the top 15 countries in world merchandised trade, and the top 9 in world trade in services. However, this is not the main reason why Singapore has often been invited to take a ringside seat at the GATT/WTO multilateral trade negotiations. Rather, it is because of the constructive role of Singapore, by exercising a moderating influence together with a group of middle-grounders, and individually through the skilful efforts of its diplomats to help find solutions to contentious issues, and paving the way to successful conclusions of GATT/WTO negotiations. This is the same formula that Singapore has used in other international fora and major international conferences such as its chairmanship of the UN Conference on the Law of the Seas and the 1992 UN Conference on Environment and Development.

For the same reasons, Singapore diplomats have often been selected or drafted as chairpersons of a number of GATT/WTO regular committees as well as dispute settlement panels such as: i) "US Safeguard Measure on Imports of Lamb Meat: Complaint by Australia and New Zealand", and

ii) "EC Trade Description of Sardines: Complaint by Peru". Singapore was the venue and chair of the first WTO Ministerial conference in 1996. Singapore has also been approached to chair committees on important issues such as the Council on Trade-related Intellectual Property Rights (TRIPs) which adopted the TRIPs Declaration on Public Health in 2003. This provided the legal mechanism that would make it easier for developing countries to import cheaper generic drugs made under compulsory licensing if they are unable to manufacture the medicines themselves. This is designed to address public health problems afflicting many developing countries such as in HIV/AIDS, tuberculosis, malaria and other epidemics.

Thus, since the Uruguay Round, Singapore has played an active role in shaping the agenda and substance of GATT/WTO trade negotiations, by acting as friends of the Chair at WTO Ministerial Conferences or as a facilitator in helping the chairman in resolving difficult issues such as on agriculture, a role which former Trade and Industry Minister George Yeo had accepted and executed brilliantly at Seattle, Doha and Cancun WTO Ministerial Conferences. Worthy of special mention was the role of Singapore and Minister George Yeo in particular in helping to launch the Doha Development Agenda (DDA) multilateral trade round at the WTO Ministerial conference held in Doha in November 2001.

The Doha Ministerial Conference (MC)

The Doha MC was held in the aftermath of the 9/11 terrorist attacks on the New York World Trade Centre, and amidst world anxieties as to what the US government would do in response and in retaliation against such terrorist attacks on American territory. In fact, security concerns about Qatar as a venue, a Middle Eastern country, were first raised by the Americans at an informal meeting of a small ministerial group held in Singapore in October 2001. As a result, and just weeks before the Doha MC, Singapore was approached to prepare conference facilities as an alternate venue. Fortunately, such a back-up plan was finally called off after the Qatar government succeeded in convincing and providing security assurances to the US government about Doha as a conference venue.

Learning from the Seattle MC experience where NGO activists and 20,000 American steel workers threatened to disrupt the conference, the

Qatar government decided to keep most of the NGOs out or place them at a safe distance from the conference venue. However, it was the disagreement over several difficult trade issues that cast a shadow over the launch of a new trade Round at Doha.

First, was agriculture. The French were particularly sensitive in view of their presidential election in the following year. Similarly, other EU farmers would not accept any definitive end to EU export subsidies. The EU declared that it could not accept an undiluted version of the phrase: "reductions, with a view of phasing out, all forms of export subsidies", and sought Minister George Yeo's help as he was the facilitator for agriculture. A deal was finally clinched when Minister Yeo managed to persuade the key agricultural exporters like Australia, Argentina, and Brazil to accept the insertion of the following phrase: "without prejudging the outcome of the negotiations".

Second, was the so-called Singapore Issues, namely: investment, competition policy, transparency in government procurement and trade facilitation. The EU had insisted on the inclusion of these four issues as well as greater market opening in non-agricultural products as a quid pro quo for the EU to make concessions in agriculture. However, there was strong resistance from some of the developing countries as they saw it as an attempt to undermine their sovereign right to regulate the predatory behaviour of MNCs. India was particularly sensitive to the inclusion of investment rules, and was prepared to block the launch of a new round at Doha over this. It was through Minister George Yeo's intervention that the Indian Trade Minister conceded to a compromise formula, applying to all the four Singapore Issues, which would postpone the decision to launch negotiations on these issues to the following Ministerial Conference that would take place in two years' time, but which would at the same time give the EU the satisfaction that a decision had virtually been made to include the four Singapore Issues in the DDA negotiations.

The third issue was rather unexpected, but it nevertheless threatened to derail the launch of the DDA Round at Doha. It simply involved an EU request to the WTO members to grant a waiver from the most-favoured-nation (MFN) provisions for the Contonou Agreement. Previously known as the Lome Convention, it would allow the EU to grant preferential treatment to the exports from the African-Caribbean and Pacific (ACP) countries till end 2007. This time, it met with strong opposition from some of the Central American countries such as Ecuador, Colombia and Honduras which were concerned that this preferential agreement would undermine their export share of bananas to the EU market. For this, the EU had requested Margaret Liang, Deputy Permanent Representative in Geneva, to chair the Working Party to resolve the differences. Whereas the Americans had helped to pacify the Central Americans, two ASEAN countries, namely the Philippines and Thailand held on to their objection over canned tuna. It was again through Minister George Yeo's personal mediatory efforts that settled the problem at the eleventh hour. The EU had no doubt that had its request for a MFN waiver not been granted, the ACP countries would have walked out of Doha. In fact, the closing plenary session had to delay its opening proceedings for three and a half hours while waiting for Margaret Liang to settle the final glitch.

After the Doha MC was over, several Ministers wrote to thank and congratulate Minister George Yeo for his role as the Agriculture facilitator and for helping to resolve the contentious issues by creating a "constructive atmosphere". One wrote as follows:

> Your personal capacities as a facilitator are, as we already knew from Seattle, outstanding. Your willingness to listen to the views of all the players, your ability to hear not only what they were saying but what lay behind the words, and the manner in which you distilled what you learnt into a possible solution proved in my view to be the key element in reaching agreement on the agricultural part of the Declaration.

It was a befitting tribute to Singapore's role at Doha in launching the DDA. There is also a self-interest element here as it is in Singapore's interest to keep multilateralism alive and to ensure a healthy and robust international trading system even as bilateral and plurilateral preferential trade agreements have taken over the role of the WTO as the central place for market access negotiations and rule-making. The ambassador of a small developing country explained to me why his country decided to join the WTO. Firstly, it would ensure that his country would be part of the main stream. Secondly, it would provide justification for economic reforms undertaken in his country. Thirdly, it would allow his small country to take on its big neighbours for dispute settlement.

He missed the fourth point, i.e. the MFN principle of the WTO would allow small nations to free ride on concessions exchanged among the economic majors.

SEE Chak Mun was Senior Advisor to the Ministry of Foreign Affairs, Singapore. He is currently an Adjunct Senior Fellow of the S. Rajaratnam School of International Studies (RSIS), Nanyang Technological University of Singapore as well as an Adjunct Senior Research Fellow of the Institute of South Asian Studies (ISAS), National University of Singapore. He joined the Foreign Ministry in August 1966. Chak Mun served as Singapore's Ambassador/High Commissioner to Australia, the Federal Republic of Germany, Italy, Greece, Turkey, Austria, Hong Kong and India. He served as the Singapore Permanent Representative to the United Nations and the GATT/WTO in Geneva from 1986 to 1999 and from 1997 to 2001. He was Singapore's High Commissioner to India from April 2002 to September 2006. At the Singapore Foreign Ministry, he had served as Director of the Political Division (1979–82), and Deputy Secretary/International (1991–94). He has written several articles on the international trading system, ASEAN/India relations, and an ISAS monograph on *India's Strategic Interests in Southeast Asia and Singapore* (2009).

Singapore and the World Trade Organization (WTO)

K. KESAVAPANY

Singapore's standing as a leading trading nation, an advocate of free trade and an open market system gave significance to a posting in Geneva. It was therefore, with a sense of pride that I assumed the post of Permanent Representative to the UN and Ambassador to the General Agreement on Tariffs and Trade (GATT), the precursor to the World Trade Organization (WTO) in December 1991.

The posting was particularly significant as the world of trade was watching when the Uruguay Round of trade negotiations (UR), commenced in 1986, would come to an end. The long suffering Director-General of GATT, Arthur Dunkel decided to call it a day and Peter Sutherland, a former Irish Minister took his place. Sutherland took over the running of an organisation which was essentially the preserve of the Quads — US, European Union, Japan and Canada and a few of the big countries like Brazil and India. The smaller countries had very little say or influence in the on-going negotiations, which were largely managed by the Green Room process i.e. a group of Ambassadors invited by the Director-General to help him with the negotiations. Nothing moved as there was no meeting of minds, even among the Quads, on the various sticking points.

It was against this stalemate that I participated as Singapore's Trade Negotiator in the UR negotiations. As I had no previous experience in the trade-related diplomacy and no knowledge of the issues holding up the completion of the Round, I had to learn fast and hold my own against my colleagues, some of whom had spent their entire careers in GATT.

I was lucky to have had a good team in the Mission including Margaret Liang, Tan Yee Woan (the present Singapore Ambassador to WTO, Ng Bee Kim (now Director-General for Trade in MTI), Rossman Ithnin, Peter

Govindasamy, Joseph Teo and Siva. Within a few months, I came to the notice of the senior Ambassadors and was appointed to the posts of Chairman, Budget Committee (1992) and Chairman of the Banana Panel (1993).

Impetus was given to the UR negotiations by the direct action taken by Sutherland. Instead of letting the Ambassadors, especially the Quads, set the pace, he dealt directly with the Ministers in the various capitals, notably Washington, DC and Brussels. Given his status as a former Minister, he had the standing to do so.

As a result, the outstanding issues holding up the conclusion of the UR were narrowed to four or five. These were resolved by Sutherland "inviting" eight Ambassadors to his office to find solutions to them. Representing the ASEAN Missions, I was one of the eight. The whole Agreement was then approved by the GATT Council.

With the negotiations concluded, the stage was set for the implementation of the Agreement at a Ministerial Conference to be held in Marrakesh, Morocco. Much to my surprise, I was chosen by the Council to chair the Implementation Committee. It was a harrowing task as every one of the 150 members had to be brought on board and their interests accommodated. While this made the governance of the international trading system more democratic, it meant a slowing down, or worse, a paralysis, of the decision making process.

Additionally, the non-governmental organisations (NGOs) closely scrutinised the WTO Agreement. Though they could not directly participate in the meetings, they could lobby their respective governments/ constituencies to have their interests accommodated.

Here I must acknowledge Arif Hussein, an experienced GATT staff member, for guiding and alerting me to pitfalls. The process was undertaken in such a smooth manner that a veteran NGO activist, Raghavan remarked, "You have done it like a thief in the night!" I took this as a back-handed compliment as he was one of the most vociferous critics of GATT/WTO on grounds that it did not safeguard Third World interests.

The stage was set for the ushering of a new world body, the World Trade Organization, into the constellation of international organisations. Much hope was placed in this new body as it was envisaged that it would promote social justice through trade. With pomp, ceremony and warm hospitality provided by the Kingdom of Morocco, the WTO came into existence on 1 January 1995.

Upon the return of the delegations from Marrakesh, the first meeting of the General Council was convened. At that meeting, I was chosen unanimously as the first Chairman of the WTO General Council. While it was a signal honour for me, more importantly, it was a recognition of Singapore's standing in the global community of trading nations.

With the UR negotiations concluded and the WTO brought into being, Sutherland decided to leave Geneva to pursue other goals. I was sorry to see him depart as we had established good rapport in the two years that we worked together. He could have done a lot to establish the WTO on a firm footing.

The task of selecting Sutherland's successor fell on me in my capacity as Chairman of the General Council. Several names were put forward, including Luis Philipe Lamperia, the Brazilian Ambassador of WTO. Following extensive consultations, Renato Ruggiero, a former Trade Minister of Italy was chosen as the second Director-General of WTO. An amiable person, he however lacked the forceful personality of his predecessor and therefore could not manage the wily Ambassadors, who resumed calling the shots. At one point, Ruggiero famously declared, "When I visit the capitals, I am received like a King. Here, I have to get the permission of the Ambassadors to even go to the toilet."

Among the issues that needed to be settled immediately by the Council was the convening of an annual Ministerial Conference (MC), as called for in the WTO Agreement. The Conference was meant to take stock of the Organisation's progress in a regular manner. The Members decided that the Conference would be held alternately in Geneva and member countries. This was aimed at giving greater visibility to the WTO, outside of Geneva. In the consultations that I undertook as Chairman of the General Council on the location of the first MC, I was pleasantly surprised that the unanimous choice was Singapore. Again, this reflected Singapore's standing in the world of trade.

When I reported to Headquarters on this desire of the WTO membership, the reaction was a mixture of joy and concern. This would be the largest international conference that Singapore would host since the meeting of the Commonwealth Heads of Government in 1971. Let alone the protocol and administrative aspects, even the venue for the Conference — Suntec City — was still under construction.

An issue of greater concern was the handling of the NGOs who would be coming to monitor the proceedings. At the best of times, Singapore has had an uneasy relationship with Western NGOs on account of various issues, such as freedom of the press! Following intensive inter-agency consultations, I was informed that I could formally announce that Singapore would be agreeable to hosting the first Ministerial Conference of the WTO. I did so at the General Council meeting, and the proposal to that effect was unanimously accepted.

With the "Road to Singapore" in their sights, the Secretariat and the Members got down to work in framing the agenda for the Conference. At this juncture, a domestic incident in Singapore threatened to derail matters in Geneva. This was the Michael Fay case where a young American citizen was charged for vandalism and punished accordingly, including caning. There was uproar in the US and all sort of pressures were applied on the Singapore Government to alter the sentence given to Fay. A principal proponent of these pressures was Mickey Kantor, then United States Trade Representative (USTR). Taking the matter personally, Kantor declared that the Ministerial Conference in Singapore would take place "over his dead body".

Aghast at the position taken by Kantor, the US Ambassador in Geneva, Booth Gardner, tried to argue that the two issues should not be linked. Kantor stood firm, with implicit support from Sir Leon Brittan, the EU Commissioner for Trade. As a way of getting around this impasse, Sir Leon suggested that the first MC be held in Geneva, and the second in Singapore. With the backing of all the other delegations, I maintained the Council's decision that the first meeting should be held in Singapore.

The issue dragged on for several months until the time came for a formal decision to be taken at the final meeting of the Council for that year. I informed Ambassador Gardner that I would be tabling a motion and added that the US ran the risk of being the "odd man out". Responding, the Ambassador told me to go ahead and table the motion. While all the other members approved the resolution by acclamation, Gardner looked the other way and allowed the motion to be carried. His Deputy, Andrew Stoller rushed up to Gardner to remonstrate but the deed was done. Gardner's gesture was a gift to a friend for which I will forever be grateful.

With this drama caused by the Michael Fay incident out of the way and Singapore confirmed as the location for the first MC, my one-year term as Council Chairman came to an end. There were suggestions from friends that in the light of the MC being held in Singapore, I should continue for another year. Declining, I said that a precedent should not be set. I was also happy that a dear friend of mine, William Rossier, the Swiss Ambassador, was in line to take over as Chairman. A suave and witty personality, William and I had worked well and I was confident that the steering of the "Road to Singapore" was in good hands.

Work started in earnest in the Council on the framing of the agenda for the Ministerial Conference. However, a shift in positions among the delegations was becoming apparent. The developed countries wanted new issues such as environmental and labour standards to be included in the agenda of the WTO. The developing countries led by India, Egypt, Pakistan, Malaysia and Kenya opposed the inclusion of the new issues. They insisted that commitments undertaken in the Uruguay pound be fulfilled first and additional market access be offered by the developed countries. The Least Developed Countries (LDC), Bangladesh, put forward their own list of demands.

This ideological cleavage hung over the entire MC negotiation process and threatened to stifle the newly formed body. Despite inputs made by Senior Officials coming from the capitals, no progress was made. As a result, there was no agreed text available to be taken to Singapore. My colleagues in HQ were none too pleased by this state of affairs.

Negotiations at the Ministerial level, chaired by Singapore's Trade Minister then, Yeo Cheow Tong, continued in earnest. The major sticking points were trade and investments, trade and competition policy, transparency in government procurement and trade facilitation. The developed countries wanted these four issues, which came to be called "the Singapore issues", included in the agenda for a new round of trade negotiations. The developing countries, led by India, Egypt, Pakistan and Malaysia, stood firm and insisted that these issues be excluded from the agenda of the next round of negotiations. They feared that additional commitments would burden the economies of the developing countries.

With time ticking away, the delegations resigned themselves to a "failed" conference, which would have been an inglorious start to the WTO. However, fate intervened in the form of Rafidah Aziz, the dynamic and rumbustious former Trade Minister of Malaysia. Much to the delight of the

Singapore delegation and to the chagrin of the Indian, Egyptian and Pakistani delegations, Rafidah remarked, at the Negotiating Council's meeting that there was no harm in the four issues being 'discussed', with the clear understanding that they would not be included in any forthcoming trade negotiation agenda.

This opening given by Minister Rafidah was enough for a Ministerial Statement to be crafted, which was then adopted at the final meeting of the Conference on 13 December 1996. Thus ended the saga of the first Ministerial Conference of the WTO.

As a gesture of appreciation, on the return of the delegations to Geneva, I offered, on behalf of Singapore, the logo used for the MC meeting, to be adopted as the logo for the WTO. The offer was accepted and thus Singapore has left an indelible mark in WTO's history.

K. KESAVAPANY was the Director of the Institute of Southeast Asian Studies, Singapore, from October 2002 to February 2012. Prior to this, he was Singapore's High Commissioner to Malaysia from 1997 to 2002. He also served as Singapore's Permanent Representative to the UN in Geneva and was concurrently accredited as Ambassador to Italy and Turkey (1991–1997). He was elected as the first Chairman of the General Council of the World Trade Organization when it was established in January 1995 and was a member of the Singapore Mediation Centre's International Panel of Mediators. Kesavapany graduated from the University of Malaya with a Bachelor of Arts (Honours) degree and obtained a Master of Arts (Area Studies) degree from the School of Oriental and African Studies, University of London. Presently, Kesavapany is Singapore's Non-Resident Ambassador to the Hashemite Kingdom of Jordan. He is also a Governor on the Board of the Singapore International Foundation, a member of the Board of the Energy Studies Institute, a Term Trustee of the Singapore Indian Development Association and President of the Singapore Indian Association. Most recently, Kesavapany has been conferred the title of Distinguished (Affiliated) Fellow at the Asia Research Institute, National University of Singapore.

Who Owns the UN?

TAN York Chor

During my Foreign Service career, I am fortunate to have been exposed to both bilateral and multilateral work in Singapore and at overseas posts. Having worked on these two key tracks of diplomacy, which require somewhat distinct skills and approaches, I can consider my diplomatic experience as quite fulfilling. Besides, I had the opportunity to work as Deputy Permanent Representative in New York, and thereafter as Singapore's Permanent Representative to the United Nations (UN) in Geneva and to the International Atomic Energy Agency (IAEA) in Vienna. New York gave me insight into how the principal UN organs worked, in particular, the Security Council and the General Assembly. In Geneva and Vienna, I learnt a lot about international organisations (IOs) including UN special agencies that carry out functional and technical work that impact on the lives of billions of people on earth.

Singapore is a small state in this universe of the UN systems. By their limited resources and capacities of influence, small states are price-takers and are generally unable to set the agenda or otherwise significantly influence outcomes. If the major powers dominate international peace and security decisions taken by the UN Security Council in New York, the developed states dominate most IOs in Geneva and Vienna where the North-South divide is clear. Notwithstanding every state's declared support for the noble missions of the UN and IOs, this universe is an arena where states push their national interests, alas, often riding roughshod over smaller, less developed states.

During the Cold War, the First World had a strategic imperative to compete with the former Soviet bloc for the Third World's support. The end of the Cold War altered the calculus of key developed States towards the developing world. Many developed states are, moreover, saddled with over-generous social systems back home that are difficult politically to reform, compelling them to be more stringent on external expenditure. In the new cold calculative approach to national interests, the "North" has not hesitated to pull harder on the purse strings of many IOs while demanding a sharper narrower focus on their specific interests. Generally, such power plays are not explicit and are kept away from public eyes.

Nevertheless, self-serving hypocrisy do at times surface openly, for example, in the Human Rights Council (HRC) in Geneva. Progress in human rights is probably better achieved through exemplary behaviour and calm reasoned dialogue than by a holier-than-thou ideological approach of hectoring and issuance of threats. However, many non-governmental organisations (NGOs)[1] and the liberal Western media would not hesitate to take Western governments to task publicly for any perceived weakness vis-à-vis countries that these NGOs target for condemnation, so Western officials are pressured to act "tough" on these countries.

By 2005, the atmosphere in the Commission of Human Rights (CHR) had grown so venomous as to render its work futile and meaningless, while risking to spill over to other areas of UN work. The HRC was established in 2006 to replace the discredited CHR, but it did not take long for the old confrontational behaviour to creep back. This should come as no surprise since the states that seek HRC membership are basically the same states that had sought CHR membership. If anything, the NGO industry has continued to blossom and pressures on Western governments have only increased.

Two instances of particular tensions in the HRC remain fresh in my mind. The first occurred in 2008 when the African Group sought a HRC Special Session on the Global Food Crisis. Poor harvests and high oil, energy and transport prices, compounded by commodities speculation and by knee-jerk actions of some big countries to augment food stockpiles. These factors led world food prices to spike sharply in 2007 through the first

---

[1] While NGOs like Médecins Sans Frontières (MSF) which, often at great risk, help the vulnerable in poor countries (e.g., among the hundreds of MSF doctors who have volunteered and worked in Ebola-afflicted zones, several have contracted Ebola and died despite taking all necessary precautions), command my respect, I see a whole industry of other NGOs that exist on championing specific causes in an ideological way.

half of 2008. Millions of people in developing countries suddenly were priced out of access to food. For unfathomable reasons, Western states were against such a Session, and Germany emerged to lead the opposition on grounds of costs and relevance. Surely, the cost of a Special Session could not be the issue since Western countries are ever so keen to call for such Sessions on country situations? Nor should relevance be an issue: an avoidable food crisis was causing millions around the world to starve. It could not be fear of being blamed for the crisis, nor fear of being committed to providing food aid. HRC resolutions, even if one was issued by the Session, are non-binding, while Western diplomats were more than capable of thwarting any unreasonable blame or demands. Quite plausibly, watched by their NGOs, Western states were just showing firmness in their categorical opposition to the very notion of right to food as a human right.

The second incident happened in 2009. The early months of 2009 saw the Tamil Tigers in Sri Lanka suffer huge setbacks but, right to the end, the Tigers gave no sign of wanting to sue for peace by laying down arms. All previous truces had not held up. As the Sri Lanka army pushed to eliminate the Tigers for good, ending 26 years of conflict that killed or wounded hundreds of thousands, some Western states suddenly became seized with humanitarian concerns about the human rights of the Tigers[2] and urgently sought a HRC Special Session. Was this a liberal knee-jerk reaction in Western capitals to save the hundreds who risked being killed in the final battles of this war? If so, it disregarded the fact that if the Tigers were once again given time and space to recuperate, the renewed conflict would kill and harm far more people. In much the same way, those who champion abolishing the death penalty often ignore the lives destroyed by crime syndicates and their arms, drugs and other activities. Behind this apparent move, some saw a cynical last-ditch attempt by an effective pro-Tiger lobby in many Western countries to pressure Sri Lanka to desist from finishing the Tigers. In the end, Sri Lanka won the understanding of a majority of member States in both the HRC and the wider UN membership. After destroying the Tigers, Sri Lanka could begin to work in peace to heal its nefarious inter-ethnic divisions. As a corollary, Sri Lanka's woes offer a lesson in the grave danger of societal divisions over race and religion. Singapore has rightly

---

[2] Western States have a second notion, disputed by many non-Western States, that only State authorities, not individuals or non-State entities, can commit human rights offences.

kept forging inter-racial and -religious relations, a work forever in progress which we must never relent on. Singapore's success in this regard has proved useful in various international discussions on non-discrimination by race or religion.

Beyond the HRC, the developed states that exploit the North's dominance over many IOs for their own narrow interests may not realise the damage they are causing to the weak governance of the global commons and, therefore, eventually to themselves. To begin with, the developed states have generally manoeuvred to dominate many IOs by blocking increases to regular budget (RB), leaving these IOs dependent on voluntary contributions (VCs) in cash and in kind that mainly only richer states and their NGOs and other donors can afford. Hence, many IOs have significantly larger numbers of experts and officials, especially at higher echelons, seconded by developed states to beef up these IOs. Developed states have also used the Global Financial Crisis to force some IOs to cut their RB by up to 20% although these states have not similarly reduced their national budgets.

Member States collectively deliberate on how the RB is to be used to the IO's main mandate, but not on how VCs are used which is generally determined by donors directly with the IO's secretariat. What is alarming is the fact that the RB of various IOs has fallen over the years to become inferior to VCs, such that it is no longer unusual for VC to now exceed RB by 3:1, as is the case for the WHO, or higher, as is the case of the Office of the High Commissioner on Human Rights.[3] Increasingly, since IOs have little left in the RB after paying for their recurring overheads, donors largely determine work programmes by leveraging on their VCs. The practical effect of the First World being mainly interested, for instance, in the tackling rich people's diseases, has led to so-called "neglected diseases", until such diseases, like Ebola, threaten to spread to affect everyone.

The ongoing Ebola crisis has drawn the world's attention to some failings of the WHO. However, a number of analysts who have examined the issues more in-depth have noted that the deep RB cuts in recent years that

---

[3] Since he who pays the piper calls the tune, that the Office derives from developed States and NGOs 80% of its resources seriously raises the question of whom the Office answers to, and it undermines the High Commissioner's credibility in addressing countries on human rights concerns.

the WHO had been subjected to were a key underlying cause of its deterio-
rated capacity.[4] As those cuts were being imposed, top WHO officials rightly
fretted that something would eventually give in terms of the WHO's
response to specific health crisis situations. The poor initial response to this
Ebola outbreak has proven them prescient. All this is not to say that the
WHO and other IOs are paragons of effective efficient use of their resources.
But my respect goes out to the many IO professionals who try their best to
do a good job for humankind under trying financial and political circumstances. Diplomats with good IO contacts have all heard enough inside
stories of manipulation by the more powerful states through all sorts of
interferences and machinations. I have also experienced attempts, in small
settings, by powerful states to intimidate Singapore, albeit to no avail.

On other issues, such as nuclear energy, the International Atomic
Energy Agency (IAEA) also has its RB constraints, within which the tussle is
constant between developed countries, which want it to focus on verifica-
tions to ensure the peaceful use of nuclear technology, and developing
countries, which look to the IAEA for useful technological applications for
their development (e.g., in industry, agriculture, medical facilities, etc.).[5]
That the First World seems only interested to advance its own interests and
has resorted to subverting the system undermine mutual trust necessary for
the world to collectively solve problems in the global commons like climate
change.

Nevertheless, ultimately, everyone needs the UN, so things will
hopefully change for the better. Where Singapore is concerned, it has tried,
where feasible, to be a voice of reason,[6] putting forth innovative ideas to
bridge divides. It has also shown empathy for and solidarity with developing countries, including through sharing its developmental experiences,

---

[4] E.g., see "An underfunded WHO is incapable of fighting Ebola" by Kishore Mahbubani in
The Financial Times, 15 October 2014, and "WHO — Too Big to Ail" in *The Economist*,
13 December 2014.

[5] This North-South divide in interests reminds me of an episode when the US delegation tried,
in all seriousness and sincerity, to propose a UN resolution on cooperation to protect critical
infrastructure. Many officials from poor developing countries were at a loss, with some asking
what this infrastructure was, while others noted the obvious need to have something before one
could protect it.

[6] We have on occasions spoken up for getting things right, rather than to save a penny on
prevention only to spend foolish pounds later to solve crises.

training over 90,000 developing countries officials since 1992 under the Singapore Cooperation Programme alone. Singapore has also done its bit to fight neglected diseases by partnering Novartis in the Institute for Tropical Diseases.

---◦◦---

TAN York Chor is, since 2011, Singapore's Ambassador to France and to Portugal. He joined the Civil Service in 1985. Until 2002, he had worked in various capacities in the Ministry of Defence and the Ministry of Foreign Affairs (MFA), including at the Singapore Embassies in Paris and Bangkok, and the Singapore High Commission in Canberra, as a Deputy Director in MFA's Southeast Asia Directorate, and as Senior Deputy Director for North America and Europe. From 2002 to 2005, he was concurrently Deputy High Commissioner in the Singapore High Commission to Canada and Deputy Permanent Representative to the UN in New York. More recently, he was MFA's Director for Europe from 2006 to 2007 and concurrently Director for International Economics in 2006, and Director for International Organisations in 2007. From 2007 to 2010, he was Singapore's Permanent Representative to the United Nations and other international organisations in Geneva and to the International Atomic Energy Agency in Vienna.

Merits of Multilateralism

Burhan GAFOOR

The United Nations (UN) is the largest arena for the exercise of "multilateral" diplomacy. At the UN, multiple countries work together not only to advance a common good but also to advance their own individual interests. For all countries, and especially for small countries, multilateral diplomacy at the UN is an essential part of their foreign policy.

Dag Hammarskjold, the second UN Secretary-General, famously said that "the UN was not created to take humanity to heaven but to save it from hell". It is worth noting that the UN was not designed to solve all the problems of the world. However, it provides a forum for countries to manage tensions in an inter-dependent world.

The UN is important to small countries, for three main reasons. Firstly, the UN embodies and entrenches a rules-based international system. Secondly, it provides a platform for small countries to build a network of friends and enlarge their diplomatic and geopolitical space. Thirdly, it provides small countries an opportunity to play a constructive role globally and thereby increase their profile within the community of nations. The three reasons are inter-related.

Multilateralism and the Rule of Law

The UN provides the framework for an international system based on the rule of law. The UN Charter establishes the basic parameters for international cooperation, such as the sovereign equality of all states, the peaceful resolution of disputes, and the principle of non-interference in the domestic affairs of states. It delegitimises the notion that "might is right" in international relations.

The UN cannot prevent the deeply ingrained instinct of larger countries to act unilaterally to advance their own interests. Neither can the UN change the reality that the world is made up of big powers and small states. But it does put the onus on all states to explain and justify their actions in terms of the UN Charter and international law. And when a state's actions violate established rules and principles, it provides legitimacy for a response from the international community.

As a small state, we have an abiding interest in strengthening the rules-based framework through the adoption of treaties, norms and guidelines. More importantly, we have a greater interest in ensuring that any treaties or rules adopted are in line with Singapore's interests or, at the least, not inimical to Singapore's interests. The UN Convention on the Law of the Sea (UNCLOS), which governs international conduct on maritime issues, is a good example of the treaty making power of the UN. Professor Tommy Koh, who was Chair of Third UN Conference on the Law of the Sea, and Professor S. Jayakumar, who later became Foreign Minister, played key roles in the negotiations and the adoption of UNCLOS.

In 2006, I made a small contribution to the adoption of a Treaty relating to simplified procedures to register Trade Marks at the World Intellectual Property Organization (WIPO). I was privileged to chair the WIPO Diplomatic Conference that negotiated, finalised and adopted the treaty in Singapore in March 2006. The treaty, known formally as the Singapore Treaty, remains to this day as the only treaty named after Singapore.

In recent years, the UN negotiations on climate change have emerged as one of the most important exercises in establishing global rules and norms. I was privileged to serve Singapore in this area, as Ambassador and Chief Negotiator for climate change negotiations at the UN Framework Convention on Climate Change (UNFCCC). As a small-island country, Singapore is vulnerable to the effects of climate change. Naturally, we have a strong interest in promoting a global agreement on climate change. At the same time, we have an equal interest in promoting a global agreement that does not penalise a small city-state with an export-oriented economy like Singapore.

For a small state like Singapore, the adoption of a multilateral agreement on climate change is a superior outcome to a regime based on unilateral actions and trade sanctions. Over the past few years, several ideas we advocated in the climate negotiations have been accepted in the negotiations. One of the lessons I learned is that, in multilateral diplomacy, it is important to explain one's proposals again and again, to gain mindshare and build support. There has to be constant lobbying and outreach, before proposals gain traction. It is a slow and patient process.

In the lead-up to the UN climate conference in Copenhagen in 2009, many developed countries wanted to impose a "cookie-cutter" solution to reducing carbon emissions. One idea advocated was to allocate carbon reduction targets to each country based on per capita GDP and/or their per capita carbon emissions. We strongly resisted this idea not only because it would penalise small countries like Singapore but also because it would relieve developed countries of their historical responsibilities for carbon emissions.

Ambassador Chew Tai Soo, one of Singapore's distinguished multilateral diplomats and the first Chief Negotiator for climate change, led the charge in defending Singapore's position. When I took over from him in 2010, I continued to argue that wealth or GDP in itself was not a good indicator of a country's potential to reduce carbon emissions. We explained that Singapore is already an energy-efficient economy with no fuel subsidies and with very little access to alternative energy and very limited potential to further reduce carbon emissions. Additionally, we are a hub-economy that serves the region and the world. For instance, Singapore has always been an important hub for the refining of petroleum, a carbon-intensive industry. Yet, very little of that is consumed in Singapore because our electricity is produced from natural gas, a much cleaner form of fossil fuel.

In the climate change negotiations, we promoted the idea of creating a framework of rules that would acknowledge "national circumstances" and allow each country to put forward its own carbon reduction targets. We argued that an approach based on "national circumstances" would raise ambition by facilitating participation and contribution from every country. We worked with other countries, including larger ones, to advance our idea. The Singapore team provided inputs and "intellectual leadership" wherever possible to advance the notion of accommodating national circumstances. Significantly, after years of lobbying, our argument became entrenched after it was endorsed by a decision adopted at the Warsaw Conference on Climate Change in 2013.

UN as a Platform for Networking

This leads me to my second point: the UN provides the platform for small countries to build a network of friends and thereby enlarge their diplomatic and geopolitical space. Through the UN, small countries can magnify their strength and influence by working with other countries. Put simply, multilateral diplomacy allows smaller countries to gain strength through numbers.

In the 1990s, a group of small-island countries banded together to form the Alliance of Small Island States (AOSIS), which till today remains a powerful force at the UN on climate change and sustainable development issues. Singapore was invited to join this group at an early stage, an invitation we did not hesitate to accept. To this day, the AOSIS countries, who are mostly from the Pacific, Caribbean and the Indian Ocean regions, remain very important friends for Singapore. Similarly, in the 1990s, Singapore took the initiative to create a grouping of small countries at the UN, known as the Forum of Small States (FOSS), which was the brainchild of then-Permanent Representative Ambassador Chew Tai Soo.

One of the key lessons in multilateral diplomacy that I have learned over the years is the importance of personal relationships. Lord Palmerston, a 19th Century British statesman, is credited with the saying that in relations between states, there are no permanent friends but only permanent interests. This is true but it does not preclude the important role of personal relationships in diplomacy. A good personal relationship based on mutual trust and confidence can help to secure the support or vote of other countries.

In 2005, as Permanent Representative to the UN in Geneva, I was involved in lobbying for support for a statement that asserted the sovereign rights of countries to impose capital punishment. We argued that capital punishment should be treated as an issue of criminal justice and not as an issue of human rights. Every year, we lobbied other countries to support our statement. There were many countries who signed up to our statement. There were several, in particular from Africa, who signed up to our statement based on their personal relationship with me. As it turned out, in 2005, we obtained the highest number of supporters for our statement. This was the result of active lobbying not only by me and my colleagues in Geneva, but also by our diplomats around the world. The lesson I learned is that personal relationships cannot be underestimated in multilateral diplomacy.

UN as a Platform for Building Bridges

Multilateral diplomacy is a messy affair. In any given negotiation at the UN, more than one hundred countries are involved. At the UN, it is never easy to find common ground acceptable to all of them. There is a saying at the UN that "nothing is agreed until everything is agreed". Added to this, there is always a dynamic of tension between countries and groups of countries (not to mention personalities), each with their own vision of a good global agreement. Inevitably, there are disagreements, divisions and delays. The landscape is constantly shifting and small countries have to navigate treacherous shoals or find themselves shipwrecked and abandoned to the sharks, to put it metaphorically.

This leads me to my third point, which is that the fractured landscape of multilateral negotiations offers small countries like Singapore an opportunity to build bridges and increase its influence. At the UN, a disinterested party is often required to bridge differences and create a common position. In many instances, Singapore has been called upon to play the role of a bridge builder. We are seen as a serious and credible country that would be acceptable as an honest-broker to different groups of countries.

There are many examples of Singapore diplomats and negotiators who have made stellar contributions as chairpersons and facilitators at UN negotiations. When Singapore diplomats play such a role, they project a positive image of Singapore at an international level. More importantly, they build influence for Singapore and help to shape the outcome of negotiations.

In 2010, when I assumed the role of Chief Negotiator for Climate Change, I was asked by the Secretariat of the UNFCCC to be the "facilitator" for negotiations on climate finance, one of the most contentious issues in the climate negotiations. Singapore was seen as a credible bridge between the positions of developed and developing countries. I made a small contribution to the process, by identifying common elements in a deeply divisive discussion. The common elements that I helped to facilitate became part of the decision adopted at the UN Climate Conference in Cancun in 2010 and led to the creation of a new climate fund, known as the Green Climate Fund (GCF). This enhanced Singapore's image as a constructive player and increased my personal influence, which in turn allowed me to better advance Singapore's interests in the negotiations.

In multilateral negotiations, small countries can enhance their influence by proposing compromise solutions. Even if one is not formally appointed as chairperson or facilitator, one could propose solutions to move the process forward. The lesson here is to continuously seek opportunities to be an active presence for Singapore in such fora. I recall one such experience in the climate change negotiations in May 2012 when the process became dead-locked because there was no agreement on the agenda for the meeting. We spent a whole week trying to negotiate a one-page agenda. As someone put it, it was a negotiation about what to negotiate.

The fight over the agenda was a proxy for deep differences over substance. As Singapore, while we had our own views on substance, the impasse on the agenda was not helpful to the overall process as it delayed the substantive discussions. I decided that I should try and help break the deadlock so that actual negotiations on substance could begin. I offered various suggestions at late-night meetings. On the last day, hours before the meeting was scheduled to end, I offered a solution that was broadly acceptable to many and grudgingly accepted by some.[1] The proposal I put forward paved the way for the adoption of the agenda. Not only did I help the meeting to end on a successful note, I also helped to establish Singapore's credentials as a constructive player in the process. Again, this helped to increase Singapore's reputation and influence in the process that served us well in the larger negotiations.

Ultimately, for small countries, multilateral diplomacy at the UN has many merits. It should be noted, however, that multilateral diplomacy is not always about building bridges and facilitating a compromise. That is just one instrument in the tool-kit of a multilateral diplomat. In any multilateral negotiation, one has to deploy a variety of approaches to advance national interests. As a rule, one has to build allies and mobilise support for one's position. However, it is also necessary to demonstrate resolve and firmness, by standing firm. From time to time, it will be necessary to block or prevent a particular outcome that is inimical to Singapore's interest.

---

[1] The compromise proposal which I put forward was that there would be a footnote to the agenda that would essentially give assurance to the different groups that their right to raise issues would not be prejudiced by the agenda. To this day, the agenda and the footnote continue to provide the framework for the ongoing negotiations at the Ad-Hoc Working Group on the Durban Platform at the UNFCCC. It can be accessed at the website of the UNFCCC as document FCC/ADP/2012/L.1

At the end of the day, multilateral diplomacy is not about achieving just any outcome, regardless of its impact on Singapore. It is about shaping an outcome that takes into account our interests and concerns, and being hard-nosed about what is in Singapore's best interests. When a diplomat has the opportunity to make a small contribution that serves his country's interests and also advances a positive multilateral agenda, the satisfaction is truly tremendous.

———————

Burhan GAFOOR is currently High Commissioner of Singapore to Australia. Prior to this, he was Ambassador and Chief Negotiator for Climate Change issues. From 2007 to 2010, he served as Ambassador to France and concurrently accredited as Ambassador to Portugal. From 2004 to 2007, he was Permanent Representative to the United Nations in Geneva and to the World Trade Organization. While in Geneva, he was concurrently accredited as Ambassador to Turkey and also served as Singapore's Governor in the Board of Governors of the International Atomic Energy Agency in Vienna. He served as Press Secretary to then-Prime Minister Mr Goh Chok Tong from 2002 to 2004. He joined the Ministry of Foreign Affairs (MFA) in 1988 and has served various assignments, including as First Secretary at the Singapore Mission to the United Nations in New York. He graduated with a Bachelor of Social Science (Honours) degree in Political Science from the National University of Singapore in 1988. He also received a Master's in Public Administration from the John F. Kennedy School of Government at Harvard University in 1997 and a diploma in public administration from the École Nationale d'Administration (ENA) in Paris in 2002. He received the Public Administration Medal (Silver) in 2001 and the Public Administration Medal (Gold) in 2013 from the Singapore Government. In 2011, the French Government awarded him a medal with the title of "Grand Officier de l'Ordre National du Mérite".

WTO: Keep the Faith

KWOK Fook Seng

The *leitmotif* of Singapore's 50 years at the United Nations would be our consistent support and defence of the multilateral system. As a small nation susceptible to the uncertainties of a globalised world, our desire to see a stable and just system of global governance has intensified, more so as geopolitical and economic complexities deepen over time. Nowhere does this hold more true for us than at the World Trade Organization (WTO), given our status and heritage as a free trading nation whose external trade is a staggering 400% of our GDP.

The WTO is a highly specialised agency of the UN system which is not well understood by many. Perhaps best known for the slow pace of negotiations in the Doha Round of trade liberalisation, many understandably express scepticism about the relevance and viability of the WTO. Yet this scepticism understates the mathematical permutations in play. Trying to bring a common interest to bear upon 160 member states in nine broad negotiating pillars with numerous sub-issues which all involve legally binding international obligations is no walk in the park. Under the surface, there is so much more at work than meets the eye.

While public disenchantment remains the narrative, the world takes for granted that the fundamentals emplaced by the predecessor of the WTO, the General Agreement on Tariffs and Trade (GATT), have prevailed and still provide the strong basis for trading relationships around the world. For governments who seek policy space to pursue national interests, there is already a set of rules which are in play, enforced and upheld by the WTO. The challenge is that new trading relationships and practices are starting to outgrow those rules, and the members of the WTO are not yet able to keep up. This is not so different from situations in domestic governance and regulation. Look at how a car sharing app like Uber can be worth billions overnight and spark regulatory dilemma around the world. What should be the new rules to regulate this 'market'? Opinions differ surely, because there are cross-generational value sets in play. The iPhone generation sees no real harm done, but the traditional industry which represents the livelihoods of hardworking taxi drivers and their dependents around the world beg to differ. If any genius can square this circle, then we have a good chance to solve some of the impasse which plagues the Doha Round.

That world trade is able to flow systematically and without major disruptions despite any number of global economic and financial crises is testament to the fundamentals built by the earlier trade rounds. This includes the seminal Dispute Settlement Understanding established under the Uruguay Round in 1994, which put in place a robust and predictable system to adjudicate trade disputes, giving businesses and investors predictability and confidence to keep our trading world going. All this certainty is quietly ensured by the WTO today, as the guardian against protectionism and other forms of unfair trade practice.

Outside of the Doha Round, WTO members meet in annual cycles of specialised technical bodies to update each other, critique each others' policies, troubleshoot problems and negotiate fixes to the implementation of existing rules and disciplines to help them withstand the test of time. Many decisions taken and implemented in such bodies will never make the news because the successful updating of phytosanitary standards, for instance, grabs far fewer headlines than the inability of world governments to reach agreement on an infinitely complex deal. There is a compelling argument to keep such technical work uncontaminated by the politics of the negotiations, but it gets increasingly hard.

In an uncommon flash of common sense, WTO members sealed the Agreement on Trade Facilitation in December 2013. When implemented, these commitments would ease red tape at borders, ports promise benefits to consumers worldwide, and is an apt response to critics who have pronounced the organisation dead. Such critics should be careful what they ask for. A world with no facilitative trade rules is a world where our iPhones and Galaxy tablets will cost many multiples of what we pay today.

To be certain, the WTO is not without its problems. Its foremost problem is a vacuum of cooperative leadership at the global level, something determined by the hard knocks of geopolitics. This is compounded by shortcomings at the national level where governments find it more expedient to attribute domestic policy failures to the vagaries of the multilateral trading system which they themselves help to paralyse. This situation plagues many international negotiations, some with stakes even higher than at the WTO.

The WTO's resources and mandate are not as expansive as the UN system of which it is a part. Yet there is great professionalism and dedication in the people who populate both the WTO Secretariat and the member economies whom they serve. The importance of trade can be measured by the quality of the human capital which countries despatch to advance and protect their complex interests. For a novice like me, it gave me a great sense of privilege to work shoulder to shoulder with some of the finest trade experts and negotiators from every corner of the world. The battles are hard fought, yet the solutions reached are often both innovative and complex — testament to the fact that WTO members can and do find agreement. Even in a dispute, it is this same constructive spirit that leads disputing parties to accept and implement the final outcomes determined by the Dispute Settlement Body.

The first rate leadership of the organisation itself can also be traced through the various Directors-General since its evolution from the GATT to the WTO under New Zealand's Mike Moore to, more recently, one of Europe's foremost technocrats Pascal Lamy and today, the highly accomplished Brazilian diplomat Roberto Azevêdo. The specialised nature of trade requires a serendipitous combination of diplomacy, technical knowledge and legal insight to forge agreements in the legislative pillar of the WTO. The Director-General as the Chair of the Trade Negotiation Committee must master these driving forces to advance negotiations. This is why the unique selection process of the WTO Director-General places far greater emphasis on technical competence and the leadership ability of the individual, over the political significance of a candidate's nationality.

To those who dismiss the WTO as dysfunctional, I appeal that they try to disaggregate the complexity. The institution is sound, but it is primarily and ultimately driven by its members. The lack of common vision and direction lies with the membership, and like-mindedness is an increasingly rare commodity among nations. The WTO is like that old friend whom we so easily take for granted because she is so dependable and loyal. It is that someone who benignly supports us as we stubbornly chart our own wilful path in life. We do not appreciate the depth of such loyalty and often even resent its well-meaning disciplines. Yet we will definitely miss that constant stewardship if it is suddenly gone. The best way to reciprocate this kind of loyal friend is to work at updating the institution, to make it fit for the purposes of our complicated times (and for the generations yet to come). May those who are empowered to represent the international trading community step up to this task, and never have to learn the remorse of ingratitude to a faithful friend.

KWOK Fook Seng is currently Singapore's Ambassador and Chief Negotiator for Climate Change at the Ministry of Foreign Affairs. His service at the Ministry included portfolios at the Singapore Permanent Mission to the United Nations in New York, as Special Assistant to the Foreign Minister, and the Special Projects Desk handling cases of international arbitration at the International Tribunal for Law of the Sea and the International Court of Justice. Fook Seng also served as Deputy High Commissioner in Kuala Lumpur and Director-General of the ASEAN-Singapore National Secretariat. From 2011 to 2014, he was Singapore's Permanent Representative to the World Trade Organization (WTO) and the World Intellectual Property Organization (WIPO) in Geneva. He presently leads the negotiating team which is working towards a new global agreement at the UN Framework Convention on Climate Change (UNFCCC).

Doing Stuff; Doing Good

FOO Kok Jwee

There is a story often told by international development workers to describe their work. It is about how a man strolling along a beach saw a boy picking up, and then throwing one starfish at a time back into the sea. The boy told the man that he was trying to save the starfishes washed up on the beach — they would die if they remained beached without water. When the man chided the boy that he could not possibly save all the starfishes on the beach, the boy looked at the man in the eye, threw another starfish back into the sea, and said "*Made a difference to that one*", and continued his task!

Development workers from the United Nations (UN) and all over the world identify with this story because they passionately believe the work they do help change the lives of people they touch. Sometimes, progress is measured by one person at a time.

Development is one of the UN's three core pillars (along with peace and security, and human rights). Yet, the UN is often derided by its detractors for being an institution that is more words than deeds. More associated with pithy speeches and meandering resolutions than 'doing stuff'. But the UN has been 'doing stuff' through its development work all these years. It has helped focus attention, marshal resources, and mobilise nations to reduce poverty, promote prosperity and protect the global environment.

One such seminal moment was when the UN brought together world leaders in 2000 to commit their countries and resources to help all nations attain the Millennium Development Goals (MDGs) by 2015. Because of the MDGs, the world has since reduced extreme poverty by half; improved access to drinking water for more than 2.3 billion people; increased political participation of women; and created conditions for development assistance to rebound, among its many achievements.[1]

Singapore may be a small country. But we are also "doing stuff" with the UN, and doing good by contributing to the UN's development agenda. We do this primarily through the Singapore Cooperation Programme (SCP). Singapore established the SCP in 1992 when we had reached a certain level of development. Singapore had benefitted in significant ways from technical assistance in our early years. We turned to the United Nations Development Programme (UNDP) for help to develop an economic blueprint after we attained self-rule in 1959. The UNDP team was headed by Dutch economist Dr Albert Winsemius, who later became the Singapore government's Chief Economic Advisor. Among his early suggestions was the creation of a one-stop investor agency — what we now know as the Economic Development Board (EDB). We also sought and received technical expertise from the UN and other international organisations like UNIDO, UNCTAD, WHO and ILO.

Having benefitted from the help we received, we are now giving something back to the international community via the SCP simply because it is the right thing to do as a responsible global citizen. We also believe that all peoples ought to enjoy some basic fruits of social and economic development. But we understood from our own experience that technical assistance is equally, if not more effective, than financial aid or loans in creating the right conditions for sustainable development. We therefore share Singapore's development experiences — our successes as well as mistakes we have made along the way — through SCP training programmes and study visits in areas where Singapore is strong in, such as Public Administration, Economic Development, Urban Planning, Sustainable Development, Port Management, Civil Aviation and Water Management. We also work with UN agencies such as the UNDP, UNCTAD, UNICEF to share our policies in economic development, trade and investment, education, science, technology and innovation with other developing UN member states.

The SCP is very well received by Singapore's friends and partners. By 2015, the SCP has trained over 100,000 officials from more than 170 countries. Singapore may not contribute billions of dollars in development aid in

---

[1] The Millennium Development Goals Report 2014.

the headline-grabbing way like advanced economies and OECD countries do. But our contributions via the SCP on a per capita basis are very respectable. The SCP is successful only because Singapore is successful. Singapore stands as a powerful example because we have shown that a small country without natural resources can survive and thrive as long as it has good leadership, political stability, rule of law, pragmatism, well-run and forward-looking institutions, and continuous investment in its citizens.

Doing good through development in the UN and international system ought to be a straightforward matter. But it is often not. The global challenges we face are numerous and complex. All nations, even superpowers and wealthy OECD members, have finite resources to bring to bear to resolve these wicked problems. So nations are forced to be selective and strategic about where and how they get involved. National interests demand that nations direct their finite development aid to best serve their own political and policy goals, regardless how they sugar-coat their intentions in the name of altruism, virtues or values.

Committing billions of dollars to build infrastructure may bring commercial benefits to companies of the donor countries, or facilitate the flow of goods to them. Helping to uplift the middle class of populous nations through education or economic development assistance could mean bigger markets and economic opportunities for companies of donor countries. Providing development aid can help prop up friendly (and pliant) regimes. Sometimes, "national interests" are even more narrowly defined. Some nations promote and project their values to other countries through "technical assistance" just to preserve their domestic base which are advocating those same values, or simply because political "values" are about the only virtues left in their diplomatic toolkit that they can credibly espouse overseas. The spectre of development aid being pulled by donors if they failed to act (or vote) the "right way" in the UN or in international fora is a real one for more than a few developing countries.

Singapore is no different. We help other countries build capacity via the SCP because it also helps Singapore. Singapore is a small state and a price-taker in international relations. We cannot prosper in a turbulent and unstable environment. It is therefore in our interests to do what we can to help others so that our region is stable, prosperous, equipped to capitalise on globalisation, and attractive to foreign investors. At a broader level,

Singapore is more secure when countries all around the world are better equipped to deal with transboundary challenges such as financial crises, terrorism, pandemics and climate change. These threats are magnified by the inter-connectedness of our world today. The SCP has also helped Singapore gain many friends whose support at the UN and other international fora are crucial when we need to advance or defend Singapore's interests.

It is also common to see developed and developing nations square off in the UN and international fora over development assistance in almost every major issue. The central argument is usually framed around developing countries pressuring their developed counterparts to provide greater quantity and higher quality development assistance without conditionalities, while the donors seek assurances of accountability and evidence of progress that their assistance is working.

Some nations deliberately demand more than they know the donors are prepared to give, just so that they can externalise their domestic shortcomings. They can then blame the donors and the international community for not giving them enough assistance and expertise to deal with their domestic problems so as to deflect criticism from their own populations.

Development work might once have been the province of humanitarians and charities. But more governments now realise that development aid can become a key pillar of their diplomacy and an effective tool to gain more allies through soft power by winning hearts and minds. Many major aid agencies such as USAID and AUSAID had thus restructured their operations in recent years to be more aligned to their foreign policy and international security posture.

But as the boundary separating foreign policy and domestic policy becomes increasingly blurred in today's world, it is also getting harder for governments to persuade their citizens that giving development aid still matters to their nation's security and prosperity. Or that it is more "cost-effective" to provide development aid to prevent major natural and man-made disasters, than to commit an exponentially larger amount to manage the crises ex-post.

This is because governments are increasingly being asked by their citizens why they are spending taxpayer dollars to improve the lives of people in the developing world when there is so much hardship at home; when their jobs are no longer secure because of globalisation and automation; when they are forced to bear the brunt of high taxes; or when they suffer from the consequences of widening income inequality and lack of social mobility? There is also greater public scrutiny on how public funds are used for development aid. Governments will have to spend more time and effort to persuade their citizens that development aid is a strategic, economic, and even moral imperative central to the advancement and defence of their national interests.

Singapore has limited resources and cannot meet all requests for development assistance. But we can do more even as our government remains focused on taking care of Singaporeans as their utmost priority. We can achieve this by providing smarter aid through the SCP by concentrating our efforts in areas where we can make the greatest positive impact; experiment with new tools such as Public-Private Partnerships, and revitalise our network of partnerships with the UN, other aid agencies and International Organisations.

We have already embarked on this path. At the 2014 3rd International Conference on Small Island Development States (SIDS), Singapore announced a 3-year package that includes customised programmes on the most important challenges faced by SIDS such as sustainable development, climate change, public health and food security. We are also collaborating with the United Nations International Strategy for Disaster Reduction (UNISDR) to jointly conduct on a training course in 2015 to help small island developing states build capacity in Disaster Risk Deduction (DRR) as a concrete outcome for the 3rd World Conference on Disaster Risk Reduction in Sendai in March 2015. Singapore will also contribute via the SCP in meaningful ways towards the post-2015 Development Agenda. Doing good and protecting one's national interests are not mutually exclusive.

FOO Kok Jwee is currently Singapore's Ambassador and Permanent Representative to the United Nations Office and other international organisations in Geneva. He is also concurrently Singapore's Resident Representative to the International Atomic Energy Agency (IAEA). Kok Jwee joined the Singapore Foreign Service in 1999 after graduating with a Bachelor in Mechanical Engineering from the National University of Singapore. He later earned a Master in Public Administration from the Kennedy School of Government, Harvard University. Kok Jwee served in Singapore's Embassy in Jakarta between 2002 and 2006, and held various appointments in MFA's Southeast Asia Directorate, Americas Directorate, and Diplomatic Academy. He ran the Singapore Cooperation Programme (SCP) as the Director-General of MFA's Technical Cooperation Directorate between 2011 and 2014. Kok Jwee was also Press Secretary to Senior Minister (and later Emeritus Senior Minister) Goh Chok Tong from 2010 to 2014.

Singapore's Contribution to the WTO Dispute Mechanism: Reflections of a Singapore Negotiator

Margaret LIANG

The establishment of a dispute settlement mechanism to preserve the rights and obligations of members and to interpret and enforce rules is fundamental to the proper functioning of the multilateral trading system. Trade disputes arise when there is a breach of multilaterally negotiated binding rules and commitments by a party. Another party, affected by such measures, could invoke the dispute settlement mechanism if such measures are deemed to have violated[1] the GATT/WTO rules and have affected their benefits/rights under the WTO.

The WTO Understanding on Rules and Procedures Governing the Settlement of Disputes (DSU) is one of the key Agreements to emerge from the Uruguay Round (UR) multilateral trade negotiations. The DSU and the administrative body it creates, the Dispute Settlement Body (DSB), replaces the old GATT dispute settlement process. In essence the DSU aims to codify the experience gained under the GATT dispute settlement procedures over four decades and also to address the shortcomings under the GATT procedures.

The WTO DSU and Uruguay Round Negotiations: Singapore's Role

Prior to the commencement of the Uruguay Round negotiations, the GATT Contracting Parties felt that the GATT dispute settlement mechanism required reform. The GATT procedures were perceived to have certain deficiencies, among them a lack of deadlines, a consensus decision-making

---

[1] To note: There could also be "non-violation" complaints.

process that allowed a GATT party against whom a dispute was filed to block the establishment of a dispute panel and the adoption of a panel report, and laxity in surveillance and implementation of panel reports even when reports were adopted, which led to delays in, and non-compliance with panel rulings.

Singapore was among those countries that strongly supported the negotiations to reform the GATT procedures and to strengthen the dispute settlement mechanism. As a small country whose economy is heavily dependent on access to the global markets, it is important to have trade rules that provide for an open and predictable multilateral trading system, where the rights/interests of small countries could be protected, in particular, by an efficient dispute settlement mechanism. It was thus in Singapore's interest to strengthen the rules on dispute settlement which would discourage contracting parties from taking unilateral actions outside the GATT. As a small trading nation with little economic clout, we needed to have strengthened dispute settlement rules which could protect Singapore against restrictive measures taken by our trading partners.

I was Singapore's negotiator for dispute settlement in the Uruguay Round. I worked closely with "like-minded" countries, such as the US, Canada, Hong Kong, Switzerland, and Uruguay, who together, helped to create the DSU which sets out a mechanism that is overall more "rules-bound" and judicial in approach than the dispute settlement mechanism under the GATT that was more "voluntary" in nature.

The need for reform of the GATT dispute settlement rules had widespread support and although there were differences in overall approach and in some details, changes in the DS procedures was amongst the "early harvest" results of the Round agreed in Montreal in December in 1988 and implemented in May 1989. Procedural issues such as strict timelines for the DS process were non-contentious and received general support. The more difficult contentious issues included the following:

a) Should consensus be maintained or should greater automaticity be introduced for the establishment of panels and adoption of panel reports?
b) Concern over unilateral measures taken outside of GATT rules. This was aimed at US Section 301 and US Super 301 legislations where the US had initiated unilateral trade actions against their trading partners.
c) Issues of implementation, compensation and retaliation.

The US, supported by Canada pressed for changes which would make panels virtually automatic and more legalistic. In contrast, both the EU and Japan sought changes to increase the use of the consultation, conciliation and mediation aspects of the DS system. Amongst the developing countries, Argentina, Brazil, Jamaica, Mexico, Nicaragua, India, Uruguay,[2] Hong Kong and Singapore were active in the negotiations. Brazil, Nicaragua and India pressed for changes to strengthen the special and differential treatment of developing countries. Jamaica, Hong Kong and Singapore advocated greater third party participation rights. A proposal was also submitted by the De La Paix[3] group to bridge the differences between the developing country hardliners and the major developed countries. Their proposals included a tighter timetable for different stages of the process, mandating the WTO Director-General to resolve differences in panel selection, removing disputing countries' rights to block any findings and introducing binding arbitration. As a result of these efforts, several changes tightening procedures and timeframe were accepted and implemented in 1989 on a trial basis.

From 1989 to 1990, negotiations focussed on the procedure for adopting panel reports, the timeline for implementation, compensation and retaliation, unilateral measures, rules for "non-violation" cases, and special and differential treatment for developing countries. The EU pushed for prohibition of unilateral actions. The proposal for an Appellate Body Review stage was pressed by the US and Canada. Several countries, including Singapore had initial reservations about introducing a Review phase as this would delay the proceedings and would likely become the rule than the exception. Finally, it was accepted that the additional time required for the Appellate Body Review would be about three months, and it would focus on narrow legal questions. The US proposal on "Reverse Consensus", supported by EU, was finally adopted which introduced greater automaticity in the panel proceedings.

Although the Uruguay Round negotiations as a whole continued until late 1993, the bulk of the work on DS was finished and included in the Draft

---

[2] The Chairman of the DS Negotiating Group was Ambassador Julio Lacarte-Muro from Uruguay.

[3] This was a 12-country coalition which included Australia, Canada, Hungary, Japan, Korea, New Zealand, Sweden, Switzerland, Columbia, Hong Kong, Singapore, Uruguay. The De La Paix group was named after the hotel in Geneva where they first met.

Final Act in late 1991. The establishment of the WTO DSU was a significant outcome. The WTO dispute settlement rules have been improved and strengthened insofar as there are now more explicit and definitive rules and procedures that will expedite the dispute settlement process, and prevent parties from blocking the adoption of panel reports and implementation of panel recommendations like in the past. Significantly, the DSU prohibits WTO Members from applying unilateral actions to address violations of trade rules. (This was apparently US' concession in exchange for the "reverse-consensus" or "automaticity" rule.)

The WTO Dispute Settlement process consists of four broad stages: (1) consultations; (2) panel process and, if requested, (3) Appellate Body Review; and (4) surveillance of implementation.

The WTO dispute settlement mechanism has thus been effectively strengthened and given more "teeth" and offers, in particular, the following improvements over the old GATT procedures.

a) Prescribed time frames

Definitive time frames have been established for each stage of the dispute settlement process. This is to ensure that parties do not block or delay the completion of the dispute settlement.

b) Automaticity of Panel Process

The DSU sets out an automatic process for every stage of the dispute settlement proceedings. The DSU reverses the past GATT practice, in a manner that prevents individual Members from blocking certain DSB decisions that are considered critical to an effective dispute settlement system. Thus, unless it decides by consensus *not* to do so, the DSB will (1) approve requests to establish panels, (2) adopt panel and Appellate Body reports, and (3) if requested by the prevailing Members in the dispute, authorize the Member to impose a retaliatory measure where the defending Member has not complied. In effect, these decisions are virtually automatic.

c) Appellate Review

The establishment of an appellate review mechanism gives disputants the possibility of appealing against panel decisions to a standing Appellate Body.

d) Strict Surveillance of Implementation

Prompt compliance with the rulings of the DSB is required. Panel recommendations are to be implemented "within a reasonable period". In the event of non-compliance within the specified time, the DSB permits retaliation.

Singapore's Participation in WTO Dispute Cases

Singapore was the first WTO Member to seek recourse under the WTO dispute settlement process, shortly after the WTO came into force on 1 January 1995. On 10 January 1995, Singapore requested consultations with Malaysia under the DSU as Malaysia had imposed on 7 April 1994 an import prohibition order on two types of petrochemicals, Poly-Ethylene (PE) and Poly-Propylene (PP). The Malaysian measure prohibited all imports of these petrochemical products unless an import licence known as an Approved Permit (AP) was granted by the Director-General of Customs, acting on behalf of the Ministry of International Trade and Industry (MITI). Malaysia was a major market for Singapore's producers of PE and PP and Singapore's manufacturers and exporters were adversely affected by the Malaysian measure.

Consultations were the first phase of the WTO dispute settlement process, which allowed for both Malaysia and Singapore to meet within 30 days of Singapore's request, and a further 30 days for more bilateral consultations if needed. If a satisfactory outcome was not reached after the 60-day consultation phase, the complainant, Singapore, could request for the establishment of a WTO dispute settlement panel to arbitrate on the dispute. The panel would then take between 6–9 months to complete its report. Its recommendations would then be implemented by the offending party, unless the case was referred further to the WTO Appellate Body.

The Singapore dispute settlement team (the AP team) comprised See Chak Mun, leader of the team (then Singapore's Commissioner in Hong Kong and formerly Permanent Representative to the WTO/UN in Geneva), Lee Sieu Kin (then Deputy Senior State Counsel, AGC), Margaret Liang (then Deputy Director/MFA), Yong Siew Min (then Deputy Director, Trade Development Board), and Julian Chong (then Assistant Director/ MTI). Then Permanent Secretary of MTI Lam Chuan Leong and then Deputy Secretary of MFA Peter Ho provided the policy guidance to the AP negotiating team.

Although the DSU provides for two consultations within the 60-days' time-frame, Singapore had an additional third round at the request of Malaysia. Singapore's dispute with Malaysia was resolved after the third round of consultations when Malaysia decided to withdraw its AP scheme and eventually replaced it with an automatic licensing system consistent with the GATT/WTO. There was thus no need for Singapore to proceed to the next phase, which was to request for a panel. This dispute case that Singapore initiated under the WTO DSU to challenge Malaysia's measure was the first time that Singapore had invoked the WTO DSU as a complainant. A key lesson learnt is that the WTO DSU is an effective tool to help WTO Members, irrespective of size and clout, solve their trade disputes within the framework of multilaterally agreed rules. It had worked well for Singapore.

Singapore Panellists in GATT/WTO Dispute Cases

Several Singapore officials have had the experience of serving as panellist/ Chairperson in both GATT and WTO dispute cases. Where a dispute is not settled through consultations, the complainant can request the DSU to establish a panel to examine the dispute. A panel normally consists of three persons, none of whom should be a national of the complaining or respond-ing members or of a third party which has expressed interest in participating in the proceedings. The panellists serve in their individual capacity. The panellists are normally nominated by the WTO Secretariat, subject to mutual consent of the parties. If the parties cannot agree to the nominated panellists within 20 days of the panel's establishment, either party could request the WTO Director-General to appoint the panel.

Given Singapore's open trading system and as Singapore is often consid-ered as not having partisan interest in many WTO disputes, Singapore has provided a useful source for the WTO Secretariat in nominating panellists. Notwithstanding Singapore's limited pool of GATT/WTO experts, several Singapore officials have been asked by the WTO Director-General to serve on WTO dispute cases either as Chairman or panellists. This is clearly one way where Singapore can contribute to the WTO system by making itself useful in helping to resolve WTO disputes.

Since the GATT days, several MFA, MTI and AGC officials have been co-opted to serve as Chairman/panellists of various dispute cases initiated under the GATT and WTO. These included Ambassadors Tommy Koh, See Chak Mun, Chew Tai Soo, the late S. Tiwari, Elizabeth Chelliah, Minn Naing Oo and Margaret Liang. *Annex 1* provides details on their involvement as Chairperson or panellists. This core of local expertise could be tapped upon in the event that Singapore is involved in WTO dispute cases with our trading partners.

Conclusion: What It Means to Singapore

Looking back over the past 14 years since the WTO came into force on 1 January 1995, the general view is that the DSU has been effective in resolving trade disputes. Whilst the major developed countries are still the main users of the DSU, developing countries have made increasing use of the system and they have had considerable success in resolving disputes among themselves as well as against developed countries. However, one major complaint about the WTO dispute settlement system that is often made by businesses is that it takes too long to get results. On average, the time taken between initiation and conclusion of panel/Appellate Body proceedings is about 12 months. Thereafter, implementation period might take another 12 to 15 months. This is attributed in particular to certain gaps in the DSU rules concerning implementation of panel/Appellate Body recommendations. Another issue here is whether WTO members promptly take the actions required to bring their measures into compliance with their WTO obligations.

Studies have shown that whilst the overall record of implementation is relatively good, there are problem areas which could be addressed in the ongoing DSU Review negotiations in the WTO. The proposals include: (i) receipt of monetary payments to replace the right to suspend concessions, (ii) such payments or suspension of concessions could be calculated on a retrospective basis, and (iii) such payments or suspension of concessions could be increased periodically over time in the event of continued non-implementation. Many of these proposals have come from developing countries. For a small nation, retaliation is difficult against a big country as they have little to retaliate with. Hence their idea of seeking monetary payments instead. However, monetary payments may not work as the rich developed countries could simply buy themselves out, and still keep those measures that have violated the GATT/WTO. What is central to the DS

System is to find means to ensure that WTO members bring their measures into compliance with their WTO obligations. This is the weakest link in the DSU System.

———•◦•———

Margaret LIANG is Consultant to the Ministry of Foreign Affairs (MFA) for WTO/Trade Issues; Adjunct Senior Fellow of the S. Rajaratnam School of International Studies; and Senior Fellow of the MFA Diplomatic Academy. She has served in Singapore Missions in Bonn and in Geneva. She was Singapore's Deputy Permanent Representative to the UN/WTO in Geneva from 1999–2002. She has been actively involved in GATT/WTO negotiations since the launch of the Uruguay Round. From 1985–1992, she was Singapore's negotiator in the Uruguay Round, inter alia, in the areas of Anti-Dumping, Subsidies and Countervailing Duty Measures, Safeguards, Dispute Settlement, GATT Articles and Government Procurement. She was panelist in Chile/EC Import Measures on Dessert Apples; US-EC Import Measures on Dessert Apples; arbitrator in EC-US Section 110(5) of US Copyright Act; Chairman in Peru-EC Trade Description of Sardines; panelist in US Definitive Safeguards Measures on Imports of Certain Steel products; and Chairman in Korea: Measures affecting Import of Bovine Meat from Canada. She conducts WTO Trade Policy, FTA and other trade-related courses under Singapore's Technical assistance programmes for Cambodia, Laos, Myanmar Vietnam and other Developing Countries. She was the Academic Coordinator for the WTO Regional Trade Policy Course for Asia-Pacific, a joint cooperation between the WTO and the National University of Singapore from 2008 to 2010.

Annex 1

List of Singaporeans who have served in GATT/WTO Dispute Cases as Panel Chairs and Panelists

Name	Panel Chair/ Member	Dispute Case	Comments
1) Ms Mary Elizabeth Chelliah	Panel Member	DS401, DS400-EC — Measures Prohibiting the Importation and Marketing of Seal Products	
	Panel Member	DS381-US — Measures Concerning the Importation, Marketing and Sale of Tuna and Tuna Products (Recourse to Art. 21.5 by Mexico)	
	Panel Member	DS286, DS269-EC — Customs Classification of Frozen Boneless Chicken Cuts	
	Panel Member	DS243-US — Rules of Origin for Textiles and Apparel Products	
2) Mr Chew Tai Soo	Panel Member	Korea — Restrictions on Imports of Beef (Korea/ US — May 1988)	GATT Panel
		Korea — Restrictions on Imports of Beef (Korea/ Australia — May 1988)	GATT Panel
3) Prof Tommy Koh	Panel Chair	DS178-US — Safeguard Measure on Imports of Lamb Meat from Australia	
		DS177-US — Safeguard Measure on Imports of Fresh, Chilled or Frozen Lamb from New Zealand	
	Panel Chair	DS113-Canada — Measures Affecting Dairy Exports	

(Continued)

Annex 1 (*Continued*)

Name	Panel Chair/ Member	Dispute Case	Comments
		DS103-Canada — Measures Affecting the Importation of Milk and Exportation of Dairy Products	
	Panel Member	DS38-US — The Cuban Liberty and Democratic Solidarity Act (US/EU)	
4) Ms Margaret Liang	Panel Member	EC — Restrictions on Imports of Dessert Apples (EC/Chile, 1998)	GATT Panel
	Panel Member	EC — Restrictions on Imports of Dessert Apples (EC/US, 1998)	GATT Panel
	Panel Chair	DS391-Korea — Measures Affecting the Importation of Bovine Meat and Meat Products from Canada	Case was withdrawn by the Parties after completion of Panel Interim Report. The Parties had reached mutually-agreed solution.
	Panel Member	DS259, DS258, DS254, DS253, DS252, DS251, DS249, DS248-US — Definitive Safeguard Measures on Imports of Certain Steel Products	
	Panel Chair	DS231-EC — Trade Description of Sardines (EC/Peru)	
	Panel Member	DS160-US Section 110 (5) of US Copyright Act (Arbitration under Art. 25) (US/EC)	
5) Mr See Chak Mun	Panel Chair	India — Import Restrictions on Almonds (India/US — June 1987)	US withdrew the complaint after consultations.
6) Mr Minn Naing Oo	Panel Member	DS403, DS396-Philippines — Taxes on Distilled Spirits	
7) Mr Tiwari Sivakant	Panel Member	DS362-China — Measures Affecting the Protection and Enforcement of Intellectual Property Rights	

UNITED NATIONS
Specialised Agencies

The Singapore–IAEA Story

CHIN Siew Fei

Singapore became a member of the International Atomic Energy Agency (IAEA) in 1967 and has had a permanent presence in Vienna since April 2010. The Permanent Mission of Singapore to the IAEA remains in Geneva. Many people often asked me, what my job entailed, over the four years I was based in Vienna. More specifically, they did not quite understand what the IAEA was about, or why a small country such as Singapore with no nuclear power plants or indeed, no nuclear weapons, would have much to do with the Agency. Some may recall the labeling of the Agency as the United Nations (UN) nuclear watchdog and that the IAEA has something to do with the nuclear dossier of Iran or the Democratic People's Republic of Korea. Few are aware of the important role the IAEA plays in our daily lives. I would like to share with you the Singapore–IAEA story and a couple of myths and facts about the Agency.

Myth: While often called the "UN Agency" in news report, the IAEA is not a specialised agency of the UN. It is an independent international organisation. Its relationship with the UN is governed by a special agreement. In accordance with the provisions of its Statute, the IAEA reports annually to the UN General Assembly and, where appropriate, to the UN Security Council.

Half myth: The IAEA is a nuclear watchdog dealing with nuclear non-proliferation issues. *Fact*: According to its website, the IAEA works for the safe, secure and peaceful uses of nuclear science and technology. Its key roles are to contribute to international peace and security and to the world's Millennium Goals for social, economic, and environment development. I am not quite sure whether the ordinary man or woman in the street quite understands this. Whenever the word "atomic" appears, many would conjure up images of the "mushroom cloud" during a nuclear bomb detonation, or that nasty radioactive thing which destroys all cells indiscriminately and kills almost immediately whenever one is exposed to it. A certain paranoia may then take hold. We have to thank Hollywood and other foreign production houses for raising our awareness of the extremely destructive nature of nuclear and radioactive material as well as nuclear weapons technology. However, we have to bear in mind that these movies provide a rather simplistic and often inaccurate description of how nuclear weapons and material work.

The Dark Side of Nuclear Technology

It is not my intention to make light of the important role of the IAEA in preventing the spread of nuclear technology for military purposes. Nuclear technology is a double-edged sword. Together with chemical and biological weapons, nuclear weapons *are* weapons of mass destruction. When the US dropped two atomic bombs on Hiroshima and Nagasaki, two cities were wiped out almost instantaneously — human lives, animals, plants, land and buildings. Those who survived suffered, inter alia, long-term health consequences. Contaminated places took decades of remediation efforts to make sure that the radioactivity was low enough to be safe again for human health, agriculture production, etc. — if ever. For a small island-state like Singapore, any detonation, whether within our territory or in the vicinity, is potentially an existential threat. All the hard work and achievements of more than 50 years could be vaporised in an instant.

For the sake of humanity, we have to work with other countries to ensure that nuclear weapons will never be used again, whether by design, miscalculation or accident. Even a "dirty" bomb, made from radioactive material which is more widely available in industrial use, and can be more easily assembled than nuclear weapons, could have a devastating impact on human health, the environment, the economy, or simply the psychology of a nation.

Our long-term aspiration should be a world without nuclear weapons. In the interim, all countries should commit not to conduct any nuclear weapons testing. Those with nuclear weapons should make a real commitment and take concrete steps to reduce their nuclear arsenal steadily to zero.

But the nuclear threat can also come from rogue states or terrorists if they acquire nuclear weapons and the capability and means to use them. This is the reason why Singapore works very closely with the IAEA, the UN, and other relevant international organisations to counter nuclear proliferation. Singapore supports the IAEA in maintaining a robust nuclear verification and safeguards system. In broad layman's terms, this means that the IAEA inspectors can verify that all the nuclear material, activities, and facilities, both declared or undeclared, within a State and its territories, are exclusively for peaceful purposes.

In addition, through the IAEA and multilateral processes such as the Nuclear Security Summits, we support greater global nuclear security by encouraging all States to secure all nuclear material, activities and facilities, whether in military or civilian holdings, so that they do not fall into the wrong hands, either by theft or through smuggling. Radioactive material, widely used for medical and other industrial purposes should also be properly secured and accounted for to prevent its use in a "dirty bomb".

The Amazing World of the Peaceful Application of Nuclear Science

We have all, at one stage or another, undergone a medical scan involving X-ray machines for purposes such as the detection of illnesses without unnecessary surgery. Radiation therapy uses high-energy particles or waves to destroy cancer cells. Radioactive material, used in controlled doses by well-trained professionals, can improve the well-being of human beings and the environment. Food irradiation, the exposure of food to carefully controlled amounts of ionising radiation, can eliminate disease-causing micro-organisms such as *E. coli* and *Salmonella*, an important contribution to food safety. It can also be used to prolong the shelf life of fruits and vegetables, as it inhibits sprouting and delays ripening.

Using the Sterile Insect Technique (SIT), populations of key agricultural insect pests can be significantly reduced. It is a form of "birth control" where wild female insects of the targeted pest population cannot reproduce as they are inseminated by the deliberate release of radiation-sterilised males. SIT has been used successfully over the past 50 years. Research is ongoing to see if similar techniques can combat mosquito-based illnesses such as malaria and dengue fever, the latter which plagues countries such as Singapore.

Singapore collaborates with the Agency to promote the peaceful application of nuclear science and technology. In particular, many developing countries do not have the expertise or the equipment to apply such nuclear techniques, or require assistance to make sure that the application of nuclear technology is done in a safe and secure manner. For example, medical health workers should have adequate training to ensure that they do not subject themselves to unnecessary exposure in the conduct of their work using nuclear technology to help others. Singapore has worked with the IAEA to provide training to many developing countries in areas where we have niche expertise such as nuclear medicine, radiotherapy and radiation protection.

Nuclear power generation has been an issue of contention. In many ways, it is a clean and sustainable energy source, compared to fossil fuels such as coal, petroleum and natural gas. However, we have witnessed the downside of nuclear power generation in three major accidents in the past 30-odd years. The older generation may recall the Three Mile Island and the Chernobyl nuclear accidents. The younger generation will remember the Fukushima nuclear accident in Japan in 2011 which was caused by a major earthquake and tsunami.

Any technology, including nuclear technology, can fail. The problem with nuclear and radioactive material is its destructive nature when released (and out of control). Chernobyl and Fukushima have demonstrated that the consequences of an accident at a nuclear power plant ignore frontiers. For many years after Chernobyl, many in Europe worried about soil contamination and the impact on human health. The whole food chain was affected. Displaced populations will, in many cases never be able to return, either to Pripyat or to the towns affected by the Fukushima nuclear accident.

It is, therefore, important for the international community to work closely together to ensure that the highest standards of nuclear safety, security and safeguards, or the 3S, are applied in all nuclear power programmes. The "3S"s do not apply just during the operation of nuclear power plants. They should be applied from the earliest feasibility study stage, site selection, to the eventual decommissioning of the nuclear power plant and the safe, long-term disposal of all spent fuel and other radioactive waste.

Given that natural disasters are increasingly severe, perhaps due to climate change, more care should be applied to site selection. Previous assumptions about the impact of natural hazards on the safe operation of a nuclear power plant, whether new or existing ones, should be reconsidered. We must never be complacent. Nuclear accidents can happen because of human error, malice or technical failure. A robust nuclear safety and security culture, and regulatory and legal infrastructure are as essential as ensuring that all staff are well-trained. In addition, as the majority of nuclear power plants were built more than 30 years ago, regular inspections should be made to ensure their continued safety and if necessary, retrofitting and technical improvements done. Narrow commercial interests about the cost implications of such improvements should not prevail over the risks a nuclear accident may pose. All possible measures should be made to prevent another accident from occurring as all experts believe that it is not a matter of "if" but "when" the next one may take place. It is with this in mind that at the IAEA and other multilateral fora, Singapore works closely with many countries to ensure that those which choose to deploy nuclear energy for power generation do so in a safe, secure and safeguarded manner so that it can benefit rather than cause harm to the people and the environment.

There is still much more for us to learn. In this regard, Singapore launched the Nuclear Safety Research and Education Programme in April 2014 which comprises two main components: (i) the Singapore Nuclear Research and Safety Initiative (SNRSI) which focuses on research and developing capabilities in nuclear safety, science and engineering, and (ii) the Nuclear Education and Training Fund (NETF) which will support education and training in these areas. Closer cooperation with the IAEA is important so that we can further benefit from the peaceful application of nuclear science and technology as well as help other developing countries along as we gain more capabilities. It is similarly important for us to understand how to respond and mitigate the consequences in the event of any nuclear accident.

CHIN Siew Fei took up her appointment as Head of Mission and Chargé D'Affaires of the Embassy of Singapore to Brazil in June 2015. She established and headed the Vienna Office of the Permanent Mission of Singapore to the International Atomic Energy Agency from April 2010–January 2015. She was appointed as Singapore's Sous-Sherpa to the Nuclear Security Summit process in 2009 and held the position for five years. She has been a member of the Advisory Board of the Vienna Centre for Disarmament and Non-Proliferation (VCDNP) since 2011. Her previous assignments at the Singapore Foreign Ministry included those dealing with International Organisations, Europe, Technical Cooperation, International Economics and Northeast Asia. Her other overseas assignments were in Hong Kong during the transition from British to Chinese rule and in Brussels with concurrent accreditation to the European Communities, Belgium, the Netherlands, Luxembourg and the Holy See. Ms Chin graduated with a second upper Honours degree in Philosophy from the Faculty of Arts and Social Sciences at the National University of Singapore after being placed on the Dean's list the year before. She holds a Masters degree in Diplomacy and International Relations from the Diplomatic School of the Ministry of Foreign Affairs and International Cooperation of Spain. Ms Chin was conferred the Commendation Medal of the 2012 Singapore National Day Awards. She speaks English, Mandarin, Cantonese, French, Spanish, and Portuguese.

Singapore and ICAO

Civil Aviation Authority of Singapore

As a small island State, Singapore is heavily dependent on international civil aviation for its link to the rest of the world as well as its socio-economic development. The connectivity that international civil aviation provides is vital to Singapore being a global city. In addition to its own contribution to Singapore's GDP in the order of 6%, aviation is a key enabler of trade, tourism, commerce, investments and other activities which are building Singapore economically.

International Civil Aviation and Singapore-ICAO Cooperation

Unquestionably critical, therefore, to Singapore is the International Civil Aviation Organization (ICAO) and its work in providing the framework for the safe, secure, efficient and sustainable development of international civil aviation. ICAO was formed as a UN specialised agency close to the end of World War II when 52 States signed the "Convention on International Civil Aviation" in Chicago in 1944. The Chicago Convention, as it is widely known, sets out international cooperation, policies and standards for the safe and orderly operations of flights across borders based on equality of opportunity. In line with its mission, ICAO has steadily advanced international civil aviation and grown its membership to 191 Contracting States.

Since joining ICAO in 1966, the aviation sector in Singapore has grown significantly under the international system that the agency has established and enhanced over time, and with the valuable assistance it has provided. Singapore Changi Airport is now one of the world's major air hubs handling over 54 million international passengers and 1.8 million tons of airfreight per annum, with about 6,500 weekly scheduled flights operated by over

100 airlines to some 300 cities worldwide. Singapore Airlines is recognised as one of the premier airlines globally, and the various Singapore carriers provide a wide range of options to air travellers. Singapore provides air navigation services of high quality for the Singapore Flight Information Region, which covers an area of 245,000 nm^2 into the South China Sea.

Having benefited from the international system, Singapore is actively giving back to the international civil aviation community through and with ICAO. At the highest level, Singapore is a member of the ICAO Council (since 2003) and a Singapore expert is part of the Air Navigation Commission (since 2005). Singapore has also been contributing experts to the ICAO Secretariat and ICAO expert bodies to help shape and develop international Standards and Recommended Practices and guidance materials on international civil aviation. Ten officers from the Civil Aviation Authority of Singapore (CAAS) are now seconded to the ICAO Secretariat at its Headquarters and Offices in the Asia-Pacific. Singapore currently participates in over 100 ICAO expert bodies covering the full spectrum of international aviation: aviation safety, air traffic management, aviation security, environmental protection, air law, air transport and aviation medicine, with Singapore chairing 17 of these bodies.

Providing Solutions

In the various areas, Singapore strives to help address issues confronting international aviation, providing solutions — both large and in small packages — that have benefited the industry. The failed terrorist plot in August 2006, where there was an attempt to use liquid explosives on some transatlantic commercial flights, led to the immediate ban by Europe and the United States on the carriage of Liquids, Aerosols and Gels (LAGs) on commercial flights; several States followed suit. This led to a patchwork of regulations and procedures differing from State to State, which brought about operational, security and facilitation problems for airlines, airports, security screening agencies, airport retailers and passengers given the transboundary nature of air travel.

It was clear that a more universal, global solution was needed. Singapore gathered a few like-minded stakeholders, including industry players and regulators from States with large airport retail markets, to work on a pragmatic solution that addresses the risk. Instead of pursuing a full-proof solution, a prototype for a tamper-evident bag with a regulated supply chain process was conceptualised, developed and tested in some of the States and refined. The finalised bag specifications and associated supply chain process were subsequently presented to the ICAO Council by Singapore on behalf of the sponsoring States, and adopted. This led to the ICAO standards for LAGs bags and related supply chain process, which are still in use today. With duty-free purchases at airports worldwide, even by transfer passengers, kept going, the air transport sector has endured another threat.

A role that Singapore played in aviation medicine was also forced upon us; this time directly and resulting in a system solution. Many would remember the harrowing effects of the Severe Acute Respiratory Syndrome (SARS) pandemic that hit the Asia Pacific, including Singapore, in 2003. Air passenger movements took a nosedive, as the travelling public's fear of the highly infectious disease became sharply acute. The airlines in the Asia Pacific had to cut their capacity, some including Singapore Airlines by as much as 70% in the worst month, and suffered revenue losses of over $6 billion. Singapore saw a drop in tourist arrivals by more than two-thirds. Undaunted, stringent control measures and processes were put in place to rein in the spread of SARS, including the use of improvised thermal scanners for screening of passengers at Singapore Changi Airport to identify potentially infected passengers. CAAS and the industry also worked in concert with public health authorities and providers to restore public confidence.

With the aim of preventing and managing the spread of communicable diseases by air travel and bringing aviation to its knees again, Singapore shared with ICAO its experiences in dealing with SARS and worked with the international organisation to establish the Collaborative Arrangement for the Prevention and Management of Public Health Events in Civil Aviation (CAPSCA) in 2006. The Head of the Singapore Civil Aviation Medical Board, Dr Jarnail Singh, was seconded to the ICAO to roll out the CAPSCA programme to assist States to develop and maintain national preparedness plans for the aviation sector in compliance with the World Health Organization's International Health Regulations and the ICAO's Standards and Recommended Practices. Launched in the Asia Pacific, the CAPSCA programme was subsequently extended to all the other regions: Africa, the Americas, Europe and the Middle East. CAPSCA has proved useful in the recent health emergencies such as the H1N1 influenza, Middle East Respiratory Syndrome and Ebola in managing the spread of these viruses by air travel.

Training for Capacity Building

Another mainstay of ICAO-Singapore cooperation is training for capacity building. Singapore is a nation built on human capital, with heavy investments made in its only asset — its people. As Singapore's first Prime Minister, the late Mr Lee Kuan Yew said, "Talent is a country's most precious asset, more so for a small resource-poor country like Singapore. … it is the defining factor." This certainly goes for Singapore aviation. The human resource and talent for Singapore's aviation industry was initially developed through training programmes made available by many, including the United Nations Development Programme (UNDP). As the aviation sector in Singapore grew in breadth, dynamism and sophistication, and training places overseas became increasingly limited, Singapore adapted the training programmes and developed new ones to meet its special needs and circumstances.

In 1958, Singapore went further to establish its own civil aviation training school. Set up in an empty hangar, a group of air traffic controllers led by the then Director of the Civil Aviation of Singapore improvised to build the school's first aerodrome "simulator". This comprised a large wooden table top with a runway and taxiways painted on it, air traffic controllers playing "pilots" manually moving small aircraft models on sticks to simulate taxiing and flight, and trainee air traffic controllers in a glass-panelled room communicating instructions to the "pilots" over telephones. Over the years, the civil aviation training school expanded, became the Singapore Aviation Academy, and grew into the renowned institution it is today. The improvised aerodrome "simulator" has been replaced with three state-of-the-art, realistic air traffic control simulators: an aerodrome control tower simulator, a surveillance/control simulator and a procedural control simulator. Unchanged is the strong involvement of Singapore air traffic controllers in developing the simulators and training methods to effectively prepare new cohorts of trainee air traffic controllers for the changing air traffic management operations and its growing complexities.

With its advancement over the years, the Singapore Aviation Academy is a key part of Singapore's efforts to help the international aviation community in the development of the necessary aviation human resource. Through a wide range of training programmes and forums and an "open door" policy, the Academy provides platforms for the exchange of knowledge, expertise and ideas among aviation leaders and professionals. To date, over 91,000 persons from 200 countries and territories have participated in the Academy's programmes and forums, with over 6,500 participants receiving fellowships from the Singapore Government available since 1990. These include fellowships under the Singapore-ICAO Developing Countries Training Programme specifically for developing countries in ICAO. In 2000, the ICAO Council conferred the Singapore Aviation Academy the 34th ICAO Edward Warner Award "in recognition of its eminent contribution as a centre of excellence in international civil aviation training". More recently in 2014, the Singapore Aviation Academy was among the first four training centres around the world to be designated an ICAO Regional Training Centre of Excellence. This is in recognition of the Academy's forte and partnership with ICAO in providing the highest quality of training for the advancement of international aviation.

Further Advancing Aviation

As the world develops economically and becomes more integrated, international aviation will continue to grow. At the same time, it will continue to face challenges; be it in aviation safety and security, air traffic management, or sustainable development. As a country reliant on air transport, Singapore is a beneficiary of the framework and system that ICAO has established for aviation's progress and through which each challenge confronting aviation is addressed. In turn, Singapore is committed to playing an active part in ICAO and the attainment of its strategic goals. Given shared interests, the close relationship and collaboration between Singapore and ICAO will certainly grow from strength to strength to the benefit of the international aviation community.

The **Civil Aviation Authority of Singapore (CAAS)** is a Statutory Board under the Ministry of Transport; with the responsibility of enabling the growth of the air hub and aviation industry, overseeing and promoting safety in the industry, providing air navigation services, and developing Singapore as a centre of excellence for aviation knowledge and human resource development. CAAS oversees Singapore's cooperation with ICAO, including our contribution and participation through the ICAO Council and Air Navigation Commission and in over 100 ICAO expert bodies and working groups to shape international civil aviation standards and recommended practices.

[Ph1] Singapore is admitted as the 117th member of the United Nations, 21 September 1965. The flag is raised the next morning.

[Ph2] The Prime Minister of Singapore, Lee Kuan Yew, visited United Nations headquarters on 21 October 1967 and met with Secretary-General U Thant. Seen here, from left: Inche Rahim Ishak, Minister of State for Education, Singapore; Prime Minister Lee Kuan Yew; Secretary-General U Thant; S. Rajaratnam, Minister of Foreign Affairs, Singapore; and Wong Lin Ken, Permanent Representative of Singapore to the United Nations. [Photo credit: UN Photo]

[Ph3] General Assembly hears address by Prime Minister of Australia and seven statements in general debate. The delegations of Singapore headed by S. Rajaratnam *(left)*, Minister for Foreign Affairs and Tommy Koh, Permanent Representative to the United Nations, New York, September 1974. Back row *(left to right)*: Michael Cheok, Lee Chiong Giam and Peter Chan. [Photo credit: UN Photo]

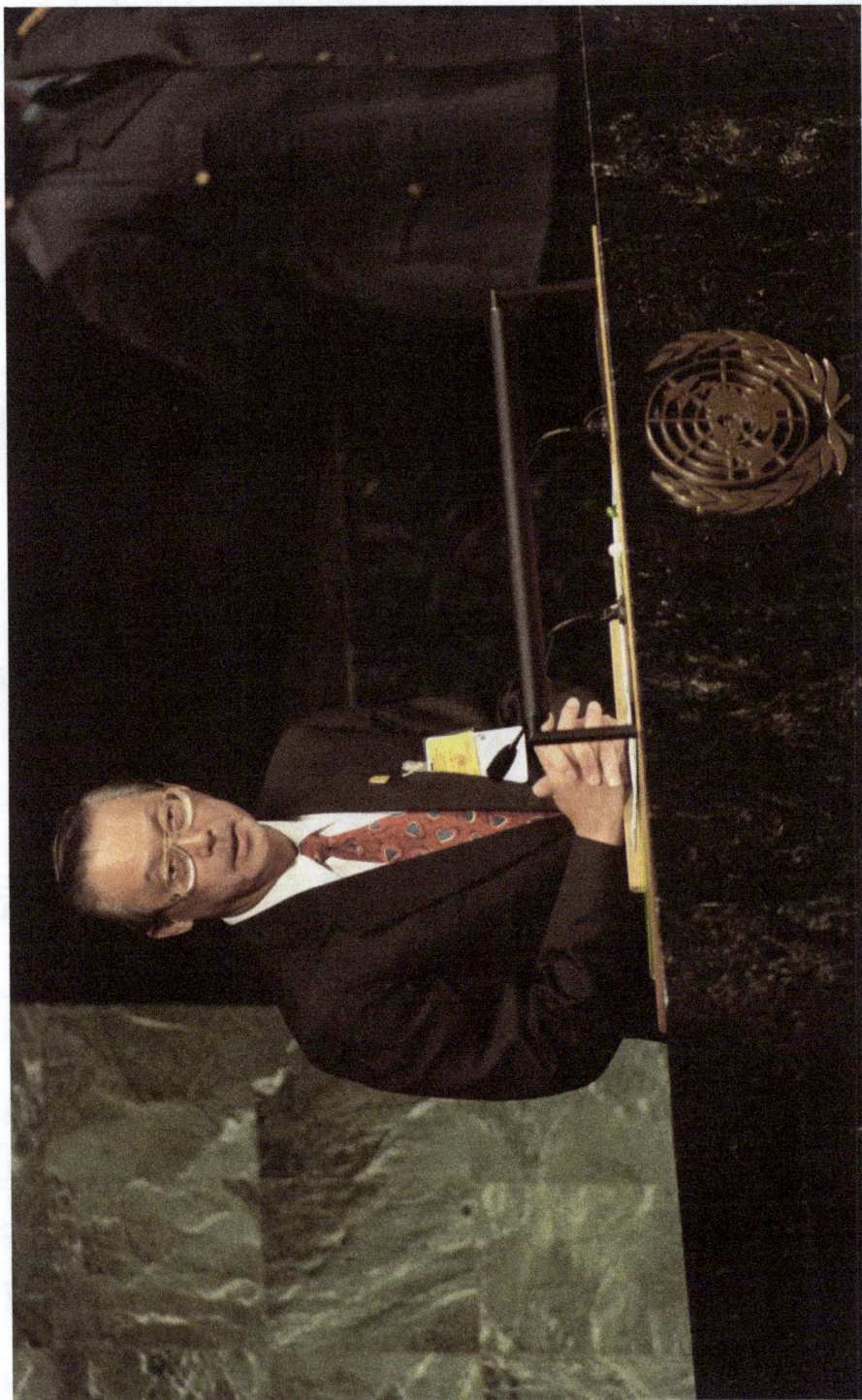

[Ph4] Goh Chok Tong, Prime Minister of the Republic of Singapore, addressed the Special Commemorative Meeting in the General Assembly Hall. On the occasion of the 50th Anniversary of the United Nations, a Special Commemorative Meeting of the General Assembly was held from 22 to 24 October 1995. Over 200 Heads of State, Vice-Presidents, Heads of Governments, Deputy Prime Ministers, Foreign Ministers, Permanent Representatives, Permanent Observers and International Delegations are addressing this special meeting at UN Headquarters (Tuesday, 24 October 1995).

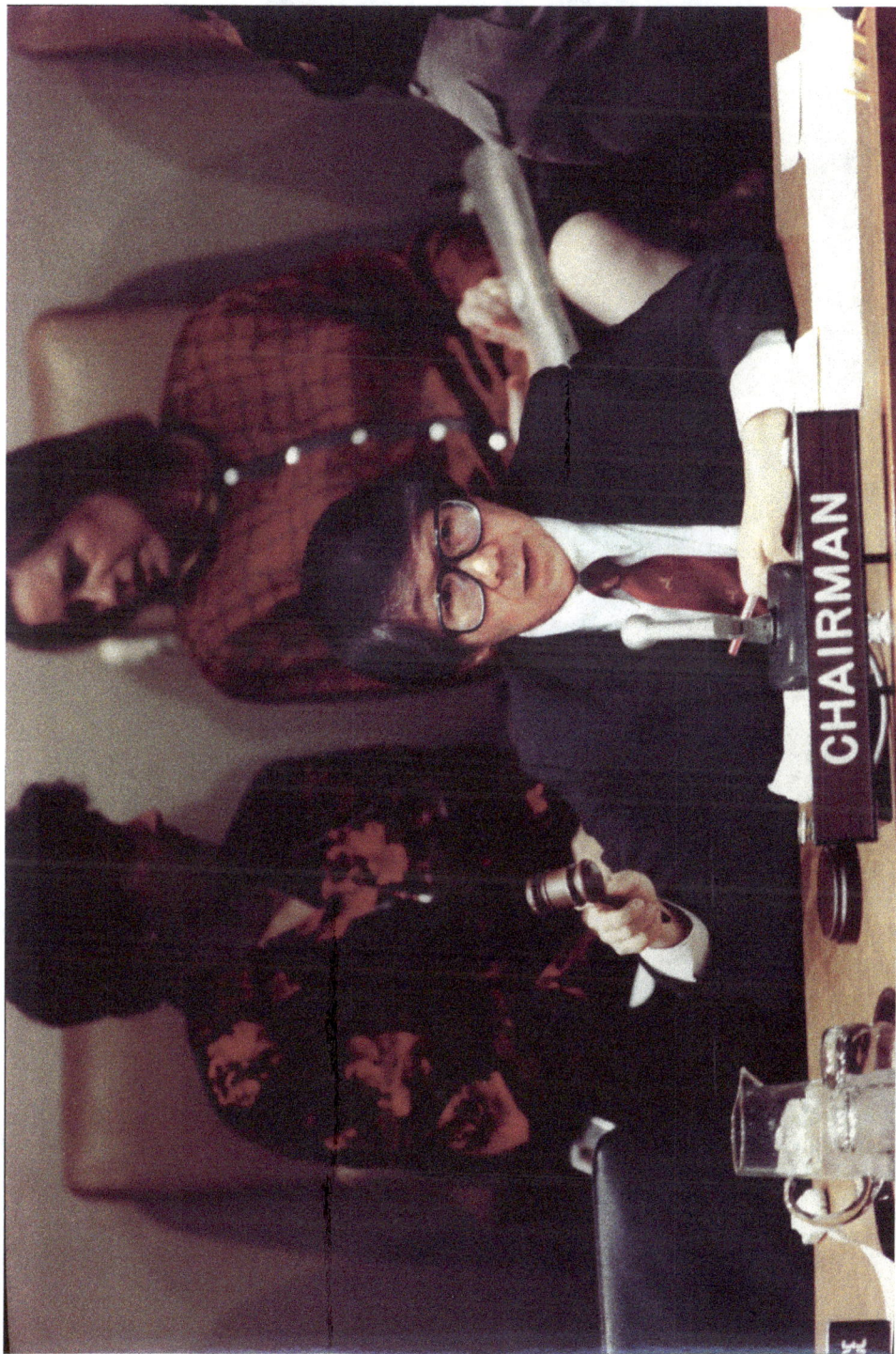

[Ph5] Tommy Koh chairing the last preparatory committee meeting of the Earth Summit, New York, April 1992.

[Ph6] S. Jayakumar presiding over a UN Security Council meeting during Singapore's presidency of the Security Council from 2001 to 2002, in May 2002.

[Ph7] Kishore Mahbubani presiding over one of the UN Security Council meetings in May 2002 when he was the Council President.

[Ph8] Chan Heng Chee addressing the UNGA. She served as the Permanent Representative of Singapore to the United Nations from 1989 to 1991. In 1996 she was appointed Ambassador to the United States.

[Ph9] Bilahari Kausikan presenting his credentials to UN Secretary-General, Boutros Boutros-Ghali on 1 August 1995.

[Ph10] Chew Tai Soo speaking at the conference to commemorate the 20th anniversary of FOSS in October 2012.

[Ph11] Vanu Gopala Menon (seated on the left of then Foreign Minister George Yeo) at the annual Global Governance Group's Ministerial Meeting in 2010.

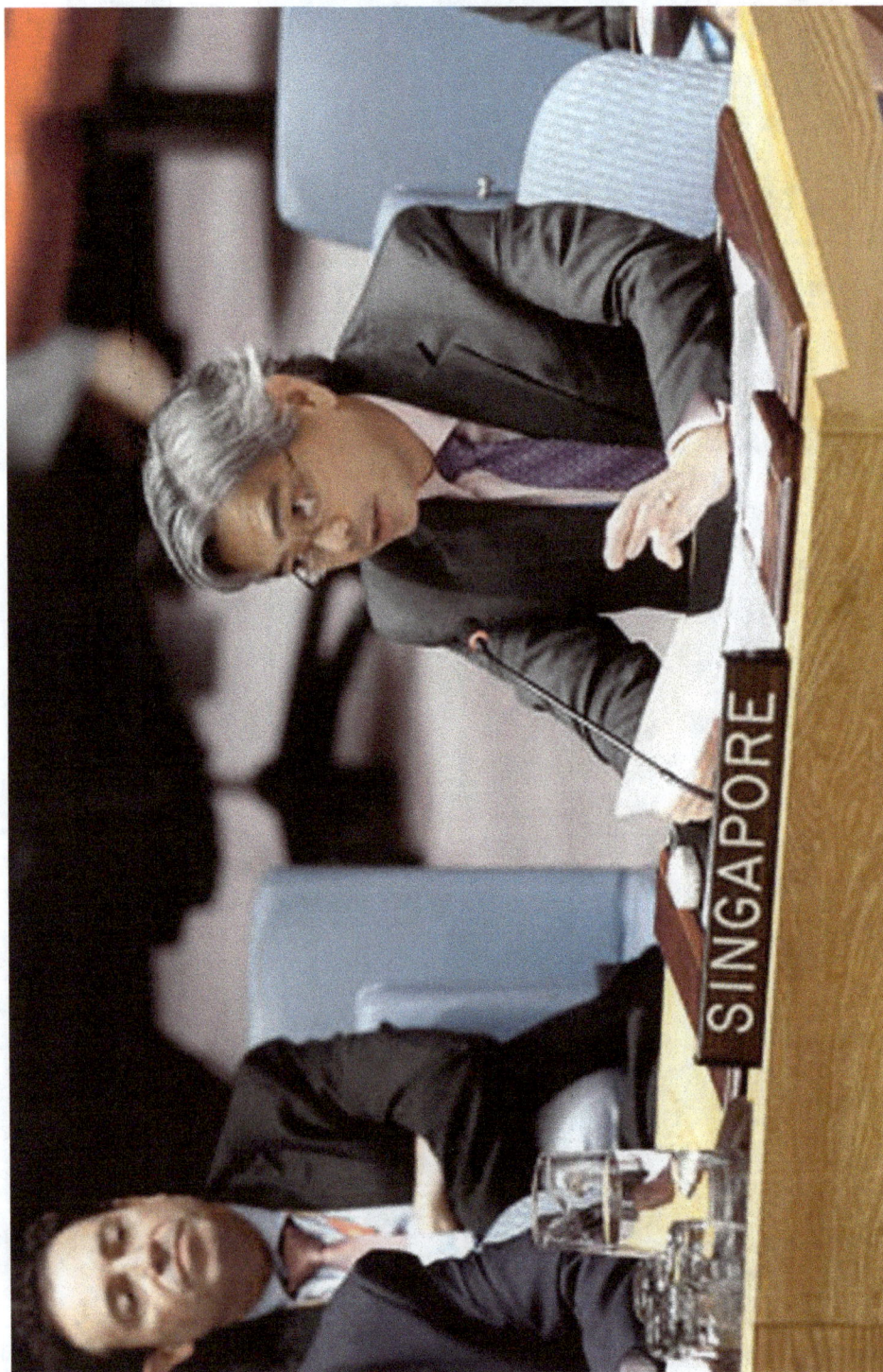

[Ph12] Albert Chua addressing the Security Council in September 2014 during the debate on ISIS. He served as Permanent Representative of Singapore to the United Nations from August 2011 to June 2013.

[Ph13] Karen Tan addressing the panel discussion on "Open Defecation and the Challenge for Women and Girls", on the occasion of World Toilet Day in 2014. She is currently the Permanent Representative of Singapore to the United Nations.

[Ph14] Singapore officials at the closing ceremony of the WTO Ministerial Conference at Doha, Qatar, on 14 November 2001. *Left to right*: Elizabeth Chelliah, First Secretary, Singapore Permanent Mission in Geneva; Margaret Liang, Singapore Deputy Permanent Representative, Geneva Mission; Chairman of the WTO Ministerial Conference HE Youssef Hussain Kamal, Minister of Finance, Economy and Trade of Qatar; See Chak Mun, Singapore Permanent Representative, Geneva Mission; with two Qatari officials.

[Ph15] K. Kesavapany, the first Chairman of the WTO General Council, together with Renato Ruggiero, second Director-General of WTO and Mounir Zahran, the last Chairman of the GATT Council.

[Ph16] The Singapore Delegation to the WTO Dispute Settlement Case against Malaysia for its import restrictions on certain petrochemical products under Malaysia's Approved Permit Scheme, March 1995. Background is the WTO Secretariat Building in Geneva, Switzerland.

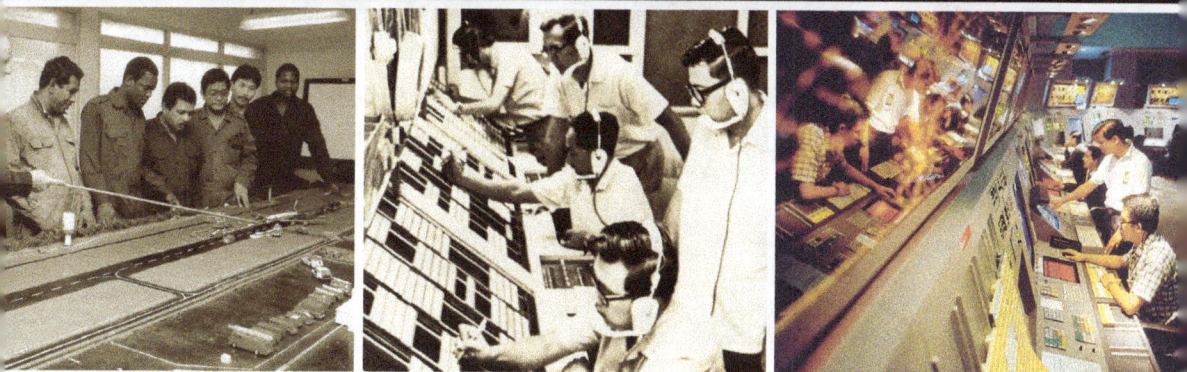

[Ph17] Progression of air traffic simulators at the Singapore Aviation Academy: from improvising with manual models in 1958 to present-day using 360°, virtual, state-of-the-art technology.

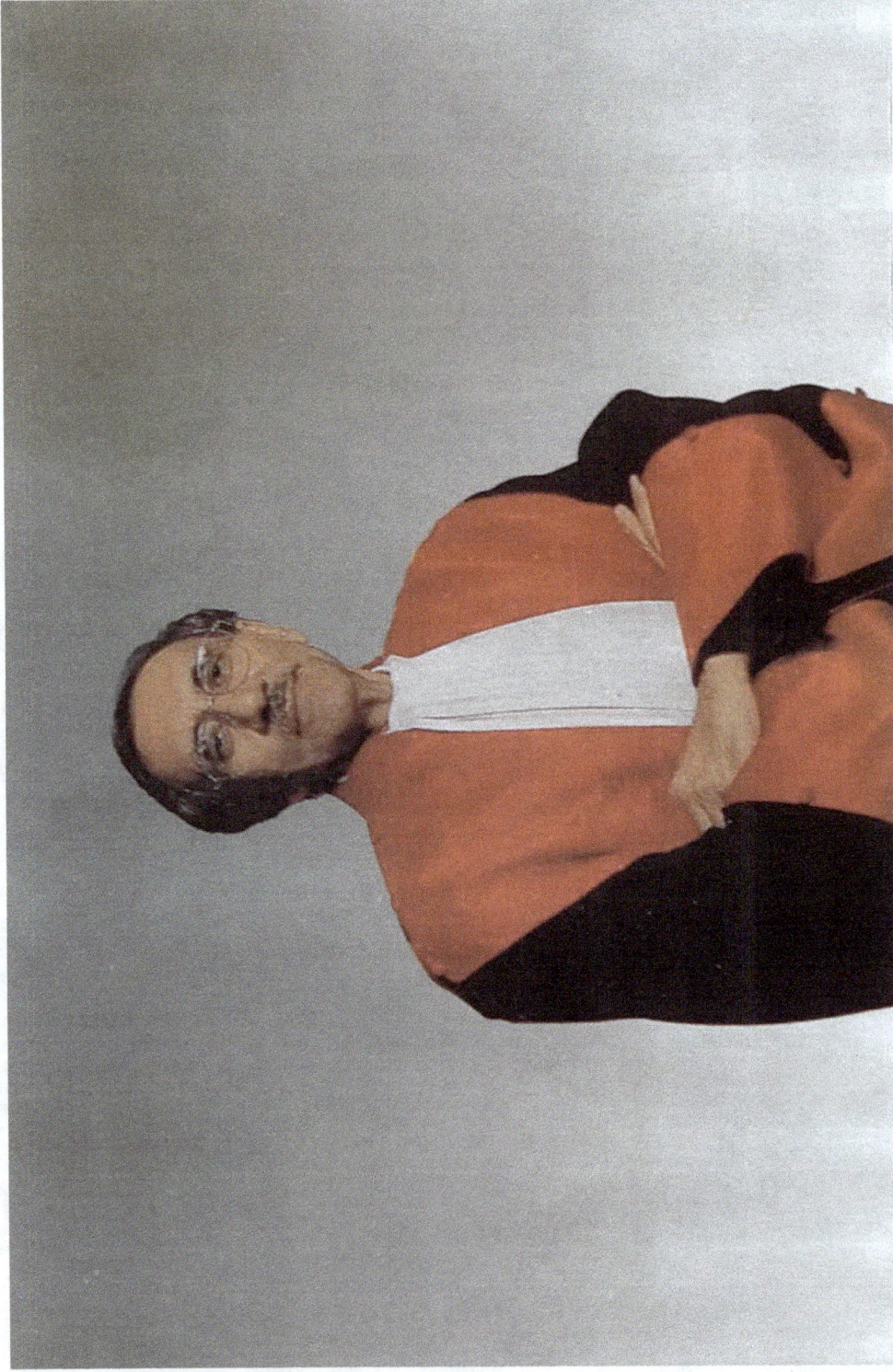

[Ph18] Amarjeet Singh, Ad Litem Judge, International Criminal Tribunal for the former Yugoslavia, from 2001 to 2005.

[Ph 19] Halimah Yacob at an International Labour Organization Meeting in Geneva.

[Ph20] Janet Lim meeting with refugee women in the Democratic Republic of Congo, November 2010.

[Ph21] Andrew Toh (in red) with Mujahideen fighters in Mazar-i-Sharif, Afghanistan, 1988.

[Ph22] Balaji Sadasivan being congratulated on his election as the Chairman of the WHO Executive Board. Margaret Chan, WHO Director-General is on his left.

[Ph23] Vernon Lee, medical epidemiologist in the WHO Indonesia country office, working with local authorities on a pandemic response simulation exercise.

[Ph24] Geoffrey Yu, second from left in the front row, accompanying the late Director-General of WIPO, Árpád Bogsch, to call on President Jiang Zemin of the People's Republic of China.

[Ph25] Personnel from the Singapore Armed Forces (SAF) as part of the United Nations Iraq-Kuwait Observation Mission (UNIKOM). The SAF participated in this peace operations from 1991 to 2003, where our personnel were tasked with monitoring a demilitarised zone along the boundary between Iraq and Kuwait, as well as the Khawr Abd Allah waterway.

[Ph26] Singapore's Police Officer, Superintendent (Supt) Sng May Yen, with the children of Timor-Leste.

[Ph27] Paul Cheung speaking at the UN Pavilion at the Shanghai Expo in 2010.

[Ph28] Shirin Hamid with children in extremely-poor urban settlement in Dhaka, Bangladesh, while visiting the UNDP Urban Partnerships for Poverty Reduction Project, September 2014.

[Ph29] Noeleen Heyzer in consultation with displaced women and children in a refugee camp. (Photo credit: UN Photo)

[Ph30] Thelma Kay, second from right in the front row, with the Governing Board of the International Institute for Educational Planning, UNESCO, Paris, December 2003. The person in the centre (seated) is then Director-General of UNESCO, Koichiro Matsuura.

[Ph31] Dileep Nair with UN Secretary-General Kofi Annan.

[Ph32] Yeo Bock Cheng with UN Secretary-General Kofi Annan.

The World's First Independent War Crimes Court — Reminiscences and Reflections

Amarjeet SINGH

I was one of a number of candidates elected by the United Nations General Assembly in June 2001 as an Ad Litem Judge to what can be called as the world's first independent war crimes court. The International Criminal Tribunal for the former Yugoslavia (ICTY) was established in 1993 as a temporary Tribunal and is located in the Hague. The ICTY had required additional judges. I was privileged to be the first international judge to be appointed to a United Nations Court from Singapore.

My candidature was premised on the Singapore judiciary's high standing in comparative international surveys and on policy grounds:

> The Singapore Government has a longstanding commitment to the maintenance of international rule of law and justice. It attaches great importance to the work of the International Criminal Tribunal Yugoslavia. The Singapore Government is convinced that Mr Singh's professional qualifications and wealth of experience in the field of criminal law would enable him to make a positive contribution to the work and effectiveness of the international Tribunal, including the development of international humanitarian law. Singapore's candidature also reflects our abiding commitment to the peace process and the establishment of a more tolerant and multi-ethnic society in all parts of the former Yugoslavia.

I arrived at the ICTY a few months later as one of five new judges called, the other four being women to bridge the then existing gender imbalance there. They were from Canada, Mali, Japan and the Czech Republic. The

ICTY, which is now projected to complete its work and close in 2017 has two distinct independent branches — prosecutorial and a judicial. The latter has three trial Chambers each presided over by three judges and an Appellate Chamber assisted by a Registry for case management. All accused are entitled to counsel if needed and their fees are paid by the ICTY.

It was formed under its Statute, empowering it to address under its Articles 2–5: (i) Grave Breaches of the Geneva Convention 1949; (ii) Serious Violations of International Humanitarian Law; (iv) Violations of the Laws or Customs of War; (iv) Genocide covering offences such as murder, abductions, rape, deportations, ethnic cleansing, use of poison, torture, desecration of mosques and churches. The Statute was a response and a product of a conflict that had engulfed the Yugoslavian federation which was composed of six states: Serbia, Bosnia–Herzegovina, Slovenia, Croatia, Macedonia and Montenegro and Serbian minority ruled Kosovo with Serbian troop presence, It was a very divided society.

A spot of complex history here might be helpful in understanding the causes and nature of the resultant war crimes. Serbia and its adjacent precincts had been invaded by the Ottoman Empire in 1389 with an influx of Turkish settlers. The Ottomans had occupied the land thereafter for many hundreds of years — marking the day of defeat ('Vidovan') for the Serbs the holiest in its calendar. Now fast forward six hundred years to 1989. Fear had gripped the constituent states which had become relatively stable under President Tito's new socialism from the nineteen sixties. Slobodan Milosevic of Serbia who became President in 1989, with extremists, was seen as attempting to create a greater Serbian unitary state by exploiting Serbian nationalism on issues of ethnicity, religion and culture. In the cross-hairs was Bosnia-Herzegovina with a mixed population of minority Bosnian Orthodox Catholics, a majority of Bosnian Muslims and Croat Christians. Orthodox Bosnians referred to themselves as being 'Bosnians' whilst dubbing the Muslims disparagingly as 'Bosniaks' — thereby drawing divisive religious and cultural lines. Slovenia and Croatia were quick to secede from the federation. Bosnia-Herzegovina followed, declaring independence in 1992 after victory in an affirmative referendum by a majority of Bosniaks and Croat voters. In reaction, the Bosnian minority from Banja Luka, their administrative capital, formed their own State — the Republica SPRSKA (Bosnian Republic). Radovan Karadic became President whilst General

Ratko Mladic took over command of the military. With Serbia it went to war with the nationals of the seceding states and ended up being bombed by NATO forces, to end the long war and the commission of war crimes.

Thereafter, Serbian-Bosnian senior politicians and army officers began to be indicted by the Tribunal for committing a litany of war crimes. Presidents Milosevic and Karadzic and General Mladic were three of the most infamous names involved in the war crimes at Sarajevo, Srebrenica and Kosovo and other places, where thousands of deaths occurred. The trials of the latter two will conclude in 2015. Atrocities were also committed by the militias and officers of the other constituent states. They too were indicted.

My appointment came historically at about an inflexion point in the development of modern international law on war crimes, grounded by the Judges on a written Code of procedural, evidential safeguards and best practices. This was to ensure the need for justice not just done, but that was seen to be done. To this end live proceedings of each trial were broadcast to the former Balkan states.

Not before, and certainly not even at the Nuremberg or Tokyo military war crime tribunals (after WWII) had such transparency and objectives underpinned trials as at the ICTY with discovery of documents, modern court room technology as live notes appearing on personal monitors of judges and counsel alongside simultaneous voice translations. Comparatively, trials by military tribunals at Nuremberg, of indicted German officers of war crimes and similarly against the Japanese at Tokyo and in Singapore after WWII relied essentially on affidavit based evidence recorded from an accused by investigators and all trials were concluded swiftly within a set frame work of less than a year. The respective Tribunals' work had established that hitherto there would be no immunity for war criminals no matter how high their standing.

I shall now briefly outline both the pioneering role that ICTY has played in developing international criminal law with a few important illustrations, the evaluation of its performance, and the lessons that can be learnt.

The Tribunal in developing international criminal law has made many ground breaking precedents. Early in its infancy it ruled that the Yugoslavian conflict was an international one, not just internal. In 1997, in the first case, one Dusko Tadic, a Bosnian, faced multiple war crimes charges, some sadistic, under the Tribunal's Statute. The Tribunal settled an important question of law relating to the legal basis of its very existence. It interpreted the defence of illegitimacy of the Tribunal raised by Tadic as impinging on the national sovereignty of his country, Bosnia, as more of a jurisdictional question, ruling that it had jurisdiction founded under the Tribunal's Statute established by the Security Council and could not look outside its bounds. The ruling raised the 'common denominator' of states subscribing to the peaceful universality of man.

I did a trial of practices that had become a pattern of forcible deportations, detentions and torture that was rampantly practised by Bosnian-Serbian para military officers and abetted by local Bosnians as instruments of seizing Muslim and Croat dominated municipalities in Herzegovina from 1992 and then enabling re-elections to be held swiftly by fielding their own ethnic candidates, thereby purporting to give legitimacy to the occupation of the territories and decisions subsequently made by such municipalities.

The judges appreciated the fact that surviving victims and witnesses of the war had waited a long time and had come a long way to tell their stories and heard them patiently. I heard witnesses slowly unfolding their personal tragedies with sorrowful insights such as: "The war brought a great misfortune on everyone. I was not so sorry for myself as I was for some others as I looked around"; "What kind of a curse had befallen us?"; "I was praying if the first shell hit Samac again that morning it should hit me"; "In fear, a day can last as long as a year"; "In a communal war you tend to be afraid even of your own friends"; "Falling shells do not discriminate between soldiers and civilians"; and finally a fear expressed that pithily unlocks the whole turmoil, "Only Muslims were Yugoslavians. Serbs were Serbs. Croats were Croats."

The Tribunal has since its early days also interpreted its empowering Statute expansively where required, to give effective force to the law creating the offences, such that rape can also constitute torture or sexual enslavement under international customary law or amount to genocide where circumstances exist for such a reasonable interpretation to be given.

Of serious concern in hostilities by highly placed military and government officers of what goes on, on the ground, is Command Responsibility the law on which has been articulated in Article 7(3) of the Tribunal's

Statute. Both the concept and the crime present complex difficulties in the interpretation of liability where such officers are for instance distance removed. The ICTY had earlier in 1998 held that a superior was responsible for the same acts as had been committed by the subordinate. However, in 2008, it departed from its earlier decision holding in the landmark *Celebici* case that the offence is *sui generis* and that an absent superior or who may be far away should only be held to be responsible for *failure* to prevent or *punish* his subordinates crimes and he is not responsible 'for the crimes of his subordinates'. In other words the particular *specie* of offence was fact sensitive to establish any particular liability.

I consider the Tribunal, now in its twentieth year as having overall, both transparently and successfully performed its obligations as a pioneer *ad hoc* instrument in laying a strong foundation for international war crimes law enforcement buttressed by a body of reasoned precedents. The permanent International Criminal Court (ICC) will no doubt benefit from its precedents. Of the 161 persons indicted before the Tribunal 141 cases have been concluded with sentences being passed ranging from 40 years down to 5 years involving all ethnicities Croatians, Bosnian Serbs and Muslims. No capital punishment is sanctioned under the Statute. About ten trials and appeals are pending. Prison facilities, which I had occasion to visit and observe, in a wing of a Dutch prison for UN war crimes, are maintained to meet a UN standard and paid for under the ICTY's budget. Prisoners are allowed reading material (Milosevic had neat stacks of perhaps a hundred books lying on his cell-floor), and limited telephones calls to their families. After sentence they have a choice to serve their sentence in prisons of countries that are approved and by agreement willing to accept them.

Some lessons from the Tribunal's work though are worth bearing in mind both from the trial processes of the Tribunal and the tragic war itself: delays by states in making arrests of indicted officers and or forwarding evidence to ICTY's prosecutors. This problem must be addressed separately by the Security Council, which has the authority to exact sanctions on countries on behalf of the United Nations as it is relevant to the success of the ICC. A Prosecutor at the ICC in November 2014, withdrew all charges against the Kenyan President Uhuru Kenyatta in respect of crimes against humanity committed by him in 2007 resulting from witnesses being tempered with and Kenya's non co-operation to provide requested evidence.

The principle of 'no impunity' is as such in jeopardy. The other short point is that only the fewest of the most serious charges — perhaps three — should be put up for trial by Prosecutors, the rest being stood down to speed up trials. Milosevic passed away during the long and arduous trial on 66 charges from ill health and his trial abated. The result rendered the Trial Chamber's work as totally unproductive. Similarly so, in the case of the extremist Vojsley Seslej who becoming too sick to be further tried in 2014 was released.

The Yugoslavian tragedy based on extreme ethnic nationalism, communalism and religion and rooted in historial hatreds serves as the latest political example for countries with such plural populations to assiduously avoid.

———•◦•———

Amarjeet SINGH started his legal career in 1962, as an Assistant Official Assignee and Assistant Public Trustee, thereafter becoming a Magistrate, State Coroner and a District Judge. From 1968 to 1991 he substantially practised criminal law, first in the firm of M/s David Marshall, in partnership, and after Mr Marshall left to become Singapore's Ambassador in France, at Amarjeet Rubin and Partners. He went on to be appointed a Judicial Commissioner in the Supreme Court in 1991, serving till 2000 and upon retirement was appointed a Judge by the UN at the International Criminal Tribunal for Yugoslavia, the Hague (ICTY) from 2001 to 2005. On his return to Singapore he was made Senior Counsel and is now a Consultant at KhattarWong LLP. Amarjeet is also a member of the Competition Appeal Board, Panel member of the Disciplinary Tribunal under the Legal Profession Act, a Neutral Evaluator for the SMC, and also serves as an Arbitrator and Adjudicator.

Singapore and the International Labour Organization (ILO)

HALIMAH Yacob

Singapore joined the International Labour Organization (ILO) in 1965. For many newly independent countries then, the ILO was an important institution which was accorded a higher priority than other UN agencies.

The ILO was established in 1919 by the Treaty of Versailles. It is a specialised agency of the UN and its goal is to establish universal peace through social justice. Setting labour standards to ensure fair working conditions and supervising their observance are the two pillars of the ILO. Labour standards set the parameters of what are acceptable and humane ways of treating labour. Some of these standards may not be immediately implementable in some countries, particularly those at the developing stage, but they are akin to the gold standards for the workplace, which all countries can aspire to achieve.

The unequal bargaining position between capital and labour and the need for regulation to ensure a balance, underpins the ILO's social justice mission. Capital, unlike labour, especially in today's highly globalised world, could move freely with the potential of pitting countries against each other. This could cause a race to the bottom, especially if countries resort to extreme measures, such as waiving compliance with labour laws or offering cheap wages in order to attract investments.

I remember years ago, being shown a brochure where a government promised investors to its country labour at wages of only US$1 per day! These extreme forms of competition have not disappeared and are still very much alive today. In some countries, health and safety standards are not enforced as there are costs involved in keeping workers safe while they work. In many places, child labour is rampant because they are cheaper and more compliant. Human trafficking and slavery are still very much alive today, despite the tremendous progress that the world has made in so many areas.

The ILO is unique as it is the only specialised agency of the United Nations that is tripartite, a partnership among government, workers and employers, as all the other agencies are represented only by the governments. Hence, to me, it is an important institution that we need to uphold and strengthen as it embodies the principles and values of democracy at work. Perhaps the horrors of the First World War awakened the world to the need for a democratic global institution where ordinary working people could have a voice. This is a task too important to be left to the government alone. As the then President of Finland, Tarja Halonen, said in 2011, "Governments alone cannot implement the ILO objectives (social justice). The tripartite system is the special nature and strength of the ILO. As all three parties have committed themselves to ILO decisions, it is easier for all parties to support and promote the national implementation processes in their own countries".

Singapore enjoys a good relationship with the ILO and has made a positive impact. In many respects, we are seen as a good development model. Although we may not have ratified many ILO conventions, we are serious in enforcing those that we had ratified. Workers' lives have improved significantly and progress has not been achieved on the backs of workers. Our skills development programmes strongly supported by the government and with a statutory levy on employers are the envy of many where fear of skills obsolescence due to rapid technological advances is a real concern. Our skills programmes are often quoted by the ILO as a good example of national initiatives to keep workers relevant. The ILO has signed the 2nd Partnership Agreement with our Ministry of Manpower (MOM) to improve HRD and workplace practices in the ASEAN region, covering several areas including tripartism and social dialogue, productivity, employability and skills development.

Our practice of tripartism, too, has gained much traction in the ILO with its key focus on social dialogue. True to its tripartite nature, the ILO believes that to achieve social justice, the three parties should meaningfully and effectively engage with each other at the national level. Hence, Singapore's tripartism has often been quoted in ILO publications as an example of effective social dialogue among the tripartite partners at the state level. In fact, in 2010, Singapore's tripartite partners were invited to share their experiences in managing the financial crisis during the ILO conference. As the ILO had observed at that time, Singapore had managed the crisis well and emerged from the recession early due to our strong tripartite partnership. It also noted that Singapore had put in place measures that were aligned to the ILO Global Pact even before it was adopted by the ILO itself.

However, there were occasional bumps too in our relationship with the ILO. In 1979, Singapore denounced the Abolition of Forced Labour Convention 105 because of disagreements over ILO's interpretation of our laws and practice. Since then, no new conventions were ratified until 2003 when a number of conventions were ratified over several years, including three important conventions on the worst forms of child labour (C138), on equal remuneration for work of equal value (C100) and on tripartite consultation (C144).

In total, Singapore has ratified 27 conventions out of a total of 189 Conventions. Although the number may seem small, Singapore takes its obligations seriously and makes strenuous efforts to comply with its obligations unlike many countries that ratify a huge number of conventions but hardly comply with them. In 2012, for example, when Singapore announced its intention to ratify C187 on Promotional Framework for Safety and Health, the MOM's Commissioner for Safety and Health, Mr Ho Siong Hin, said that even before ratifying C187, Singapore had already embarked on a comprehensive National WSH Strategy 2018 to provide a strategic and long term approach to achieve sustained and continuous improvement in WSH Standards. This shows just how seriously we take our commitments under the conventions that we ratify.

I was the first Singaporean to sit on the ILO Governing Body (ILO GB) when I was elected as a Deputy Member of the Workers Group in 1999. I was subsequently re-elected three more times and had served on the ILO GB for a total of 12 years before I left the National Trades Union Congress (NTUC) to join the government. Ms Mary Liew, NTUC Central Committee Member and former Nominated Member of Parliament, now represents workers on the ILO GB. In 2005, the MOM was also elected as a deputy member to the Governing Body and in 2008 the Singapore government was elected as the titular member. The Singapore National Employers Federation (SNEF), representing Singapore employers, was elected as a Deputy Member for the first time in 2005. Each term is for a period of three years.

ILO Convention on Decent Work for Domestic Workers

As a Deputy Member of the ILO Governing Body, I represented the Workers' Group on many key committees, including the Committee on Legal Issues and International Labour Standards, the International Institute of Labour Studies, the Standards Committee, the Technical Assistance Committee as well as acted as the Spokesperson for the Workers' Group in negotiating several ILO instruments including ILO convention 189 on Decent Work for Domestic Workers. Helping the Workers' Group to clinch C189 was one of my most fulfilling tasks in the ILO. After negotiating for two years, we finally secured two instruments for domestic workers, a Convention and a Recommendation on Decent Work for Domestic Workers. A Convention which, once ratified is binding, provides the broad principles whereas a Recommendation provides greater details on the government's duties and obligations. It was a most significant moment in ILO's history as the Workers' Group had tried for more than 40 years to secure such a standard without success.

The two-year negotiations from 2010 to 2011, was a really trying period. The first year of the negotiations was the hardest as the Employers' Group opposed the Convention and used every tactic imaginable to try and thwart our efforts. Despite the en bloc veto by the Employers' Group, we had the support of an overwhelming majority of the governments from both the sending and receiving countries which helped us to conclude the report. This was subsequently adopted by the ILO General Assembly, paving the way for the discussion on the text of the Convention in the following year.

It was an invaluable experience for me in the art of negotiations, which involved thorough preparation of facts, figures and arguments, persuasion, lobbying and also compromise. Representing the Workers' Group was also no easy task as workers' organisations from different parts of the world, developing and developed, sending and receiving countries, had vastly different situations and expectations, and we had to first get them to agree to some common grounds among ourselves, before we could negotiate at the tripartite committee. I was grateful for the trust and confidence that they had in me.

We also had the strong support and presence of many domestic workers' organisations from all over the world, who attended the proceedings, including many women who had worked as maids in appalling and abusive conditions. They were crucial in creating a supportive environment for our work. It was an example of how interconnected the world had become and how global labour action had benefitted the workers. It was indeed a historic moment for the ILO and the international labour movement.

What is the future of the ILO? The situation is not smooth sailing. ILO faces challenges which, if unaddressed, could undermine its effectiveness. Governments need to accord greater priority to the work of the ILO as it is one of the key institutions present today that can help to address the extreme inequalities that we are facing and which is tearing the world apart. Governments should not view ILO's scrutiny of a country's labour standards as an encumbrance but rather as an opportunity for it to work closely with its tripartite partners to improve the living standards of its people. Governments should also take advantage of the technical assistance programmes that the ILO provides to help them improve their labour standards.

There are also mounting challenges from employers, manifested through the Employers' Group direct challenge to the ILO's Committee of Experts view that C87 on Freedom of Association includes the right to strike. For a long time, the right to strike, although not expressly mentioned in the convention, has been implied as part of the bundle of rights that workers have in order for freedom of association to be meaningful. As a result of this challenge, for the first time in ILO's history, there was no meeting of the Committee on the Application of Standards at the 101st session of the International Labour Conference (ILC) in 2012 and no conclusions were adopted for 19 cases of the most serious violations of human and trade union rights at the 103rd session of the ILC in 2014.

The ILO constitution provides that if the tripartite constituents failed to reach consensus to resolve an issue, the matter should be referred to the International Court of Justice for an urgent advisory opinion. The ILO Governing Body will be meeting in March 2015 on whether to do so and I hope that good sense will prevail and the matter will be resolved through the ICJ if further discussions do not lead to a consensus.

If such disputes over fundamental issues are not resolved, in the long run the effectiveness of the ILO as a tripartite agency and one that ensures fair labour standards throughout the world will be weakened and considerably undermined. It is therefore absolutely crucial that all three parties negotiate with each other in the ILO in good faith and equally important too for the rules of engagement to be clear and are adhered to.

I also hope that Governments could play a more involved part and should not stay neutral particularly when core principles of the ILO are involved, otherwise over time the reasons for the establishment of the ILO will disappear. ILO exists to create a fair and just society through ensuring that prosperity is not achieved on the backs of workers, usually one of the weakest groups in any country. With increasing concern over the impact of globalisation, the role of the ILO is even more important.

Finally, it is imperative that the ILO remains relevant to the needs of its constituents. The Decent Work Agenda was an example of an ILO strategy that was relevant, necessary and provided a basis for the constituents to examine their own national policies and programmes on job creation. Decent Work refers to the availability of employment in conditions of freedom, equality, human security and dignity. In short, the ILO needs to constantly examine its policies, structure, manpower and competencies to ensure that it can guide and provide good support to its constituents, and remain a key global institution standing for social justice.

———•◦•———

HALIMAH Yacob was elected Member of Parliament for Jurong Group Representation Constituency (GRC) since 2001. She had previously served as the Minister of State in the Ministry of Social and Family Development. She was elected as Speaker of Parliament in January 2013. Halimah started her career with the National Trades Union Congress in 1978, and held various positions, such as Director of the Women's Development Secretariat, Director of the Legal Services Department, Executive Secretary of the United Workers of Electronics and Electrical Industries, and Deputy Secretary General. She also sat on various Boards including the Geneva-based International Labour Organisation, Tripartite Alliance on Fair Employment Practices, Young

Women's Muslim Association, Malay Teachers' Co-operative, Comcare Supervisory Committee and Mendaki Sense. In recognition of her effort in promoting better opportunities for women in the workforce, Halimah was conferred the Berita Harian/McDonald's "Achiever of the Year" in 2001 and the *Her World* magazine "Woman of the Year" in 2004. Halimah graduated from the National University of Singapore (NUS) with a Bachelor of Laws (Honours). She was called to the Singapore Bar in 1981. In 2001, she attained a Master of Laws from NUS.

Singapore and the International Monetary Fund (IMF)

CHIA Der Jiun*

On 23 September 2011 in Washington, DC at the headquarters of the International Monetary Fund ("IMF"), there was a sombre and purposeful mood among the few dozen dark-suited figures that filed into the room and took their seats at the table. Among the group of Finance Ministers and Central Bank Governors were Timothy Geithner, US Treasury Secretary, Jean-Claude Trichet, President of the European Central Bank, Wolfgang Schauble, Germany's Finance Minister, Francois Baroin, Finance Minister of France, George Osborne, UK Chancellor of the Exchequer, Mario Draghi, Chairman of the Financial Stability Board, Jun Azumi, Finance Minister of Japan and Zhou Xiaochuan, Governor of the People's Bank of China. Taking their seats at the head of the table were IMF Managing Director Christine Lagarde and Singapore's Deputy Prime Minister (DPM) and Minister for Finance, Tharman Shanmugaratnam, who just six months before had been selected by his international peers to be Chairman of the International Monetary and Financial Committee of the IMF (or "IMFC").

The IMFC was meeting at a critical time. In the Euro-area, a mood of panic in the financial markets about sovereign debt in Greece and the periphery was spreading to more countries in the Euro-area; growth had decelerated in the US amidst ongoing deleveraging in the banking system, a weak housing market and political impasse over the US deficit that, if not overcome, would result in a "fiscal cliff"; and Japan had just suffered a devastating earthquake and tsunami. In frank and often hard-hitting discussions over two days, the IMFC came to consensus that the global economy had entered a dangerous phase that needed bold action by all the major

*The author acknowledges the contributions of Kenneth Koh and Rishi Ramchand in the preparation of this essay.

actors. It called on the Euro-area countries to take significant steps to strengthen its crisis management mechanisms and capability, and on the IMF to actively support this effort as part of its global role. It also called for advanced countries to restore sustainable public finances, whilst implementing structural reforms to boost jobs and their economies' growth potential in the medium-term.

Steering International Policy Coordination

Over the last few years, these closed-door IMFC discussions have been instrumental in developing global economic and financial policy thinking and actions. The IMFC is the policy steering committee of the IMF and comprises 24 Finance Ministers and Central Bank Governors who represent the largest countries and groups of countries. Collectively, they channel the views of 188 member countries and meet twice a year at the Spring and Annual Meetings of the World Bank and IMF. The IMFC's discussions represent both a commitment to policy coordination by its member countries and a key policy input to the IMF's policy advice to member countries. Issues discussed have frequently been contentious and difficult, such as the suitability and timing of fiscal austerity in resolving the crisis in the Euro-area, and the appropriate policy responses to the large and volatile cross-border capital flows resulting from highly accommodative monetary policy in developed countries. As the IMFC's chairman, DPM Shanmugaratnam had the task of steering discussions and forging agreement among member countries, often amidst initially divergent views. On the issue of fiscal policy for example, the IMFC has advocated growth-enhancing structural reforms and credible medium-term fiscal consolidation plans over short-term fiscal austerity.

What enabled DPM Shanmugaratnam to chair these and other difficult discussions and successfully build consensus? I believe the success factors revolved around both national and personal credibility: a track record of sound economic and financial policies in Singapore; a strong understanding of international economic and financial issues; a solid international network of relationships with Ministers and senior officials; and a posture of being objective and fair to differing views at all times. In an unusual request, IMFC members asked DPM Shanmugaratnam to serve beyond his three-year term for a fourth year, until March 2015. Singapore's reputation as an objective and credible voice, able to bridge differences and forge consensus at international forums, was further strengthened.

DPM Shanmugaratnam also strengthened the inclusiveness of the IMFC by inviting more non-member participants to the discussions and developing a close partnership with the G20 when this could increase the effectiveness of international cooperation. For example, a joint IMFC-G20 meeting was convened during the April 2014 Spring Meetings to address the continued delays in the implementation of the 2010 IMF Governance reforms. Notably, the United States had been unable to secure the agreement of Congress to ratify the 2010 reforms. The 2010 reforms sought to realign the voting shares and influence at the IMF to better reflect the increased importance of emerging market and developing countries in the global economy. There was considerable tension at the meetings as members who were disappointed with the delays had different views on the way forward. In this difficult situation, DPM Shanmugaratnam successfully rallied IMFC and G20 members around an agreement to give the United States more time, but also laid down an end-December 2014 deadline after which alternative and interim options to achieve the 2010 reforms would need to be discussed. After the United States failed to ratify by the deadline, alternative options were indeed developed and discussions underway in early 2015.

Of course, Singapore's engagement and partnership with the IMF began much earlier than 2011. Singapore became a member of the IMF in 1966 and in those early years of independence received technical assistance from the IMF on a range of financial issues. Over the years, Singapore like other member countries has contributed to the borrowed and quota funds that enable the IMF to lend to crisis-hit countries.

Supporting the IMF in Crisis Management

The IMF is a key international institution that upholds the stability of international trade and capital flows. It does this in two ways. First, as an international economic policy advisor, it conducts surveillance of member countries and the global economy and provides policy advice. Second, as a global crisis manager, it lends to crisis-hit countries. As a small open economy and an international financial centre dependent on trade and capital flows, Singapore has a strong stake in a stable global economy and financial system. Partnering and supporting the IMF advances our common interests. For example, the Euro-area crisis was not a faraway event; Singapore's trade was hit. During the Asian crisis in 1998, our economy entered into a technical recession with full-year growth slowing considerably. These events underscored the vulnerability of Singapore's open economy to external developments even when our fundamentals were strong. If the international responses led by the IMF to both the Asian crisis and the Euro-area crisis were insufficient, Singapore would not escape the consequences.

Our interest in the stability of Indonesia and ASEAN led Singapore to participate in the IMF-led programme for Indonesia in late 1997. The rupiah exchange rate had collapsed dramatically over a short period of time and a full-scale flight of capital threatened amidst growing stress in the corporate and banking sectors. The IMF, together with the World Bank and ADB put together an USD$18bn loan programme for Indonesia. Singapore together with several other partner countries from within and outside our region contributed towards a second line of financing for Indonesia, which was not used.

The policy conditionality of the IMF programme later became the subject of disagreement. But the important point here is not whether the IMF made mistakes in Indonesia; they did, have acknowledged it and drawn lessons for subsequent programmes. The point is that well-formulated reforms are integral to getting a country out of crisis, and to mobilising resources and support from the international community. Without serious and sustained reforms which restore the confidence of lenders, investors, corporates and the public, bailout money can be burned through quickly and crises recur — as recent experiences elsewhere show. Even now, the IMF remains the only international institution that has this ability to mobilise resources quickly and restore confidence by requiring reforms.

Partnership in Training

In the immediate aftermath of the Asian Financial Crisis, the Singapore Government and the IMF jointly set up the IMF-Singapore Regional Training Institute (STI) in May 1998. The STI is the training hub of the IMF in the Asia-Pacific region and its role is to provide training to economic and financial officials from this region in areas of macroeconomic management, statistics, public finances, banking and financial supervision. We saw this as a win-win-win opportunity. For Singapore and the IMF, this was an effective way to deliver high quality training to countries in the region that benefits their development as well as contributes to the stability and growth of the region. For regional countries, the IMF's expertise in macroeconomic management was much respected and training was welcomed as a way to tap into this expertise without the "stigma" of an IMF programme. Demand for the STI's courses has been strong, and since its establishment, more than 10,000 officials from more than 40 different countries in the region have been trained.

Hosting the Singapore 2006 Meetings of the World Bank and IMF

Another major milestone in our partnership with the IMF took place in 2006 when Singapore hosted the Annual Meetings of the World Bank and the IMF. These annual meetings are held outside of Washington DC only once every three years, and there is usually strong interest from various member countries to host these meetings. At these Annual Meetings, there is an extraordinary congregation of Finance Ministers and Central Bank Governors, leading academics and opinion leaders, business leaders and heads of financial institutions, and of course the global media. The prevailing economic and financial issues of the day are debated, global policy responses are discussed and coordinated, relationships and communications are strengthened, and private sector deals are struck. It is also an unparalleled opportunity for the host country to showcase its capabilities to the global economic and financial decision-makers, and draw their attention to the challenges and opportunities of the host country and region.

Singapore expressed our interest to host early, and worked hard to solicit support from member countries. When Singapore was selected to host the 2006 Annual Meetings, that was only the start of four years of preparation that involved coordination across many Government Ministries and agencies and which also involved private sector partners and many members of the public who volunteered to show our visitors the best of Singaporean hospitality and efficiency. Over a period of eight days, Singapore hosted 20,000 participants, five times larger than the WTO Ministerial Meeting hosted in 1996. Singapore acquitted itself well and received kudos and compliments from participants about the content of the programme and the efficiency and hospitality experienced. One of the highlights of the 2006 Annual Meetings was the IMF Board of Governors' adoption of the "Singapore Resolution". This called for the completion of a IMF governance reform package within a two-year period. The resulting completion of the reforms in 2008 represented the first significant step towards strengthening the voice and representation of emerging market and developing countries in the IMF.

A Deeper and Broader Relationship

In sum, the relationship between Singapore and the IMF has expanded across more areas and deepened in engagement over the years. As a small open economy with a deep interest in global stability and growth, Singapore can find common cause with the IMF on many fronts. We have done this through partnerships in lending and capacity building, and now through leadership in global policy coordination. In so doing, we have served not just our shared interests but also raised the profile of Singapore internationally as a credible and valued partner to the international community.

———•◦•———

CHIA Der Jiun is an Assistant Managing Director and Head of the Markets and Investment Group at the Monetary Authority of Singapore. In this role, he oversees the management of the Official Foreign Reserves and the implementation of monetary policy. From 2011 to 2013, Der Jiun served as Executive Director for Southeast Asia at the International Monetary Fund in Washington DC. During his two-year term, he represented the interests of the 10 ASEAN countries and three others on the Executive Board of the IMF and observed at close quarters the key policy meetings of the International Monetary and Financial Committee.

Singapore in the International Maritime Organization (IMO)

Mary SEET-CHENG

The IMO was established in 1959 with its headquarters in London. It is a specialised agency of the United Nations (UN) and is recognized as the competent authority for setting safety and pollution prevention standards for international shipping. 90% of world trade is carried by sea. The IMO thus plays a critical role in facilitating the continued progress of world commerce by regulating for safe and secure shipping.

As a major flag State, port State, and coastal State of a vital shipping lane; Singapore has varied and substantial shipping and port interests. The regulations on shipping that come out of the IMO have major implications for Singapore. This is why we have been an active participant and contributor at the IMO since we became a member in 1966. We are a major flag State being amongst the ten largest ship registries in the world with more than 4,000 vessels in our merchant fleet totalling 73.6 million gross tonnes (GT) in 2013. As membership contribution to the IMO is primarily pegged to the tonnage of ships on a member's register, Singapore is one of the largest contributors to the IMO's annual operating budget. We are a major hub port with vessel arrivals by tonnage reaching 2.36 billion GTs and handling 32.6 million Twenty Foot Equivalent Units (TEUs) containers in 2013. We are also a coastal State bordering the busy shipping lane of the Straits of Malacca and Singapore (SOMS) through which 40% of world cargo passes.

Ensuring Safe Transit Passage Through the SOMS

One of Singapore's key roles in the IMO is to help ensure safe transit passage for shipping through the SOMS. The UN Convention on the Law of the Sea (UNCLOS) requires States bordering a strait used for international navigation

(SUIN) not to hamper transit passage of vessels through the strait. UNCLOS also allows these littoral States to propose necessary rules and regulations for safe navigation and to prevent pollution from ships using these straits. As States bordering the SOMS, Singapore, together with Indonesia and Malaysia, were responsible for the proposals for a traffic separation scheme (TSS) to govern shipping through the SOMS. UNCLOS requires that such proposed TSS be referred to the competent international organisation (i.e. the IMO) for adoption. [UNCLOS, Part III, Section 2, Article 41]. To further enhance safety of navigation, the littoral States also proposed a mandatory ship reporting system called STRAITREP, which came into effect in 1998. STRAITREP is important for enhancing safety of navigation, protecting the marine environment, facilitating the movement of vessels, and supporting search and rescue and oil pollution response operations.

Two Decades of Active Contribution as Member of IMO Council

The IMO is governed by an Assembly of its 170 member states. The Assembly meets biennially. In between, the IMO is run by a 40 member Council that is elected at each Assembly meeting. In view of our expanding maritime interests with our growth as an international maritime centre, we sought election to the IMO Council in 1993. As the Council is the executive organ of the IMO, Council membership would allow us to take part more directly in the decision-making processes of the IMO.

In the two decades since we have been a Council member, we have participated actively in the IMO. Singapore's official representative at the IMO is the Maritime and Port Authority (MPA). MPA officials have served in several important technical and rule-making bodies of the IMO. In 1999 when I was in MPA as the Policy Director, I chaired Committee 1 of the 21st Session of the IMO Assembly in 1999. Mr Chen Tze Penn, then Director General of the MPA was Chairman of the IMO Council from 2001 to 2003. At various times, other MPA officers took up the posts of Chairman of the Sub-Committee on Bulk Liquids and Gases, Chairman of the Sub-Committee on Flag State Implementation, Vice-Chairman of the Marine Environment Protection Committee (MEPC), and Vice-Chairman of the Sub-Committee on Standards of Training and Watch Keeping. Currently, MPA Assistant Chief Executive, Captain M. Segar is serving as Vice-Chairman of the

Maritime Safety Committee (MSC). Nevertheless, as many IMO issues require a whole of government approach, officials from the Ministry of Foreign Affairs, Ministry of Transport, Ministry of Environment and Water Resources, Attorney General's Chambers and National Parks Board have also contributed to our participation at the IMO.

Since 1993, we have sought re-election every two years for a seat on the Council. We are grateful for the strong support we consistently receive at the elections. This shows that the member States recognise the relevance and value of Singapore's contribution as an IMO member.

The following principles have guided us in our participation in the decision making at the IMO Council and its other rule making bodies:

a) To promote safe and secure shipping and to minimise the risk of marine pollution from ships, through the formulation of practical and effective regulations and measures within the IMO framework.
b) To achieve a global framework of rules and standards governing international shipping. We are against unilateral measures imposed by one country or region.
c) To strike a balance between the rights of coastal States, flag States and port States, especially in sustaining the principle of the freedom of navigation. We work to safeguard the provisions of UNCLOS against any measures that would impede the freedom of navigation for international shipping.
d) To encourage universal and uniform implementation of IMO regulations by helping countries through capacity building programmes.

Singapore's unique circumstance of being a major flag State, port State and coastal State of a key waterway enables us to appreciate the varied interests in international shipping and bring a balanced perspective to maritime issues at the IMO. From this unique position, we are able to take an inclusive approach to decision-making, ensuring that the views and interests of all parties are taken into account in the work of the IMO.

Singapore's Contributions to the IMO

Memorandum of understanding on third country training programme

Singapore has actively supported IMO's Integrated Technical Co-operation Programme (ITCP), which aims to equip developing countries with the capabilities to implement IMO regulations and standards. In 1998, Singapore was the first Member State to sign a Memorandum of Understanding (MoU) for a Third Country Training Programme (TCTP) with the IMO to provide technical assistance and sponsor training programmes for developing countries. Under the MoU, experts from Singapore can also be sent to participate in or conduct training on behalf of the IMO. The geographical scope of the MoU on TCTP now covers countries in the Asia-Pacific, Africa, Latin America and the Caribbean. Following our example, several other IMO member States have adopted similar TCTP arrangements with the IMO, thus enhancing the IMO's ability to provide technical assistance. To date, we have conducted 65 training courses under the TCTP programme, training around 1,600 officials from more than 80 maritime administrations.

IMO's "Protection of Vital Shipping Lanes" initiative in the SOMS

The "Protection of Vital Shipping Lanes" initiative was launched by then Secretary-General of IMO, Efthimios Mitropoulos in 2004. It aimed to promote a comprehensive approach to address safety, security and pollution control in critical shipping lanes around the world. We worked with the IMO to start the initiative in the SOMS.

Under the auspices of the IMO, the littoral States, user States, and other stakeholders, met together in Singapore from 4 to 6 September 2007 to adopt a ground-breaking framework for cooperation in enhancing navigational safety and marine environment protection in the SOMS. Known as the Co-operative Mechanism, this framework represents a historic milestone in international maritime cooperation in the implementation of Article 43 of the UNCLOS. Article 43 of UNCLOS requires user States and States bordering a SUIN to cooperate on navigational safety and pollution prevention. The Singapore meeting was preceded by successful meetings in Jakarta in 2005 and Kuala Lumpur in 2006. The littoral States take turns to host the annual series of meetings under this framework.

Under the Co-operative Mechanism framework, Singapore has worked jointly with Malaysia, Indonesia and the IMO on projects to further improve the safety of navigation within the SOMS. One such project was the Marine Electronic Highway (MEH) Demonstration project, which was successfully test bedded in the SOMS by the three littoral States and the IMO. MEH links shore-based marine information and communication systems to those on board ships, allowing ships to incorporate both safety and marine environmental management systems into their sailing plans. A permanent MEH working group has now been established under the Co-operative Mechanism framework, with Singapore leading the recently completed concept study of real time under keel monitoring in the SOMS. Additionally, Singapore has worked closely with Indonesia, Malaysia and the Baltic and International Maritime Council (BIMCO) to launch the pamphlet for Safe Passage in the SOMS at the 93rd session of the IMO MSC in 2014. The pamphlet is a handy guide and advisory on safety measures and the unique conditions of the SOMS.

Singapore also proposed and implemented the "Three Green Light Night Signals" measure for safe crossing in the TSS and precautionary areas in the Singapore Strait. We brought this to the IMO to share the benefits of this safety measure with the rest of the international maritime community. The measure was adopted by the IMO as a recommendatory measure with effect from 1 June 2013.

Tackling piracy worldwide with the IMO

The IMO has been playing a leading role in the initiative to establish a framework for regional anti-piracy cooperation around the world. The Regional Cooperation Agreement on Combating Piracy and Armed Robbery Against Ships in Asia (ReCAAP), the first regional government-to-government initiative to promote cooperation against piracy and armed robbery against ships in Asia, was a response to an initiative from the IMO. The ReCAAP Information Sharing Centre (ISC) was established as an international organisation in Singapore in 2006 with Singapore providing host country funding and support. The objectives of the ReCAAP ISC include information sharing, capacity building, and fostering greater cooperation amongst ReCAAP members to tackle piracy and armed robbery against ships in Asia. Twenty States have become Contracting Parties to ReCAAP, with the USA being the most recent in September 2014.

The success of ReCAAP became a model for countries working to cooperate against piracy in the Horn of Africa. The Djibouti Code of Conduct Concerning the Repression of Piracy and Armed Robbery Against Ships in the Western Indian Ocean and the Gulf of Aden, was signed in January 2009. The ReCAAP ISC continues to work with the IMO to contribute towards developing anti-piracy capacity building efforts under the Djibouti Code. Beyond these efforts at the IMO, Singapore has contributed to the fight against piracy in the Gulf of Aden through participating in the multi-national Combined Task Force (CTF) 151.

Working in the IMO on new environmental challenges

Singapore has always been in the forefront to support and implement new IMO regulations, such as the International Ship and Port Facility Security (ISPS) Code, to enhance port and ship security post 9/11 and the Voluntary IMO Member State Audit Scheme (VIMSAS), now institutionalised as the IMO Member State Audit Scheme, to eliminate substandard shipping. Through our TCTP programmes we have also assisted other countries in their implementation of these regulations.

With global warming, the IMO was also under pressure to ensure that international shipping reduced their emissions of greenhouse gases (GHG). Singapore contributed actively at the MEPC to help reach compromise agreements to reduce GHG emissions through the Energy Efficiency Design Index (EEDI) for new ships and the Ship Energy Efficiency Management Plan (SEEMP) for operating vessels. To bridge the divide in negotiations, Singapore submitted a proposal for the phased implementation of the EEDI regulations. The aim was to provide sufficient time for effective and sustainable implementation by the international maritime community. Singapore's proposal received widespread support at MEPC which helped to bring about an agreement on these measures. This was the first set of legally-binding measures that the IMO adopted to address GHG emissions from international shipping.

Given Singapore's status as a major maritime nation, the IMO is one of the most important UN bodies for Singapore, as it sets the global framework of rules and standards governing international shipping. We have been vigilant to ensure that Singapore is in the forefront of supporting the uniform and universal implementation of these rules and standards and in helping others do so through our capacity building efforts. As a Council member of the IMO since 1993, we have added value to the decision and rule making process by offering our unique perspective as a major flag State, port State and coastal State of the strategic sea lane of the SOMS. Going forward, Singapore will continue its efforts in contributing to the IMO.

Mary SEET-CHENG is Senior Specialist Advisor in the Ministry of Foreign Affairs (MFA). She is concurrently non-resident Ambassador of Singapore to Panama and Cuba. She is the Chairman of the PEMSEA Partnership Council. PEMSEA is a regional organisation promoting the sustainable development and protection of the marine environment in the Seas of East Asia. She served as a diplomat in the Ministry of Foreign Affairs of Singapore from 1973 to 1997, holding a wide range of portfolios and had postings in Canberra and London. From January 1993 to June 1996, she was Singapore's Ambassador in Brussels from which she was concurrently accredited to the three Benelux countries (Belgium, the Netherlands and Luxembourg), the European Commission and the Holy See. In 1997, Mary was seconded to the Maritime and Port Authority (MPA) of Singapore as Director, Policy, where she oversaw policy and strategic planning, port industry development and regulation, economic research and international affairs. During this period, she regularly represented Singapore at the International Maritime Organization meetings in London. She remains a Special Adviser to MPA. She returned to MFA in 2006. Mary holds a Bachelor of Business Administration (Hons) Degree from the University of Singapore and a Master of Arts Degree in International Relations from the Fletcher School of Law and Diplomacy, Tufts University, Massachusetts.

Singapore and the International Telecommunication Union: 1965–2015

LEONG Keng Thai

The year 2015 is an important year for both Singapore and the International Telecommunication Union (ITU). As Singapore celebrates its Golden Jubilee, the International Telecommunication Union (ITU), which is the world's oldest international organisation, celebrates its 150th anniversary this year. At this milestone year, it is fitting to reflect on the relationship that Singapore and the ITU have shared over the last half a century.

Laying the Foundations

Singapore joined the ITU soon after its independence in 1965. The first task for the then newly independent nation was relatively straightforward — for the ITU to allocate to Singapore an international country code. The country code was an important symbol that recognised Singapore as an independent nation state. Coincidentally, Singapore was allocated the country code "+65", which corresponds to the year of Singapore's independence, and also the year of Singapore's membership to the ITU.

The ITU played an important and pivotal role in the early days of our nationhood, especially in building up the local telecommunications market. The most pressing need at that time was to ensure Singapore's economic survival, which was dependent upon, inter alia, an efficient, affordable, and reliable telecommunications network. The setting up of the then-Telecommunication Authority of Singapore (TAS) was the first significant collaboration between the ITU and Singapore. The discussions began as early as 1969, when the Government of Singapore enlisted the assistance of the ITU to conduct an evaluation of Singapore's existing telecommunication administration. The telecommunications administration of Singapore then consisted of the Singapore Telephone Board (STB), which operated the domestic telephone service, and the Telephone Department, which operated the trunk and international telephone services.[1]

In its report, the ITU noted that in telecommunication services, the most capital intensive sector was the national telephone services, where the returns were usually marginal. Further, the ITU pointed out that the main revenue surpluses were in the international telephone and telecommunication services. Given so, the ITU recommended a merger between the STB and Telephone Department, as the merged entity could better facilitate the raising of future loan capital and allow for more efficient operations and planning.[2]

The Government of Singapore accepted the findings of the ITU and its recommendations, beginning with transforming the Telephone Department into the TAS in 1971 and ending with the creation of the Infocomm Development Authority of Singapore (IDA) in 2000. The series of consolidations began with STB being incorporated into TAS in April 1974 and with TAS subsequently merging with the National Computer Board (NCB) to form IDA. This essentially brought four functions under one roof, namely the development of the ICT industry, the Government Chief Information Office, sector transformation and people sector enrichment functions. Without the report of the ITU, and the recommendations that it put forth, the telecommunication landscape of Singapore would probably be very different from what it is today. In addition, the spirit of the ITU report, which focused on creating efficiencies in operations and emphasised foresight in planning, continued to influence many of Singapore's telecommunications and Information and ICT policies today.

The Singapore Telecommunication Training Centre (Telecentre) is another example of collaboration between Singapore and the ITU which was instrumental in the set up of modern Singapore. The Telecentre was a

---

[1] National Library Board, (12 October 1993), Singapore Telecom Goes Public, History SG. Retrieved from: http://eresources.nlb.gov.sg/history/events/bad4f49b-de48-4f5c-8f12-70dd31addfd7

[2] A hundred years of dedicated telephone service in Singapore, 1879–1979 (pp. 13–14) (1982). Singapore: Public Relations Department of the Telecommunication Authority of Singapore.

capacity-building project between the United Nations Development Programme (UNDP) and the Government of Singapore, and was executed by the ITU and TAS in 1972. The UNDP funded 40% of the S$8.6 million project in the form of equipment purchases, fellowships and provided experts to teach at the Telecentre. The Government of Singapore contributed the rest of 60% and this went to the provision of land, buildings and equipment.[3] The Telecentre was sited at the junction of Hillcrest Road and Bukit Timah Road, and it provided courses in the use of the latest ICT technology. Students were able to practise what was taught in the Telecentre through the use of actual field equipment. The Telecentre was an early example of Singapore's continuing emphasis on skills upgrading. It was also at the Telecentre that many of Singapore's early telecommunication professionals and pioneers were exposed to the latest technology and trained in skills relevant to the then-emerging telecommunications and ICT sectors.

Spearheading Singapore's ICT Interests

By the time I joined the TAS in 1980, most of the necessary foundations had been laid for the telecommunications market in Singapore to grow. The focus for TAS then shifted to ensuring the success of the telecommunications industry for the longer term. The ITU's work in the 1980s was focused much in this same direction, and it created various platforms which were important to connect resource-scarce Singapore to the wider regional and global industries.

The ITU's "Telecom" events, which started in 1971, were undoubtedly one of the key platforms that allowed ICT officials from Singapore and the industry to network with and meet their regional and global counterparts on an annual basis. This continues to be the case today. Singapore was not just another participant in Telecom events, which were then held every four years in Geneva. We also played host to all of the regional "Asia Telecom" events between 1985 and 1997, before the Telecom series morphed into the "ITU Telecom" events in 2000.[4] Today, Telecom events are known as the "ITU Telecom WORLD", an annual global platform for high-level debate,

---

[3] A hundred years of dedicated telephone service in Singapore, 1879–1979 (p. 115). (1982). Singapore: Public Relations Department of the Telecommunication Authority of Singapore.
[4] Singapore hosted Asia Telecom in 1985, 1989, 1993, and 1997.

networking, innovation-showcase and knowledge-sharing across the global ICT community. The ITU Telecom events have contributed to a diverse and thriving telecommunications and ICT industry both regionally and globally.

The ITU's policy and treaty-making conferences were also platforms where Singapore actively pursued our national ICT interests. The ITU handles key radiocommunications issues such as global spectrum allocation and satellite filings. It is responsible for the rational, equitable, efficient and economical use of radio-frequency spectrum by all radiocommunication services, including those using satellite orbits.

Being a small country surrounded by bigger neighbours, frequency coordination of the use of spectrum is especially important to Singapore, so as to minimise radio-interference for wireless services, and to ensure the optimal use of spectrum resources. Since the early 1980s, Singapore has participated in the ITU's World Radiocommunication Conferences (WRC), which was the ITU platform tasked to review the International Treaty (Radio Regulations). The Radio Regulations determines the use of spectrum and satellite orbits for the global international community. Through the WRCs, Singapore was able to be actively involved in the ITU's process of allocating spectrum for various wireless services and harmonising spectrum use across jurisdictions. Global harmonisation of spectrum for wireless services promotes economies of scale and benefits consumers and users of wireless services, for example, to facilitate mobile roaming across different countries on a single mobile device.

The United Nations convened the World Summit on Information Society (WSIS) in 2003 and 2005 respectively to address the digital revolution and the opportunities that it brought, and to help countries make their transition to the Information Society. The ITU was the UN agency leading the organisation of the Summits. Singapore, as one of the key advocates of WSIS and its initiatives, participated actively. Having benefitted economically from the early adoption of ICTs since the 1980s, Singapore firmly believed that widespread and pervasive use of ICTs, like the Internet, was critical for economic progress.

In the lead-up to both WSIS Summits, the Internet governance issue was a contentious topic as countries were espousing polarised views on the role of governments in key internet functions like the management of the

Domain Name System (DNS), numbering and protocol systems. Singapore recognised the need for a light-touch approach towards Internet governance to preserve the traits that made the Internet so useful and pervasive in modern times. At the same time, Singapore held the view that governments had legitimate interests in public policy issues concerning the Internet. We therefore took a position to call for evolutionary and incremental approaches to changes to existing systems and frameworks, for instance, in the management of country code Top Level Domains (ccTLDs). Through the WSIS platform, Singapore was recognised as a voice of moderation and an honest broker internationally.

Sharing the Singapore Experience

By the time the Infocomm Development Authority (IDA) was formed in 2000, Singapore had surpassed many of its developmental goals. Singapore then went from being a recipient of technical cooperation, to a contributor of ITU's capacity building programmes and initiatives. Singapore started sharing its experiences in using telecommunications and ICT as an enabler of economic and social growth at various ITU forums. These experiences drew lessons from the collective ITU-Singapore history of building the foundations for telecommunication in Singapore, and enabling the growth of the telecommunications industry both locally and regionally.

To more formally share the experiences that Singapore had accumulated over four decades in ICT policy and regulations, IDA and ITU together launched the Telecom Regulatory Course (TRC) in 2007. From its inception until 2014, this annual executive training programme has trained 213 participants from 39 countries. In late 2013, IDA and the ITU also began conceptualising the organisation of a Regulators' Leadership Retreat (RLR) which seeks to establish a "Leadership Community" among ICT leaders as well as a place for them to exchange experiences and share knowledge in a candid manner. The inaugural RLR was held in late March 2015.

In 2010, the ITU and the United Nations Educational, Scientific and Cultural Organization (UNESCO) set up the Broadband Commission (BBC) to place the issue of the widespread adoption of Broadband on the international policy agenda. The BBC firmly believes that its work would accelerate progress towards all 193 ITU Member States meeting the United Nation's

(UN) Millennium Development Goals. I am deeply privileged to be invited to be a Commissioner of this esteemed Commission. Through the Commission's work, I have been able to share about Singapore's experiences in implementing the Singapore Next Generation Nationwide Broadband Network (NGNBN), as well as numerous digital inclusion initiatives which IDA had undertaken. The UN Summit in 2015 will be endorsing a new set of Sustainable Development Goals and Singapore, through our involvement in the BBC would continue to highlight the importance of ICTs in the global development agenda.

The Road Ahead

The first 50 years of cooperation between ITU and Singapore have been important not just for Singapore, but for the regional and global ICT community. Beyond laying the telecommunication industry's foundations for a then-newly independent sovereign state, the collaborations between Singapore and the ITU paved the way for the ICT industry in Singapore to thrive. Consequently, these enabled Singapore, still a small nation, to contribute to advancing the global ICT agenda. Yet, the road ahead is not without its challenges. As Singapore gears up to become one of the world's first Smart Nations, its collaborations with the ITU need to become deeper, stronger and game-changing. This will ensure that the benefits of ICTs can be harnessed to the greatest extent possible for the benefit of both Singaporeans and global citizens.

LEONG Keng Thai is the Deputy Chief Executive & Director-General (Telecoms & Post) of the Infocomm Development Authority of Singapore (IDA). He has more than 25 years of experience in the telecommunications industry. In his position as Director-General of Telecommunications since 1996, he has played a key role in significant milestones of the industry, including the full liberalisation of the sector, the introduction of a competition regulatory framework, and the deployment of the Next Generation Nationwide Broadband Network. Keng Thai is concurrently holding the appointment of the Chairman of the Personal Data Protection Commission (PDPC), the statutory body set up to administer the Personal Data Protection Act (PDPA). In addition, he is also appointed as a Commissioner to the UN Broadband Commission for Digital Development. Keng Thai graduated with a Bachelor of Engineering (Honours) from the University of Singapore and obtained a Master of Business Administration from the University of Southern California, USA. He also attended the Advanced Management Programme at Harvard Business School.

Singapore and UNCITRAL

Jeffrey CHAN Wah Teck

Singapore is a major trading nation. Much of our prosperity and growth depends on international trade. This has been the case for much of the 700 years of Singapore's history. As a nation that is highly dependent on international trade, enhancing international trade by removing obstacles that impede trade are imperatives for Singapore.

A major obstacle to international trade is the fact that every country has its own laws and regulations that differ from those of other countries. A transnational trading transaction involves two or more states, each of whom have their own peculiar laws and regulations. Every one of these apply to an international trading transaction that crosses territorial boundaries. Persons engaging in international transactions must factor these into their transnational activities as otherwise they would have no certainty as to what their rights and liabilities are. They may also inadvertently contravene regulatory provisions which may nullify their transactions. Such legal uncertainties can discourage transnational trading transactions. At the very least they increase the cost for that transaction. Increased cost is a major factor in discouraging or stunting the growth of international trade. Removing or at least ameliorating such uncertainties and facilitating greater legal certainty would reduce cost and in this way encourage the growth of transnational trade.

This can be achieved through harmonisation, or convergence or unification of laws such that states where a transaction takes place would have identical, or at least similar legal rules governing that transaction. Apart from this, as the world is constantly evolving and trade practices are increasingly challenged by new paradigms as well as new technologies, there is a need to ensure that the commercial laws of states are kept abreast of developments in other areas. These two objectives are complementary and the ideal situation would be for trade laws to be modernised in a harmonized or unified manner.

For the past century or more, a number of international agencies whose members are states have devoted themselves to resolving legal uncertainties that impact persons or their activities, including trade, as they cross international boundaries. The oldest such agency existing today is the Hague Conference on Private International Law (HCCH). It was established in 1893. The HCCH formulates treaties on various aspects of private international law all designed to bring about greater certainty and ease of operation for persons and entities who cross national borders. These include recognition of divorces, service of judicial processes, taking of evidence, civil aspects of child abduction, abolition of requirement of legalisation and enforcement of judgements of courts chosen by parties to a dispute.

Another major international agency is the Institute for the Unification of Private Law (UNIDROIT). This was established in 1926 as an auxiliary organ of the League of Nations. UNIDROIT has over the years formulated a number of Conventions and Model Laws dealing largely with commercial matters with a view to harmonising the various national laws on these issues. These included texts on franchising, security interests in high value mobile equipment and also principles for international contracts.

When the United Nations was established, one of its objectives was to achieve world peace through the promotion of world trade. Removing obstacles and legal uncertainties that affect trading activities was very quickly identified as a major impediment to the continued development of world trade. It was known that there were other international agencies existing at that time seeking to achieve this same objective. However, it was noted that all these other agencies were Euro-centric in nature. That was because most of their members at that time were states in Europe or the Americas. There was a strong sentiment at that time that there was a need to provide developing countries with a voice in the harmonisation or unification of international trade law. This would then ensure that the interests of developing countries are provided for and that these countries are fully engaged in such work and committed to its outcomes. This in turn would complement further the ultimate objective of the United Nations of ensuring world peace. To this end, in 1966, the UN General Assembly established the United Nations Commission on International Trade Law (UNCITRAL). The first Secretary of UNCITRAL was William Vis, who until that time was the Secretary-General of UNIDROIT.

UNCITRAL was intended to be the lead international agency for the harmonisation and unification of international trade law. But as the HCCH and UNIDROIT continued to make substantial contributions to this subject area, it is now common to refer to UNCITRAL as the core legal body of the UN system in the field of international trade law. UNCITRAL's membership comprise states who are members of the United Nations and who are elected to be members of UNCITRAL for six year terms. Membership terms are staggered with half of the members' terms expiring every three years. As with nearly all UN agencies, membership is determined by the regional groups within the UN, e.g. Western Europe and Others Group (WEOG); Latin America and Caribbean; Eastern Europe, Africa, and Asia and Pacific (not including Australia and New Zealand who are in the WEOG). Membership in UNCITRAL is highly sought after in recent times. As a result, the General Assembly has expanded UNCITRAL membership from the original 29 to the present 60 states. These comprise 14 African states, 14 Asian states, 8 Eastern European states, 10 Latin American and Caribbean states and 14 states from the WEOG.

UNCITRAL describes its mandate as "... *to further the progressive harmonisation and modernisation of the law of international trade by preparing and promoting the use and adoption of legislative and non-legislative instruments in a number of key areas of commercial law.*" UNCITRAL seeks to give effect to its mandate by formulating treaties, model laws and legislative guides which provide harmonised rules for international trade and matters that impact on international trade. These are initially formulated by Working Groups (WGs) established and mandated by the Commission. The outcomes of the work of these WGs are then deliberated and confirmed by the UNCITRAL Commission at its yearly meetings. For international treaties, these are then endorsed by the UN General Assembly. In certain instances, a diplomatic conference may be convened to adopt a treaty formulated by UNCITRAL.

Notable achievements by UNCITRAL over the years include the 1980 UN Convention on Contracts for the International Sales of Goods (the "CISG"); the 1985 UNCITRAL Model Law on International Commercial

Arbitration; the UNCITRAL Arbitration Rules; the 1978 UN Convention on the Carriage of Goods by Sea ("the Hamburg Rules"); the 1996 Model Law on Electronic Commerce and 2001 Model Law on Electronic Signatures; the 2005 New York Convention on the Use of Electronic Communications in International Trade ("the Electronic Communications Convention") and the 2008 UN Convention on the International Carriage of Goods wholly or partly by Sea ("the Rotterdam Rules").

Singapore joined the UN in 1965. It was at that time the smallest and youngest UN Member and had very little presence in the international arena. As a major trading hub, with a strong interest in the promotion of international trade, Singapore naturally had a very strong stake in initiatives that would lead to expansions of international trade. Singapore thus was a natural stakeholder in the work of UNCITRAL. A suggestion was thus made by the then Permanent Representative of the UN, Professor Tommy Koh, to the then Attorney-General (AG) Tan Boon Teik that Singapore should offer itself as a Member of UNCITRAL. The AG agreed to this and Singapore was duly elected as a Member of UNCITRAL in 1973.

Since 1973, Singapore has played a major role in UNCITRAL's work. Singapore delegates to UNCITRAL deliberations take their work seriously. They prepare well for the discussions and consult widely to identify the issues that are critical to Singapore. They do not confine themselves, like many delegations do, to only making country reports but participate fully in the open discussions at UNCITRAL forums, contributing ideas and challenging views and arguments put out by others. In this way they contribute to both the intellectual rigour as well as the vitality of UNCITRAL's processes.

Given the high level of participation of Singapore delegation in UNCITRAL's deliberations and the expertise that these delegates bring to the discussions, Singapore enjoys a high standing in UNCITRAL forums. Despite our small size and limited talent pool, Singapore has provided three UNCITRAL Chairmen since 1973. They are Justice (retired) Warren Khoo Leng Huat; Mr Goh Phai Cheng, SC (1995) and Deputy Solicitor-General Jeffrey Chan Wah Teck, SC (2000). Justice (ret) Warren Khoo was the Chairman of the Diplomatic Conference that adopted the CISG in 1980. Additionally, Mr Jeffrey Chan, SC, chaired the UNCITRAL Working Group on Electronic Commerce which formulated the 2005 UN Electronic

Communications Convention and also chaired the delibrations at the 2005 UNCITRAL Commission session that endorsed this Convention. He is presently the Chair of the UNCITRAL Working Group on Online Dispute Resolution.

Singapore was a major supporter and also a beneficiary of UNCITRAL work. Singapore has adopted and enacted into our domestic law the provisions of the UNCITRAL Model Law on Arbitration and the Model Law on Electronic Commerce and Electronic Signatures. The arbitral rules of the Singapore International Arbitration Centre draw very largely from the UNCITRAL Arbitration Rules. Singapore was the first nation to ratify the 2005 Electronic Communications Convention and enact it as domestic law. This Convention updates the earlier UNCITRAL Model Law on Electronic Commerce.

Singapore continues to engage actively with UNCITRAL and to support the various UNCITRAL initiatives to remove obstacles to international trade by harmonising and modernising the legal regimes that apply to transnational commercial transactions. Given our limited resources, we seek to optimise our efforts here by focussing on UNCITRAL's initiatives that are likely to yield cogent results in the fulfilment of UNCITRAL's mandate. The seriousness that we view UNCITRAL's work, the emphasis that we placed on UNCITRAL remaining true to its mandate, and the contributions that our delegates made at UNCITRAL deliberations have earned for Singapore much respect among our peers in UNCITRAL.

The regard that others have for Singapore in UNCITRAL can be seen by the fact that the Singapore delegation is often consulted on the different issues dealt with by UNCITRAL WGs and by the Commission itself. Singapore has also regularly been invited to participate in Experts Meetings convened by the UNCITRAL Secretariat to obtain more information and explore options to resolve difficult issues. Additionally, the UNCITRAL Secretariat often requests Singapore delegates and other Singapore's lawyers to speak on various topics at numerous international fora organised by UNCITRAL or related to its work.

When UNCITRAL considered establishing UNCITRAL regional centres around the world, Singapore was a preferred choice as the centre for the Asia-Pacific Region. The Ministry of Law and the Economic Development Board worked with the UNCITRAL Secretariat in Vienna to explore this opportunity. However, South Korea made a very generous offer to the UN for the UNCITRAL Regional Centre for Asia and the Pacific to be established in Incheon, South Korea. Thus the UNCITRAL Regional Centre for Asia and the Pacific (RCAP) is now located and operates from Incheon, South Korea.

UNCITRAL is one venue where Singapore has shown that notwithstanding its small size and limited resources, it can and has made substantial contributions to the international community. As a small country that is easily buffeted by the winds of international affairs, it is important that Singapore keeps itself visible and relevant to the international community. This would enable us to not just make friends but also be of value to all, even those who are not our friends. This would contribute to our security as a small nation. It would also be a source of pride for our people and an important element in forging a national identity for all Singaporeans.

—————

Jeffrey CHAN Wah Teck, SC, PPA (P), PPA (E), PBS is a Deputy Solicitor-General at the Attorney-General's Chambers. He read law at the then University of Singapore on a President's Scholarship, graduating in 1973 as the Gold Medallist of his class. His many appointments in the Singapore Legal Service included as a DPP, State Counsel, Assistant Registrar of the Supreme Court, Magistrate, Director Legal Service MINDEF and head of the Civil and then the International Affairs Division of the Attorney-General's Chambers. He was the first Chief of Staff of the Singapore Legal Service. He retired in 2013 and has been re-employed on contract. His previous appointments included member of the Military Court of Appeal, the National Committee on Heritage, the Preservation of Monuments Board, the National Archives Board, the Bioethics Advisory Committee and the Law Reform as well as the Professional Affairs Committee of the Singapore Academy of Law. He was also the Chairman of the United Nations Commission on International Trade Law (UNCITRAL) and Chairman of its Working Group on Electronic Commerce. His work included frequent litigation in the courts, legal advice, preparation of legal documents, negotiating international agreements and attending to other international, regional and Commonwealth matters. Jeffrey was

Singapore's Chief Negotiator for the Treaty on Mutual Legal Assistance in Criminal Matters as well as the Extradition Treaty with Indonesia and a Member of the ASEAN High Level Legal Experts Group. Currently he is the Chairman of the UNCITRAL Working Group on Online Dispute Resolution. He is a frequent speaker at different forums locally and abroad on a wide range of legal topics.

Singapore and the United Nations Environment Programme (UNEP): Working with the Global Environment Steward

HAZRI Hassan and Miak AW Hui Min

Early on, Singapore's founding fathers realised the importance of protecting the environment even as we pursued growth. Having to balance environmental issues with economic progress is a challenge for all countries, and a key element of achieving sustainable development. However, environmental issues know no boundaries. The quality of our air, land and water is affected as much by what happens within Singapore as what goes on beyond our borders. We live in an interdependent world and many environmental problems cannot be resolved by any one country alone. Small countries like Singapore are particularly vulnerable, especially if they share a common border or are situated in close proximity to other countries. Cooperation among countries is therefore key to tackling environmental issues in a holistic manner. It is from this perspective that Singapore seeks to be a proactive and constructive global partner responding to the multi-faceted environmental challenges that confront the planet.

The Earth Summit

Singapore's foray into the international environment scene was apparent in 1992 when Professor Tommy Koh — our former Permanent Representative to the UN — was elected to chair the main committee at the UN Conference on Environment and Development (UNCED), also known as the *Earth Summit*. The Earth Summit, held in Rio de Janeiro, Brazil, was one of the largest international conferences in the history of the UN. More than 100 world leaders gathered for the first time to reaffirm that the environment was an integral part of development. The Singapore delegation was led by the then Minister for the Environment, Dr Ahmad Mattar.

The mission of the Earth Summit delegates was to develop an action plan to achieve sustainable development worldwide, by rethinking economic development and finding ways to halt the destruction of irreplaceable natural resources and pollution of the planet. Negotiations were difficult, long-drawn and continued late into the night. Even at the final stretch, it was not clear if the Earth Summit would succeed or fail. However, Professor Koh pressed on, and as chair of the meeting, he managed to broker a deal among 179 UN member states. The Earth Summit gave birth to the following landmark decisions: *Agenda 21*, a global plan of action for sustainable development, and the *Rio Declaration on Environment and Development*. The Summit also brought into being what still remain as the important environment conventions of today — the *UN Framework Convention on Climate Change (UNFCCC)*, the *UN Convention on Biodiversity (CBD)* and the *UN Convention to Combat Desertification*. The Earth Summit was crowned a success. Singapore is privileged to have played a key role in putting in place the international architecture for environmental policy, action and cooperation, despite being a tiny country. As our further commitment, we also released our Singapore Green Plan 1992 at the Summit, which was our first domestic blueprint to achieve sustainable development.

I was not present at the Earth Summit but I had the honour to be with Professor Koh when the UN commemorated the 10th anniversary of this historic event by convening another summit at the Head-of-State level, the *World Summit on Sustainable Development*, in Johannesburg, South Africa in 2002. Many delegates there still remembered Singapore's role at the Earth Summit ten years earlier, and came over to congratulate Professor Koh. The Singapore delegation at the World Summit, led this time by then Minister for the Environment, Mr Lim Swee Say, launched the revised Singapore Green Plan 2012 which highlighted our achievements in the various programmes under the Agenda 21, as well as set out our strategic directions in environmental management, protection and sustainability.

The United Nations Environment Programme — Its Role and Mandate

Singapore sees the United Nations Environment Programme (UNEP) as an important partner. UNEP is regarded as the voice for the environment in the

UN. It also provides the platform for Singapore to support collective efforts in tackling global environmental problems. The UNEP was created in 1972 by the UN General Assembly, in response to the need for the UN to have a lead environmental agency that sets the global environmental agenda. This was the same year Singapore's Ministry of the Environment[1] was set up as a full-fledged ministry, bringing all aspects of pollution control and environmental health in Singapore, previously dealt with by other agencies, under a single organisation.

UNEP's main office is in Nairobi, Kenya, making it the first major UN organisation to be headquartered in a developing country. I recall making my first trip to the heart of Africa in 2001 to attend the Global Ministerial Environment Forum, a platform created by UNEP to allow Ministers, officials, representatives of intergovernmental organisations and civil society to discuss environment challenges facing the world. Some of the more pressing issues discussed were the environmental impacts of energy, the link between pollution and poverty, the increased intensity of natural and man-made disasters, and international environmental governance. Apart from the Forum, the trip to Nairobi itself was an eye-opener to the challenges faced by developing countries in balancing economic growth, social development, and environmental protection.

In the four decades since its creation, UNEP has played a pivotal role in spearheading many important institutions and environment initiatives. This includes being involved in developing international conventions such as the UNFCCC, the CBD, the Convention on International Trade in Endangered Species (CITES), and the Montreal Protocol on Substances that Deplete the Ozone Layer. UNEP, jointly with the World Meteorological Organisation (WMO), also established the Intergovernmental Panel on Climate Change (IPCC), the leading global body on climate science. All these were made possible by another principal role of UNEP — the coordination of monitoring and assessment of the environment. Singapore supports UNEP's approach — to use a sound, scientific basis to draw countries' attention to emerging environmental problems, and bridge them with strong policies to support sustainable development.

---

[1] In 2002, the Ministry of the Environment has been reorganised and renamed as the Ministry of the Environment and Water Resources.

Singapore and UNEP

From the outset, Singapore has always been supportive of UNEP's activities. A well supported UNEP means strong global environmental governance. Singapore joins other countries in protecting the global environment by being party to the multilateral environmental agreements (MEAs) under UNEP. These MEAs establish rules that govern how key environmental issues are addressed, often in areas where there are transboundary implications. This allows each country to be responsible global citizens in protecting our shared environment.

Singapore takes our MEA commitments seriously, and ensures that we have measures in place to meet our obligations. UNEP had noted that Singapore successfully phased out ozone-depleting substances within six years from Singapore's accession to the Montreal Protocol in 1989 — well ahead of the time-frame set for us. That said, ensuring that our national policies are in line with international norms is not easy. Therefore, besides cooperation from our industry, the technical support rendered by international organisations, such as UNEP, is important to help smoothen the process.

Doing More with UNEP

Our engagements with UNEP extend beyond the MEAs. To name one of our more interesting collaborations, Singapore partnered UNEP for three years (2006–2008) to host *Champions of the Earth*, UNEP's global environment award launched in 2004 to recognise the outstanding achievements of individuals and organisations in protecting and improving the environment. These "green" leaders were conferred the Award at a ceremony and gala dinner hosted by the Ministry of the Environment and Water Resources and the Singapore Tourism Board in Singapore.

I still remember vividly the first ceremony we hosted in 2006. Held at the Shangri-La Hotel, the event was graced by then-Singapore President S. R. Nathan and Mrs Nathan, with about 500 international, regional and Singapore-based guests from the environmental community, diplomatic corps and the business sector. A hybrid orchid was specially created for this event by our National Parks Board, and named *"Dendrobium UNEP Champions of the Earth"*. This orchid, with its rare earthly orange-brown hues, was a symbol of the close bonds forged between Singapore and UNEP through this memorable event.

Among the illustrious individuals conferred with the Champions of the Earth award was our own Professor Tommy Koh for his lifelong contributions to the global environment, especially as chair of the Earth Summit and the United Nations Conference on the Law of the Sea. Egypt's Mohamed El-Ashry was bestowed the award for championing the wise use of natural resources and helping developing countries fund sustainable development projects in his capacity as head of the Global Environment Facility. El-Ashry later became the Director-General of the International Atomic Energy Agency. Iran's first female Vice President Massoumeh Ebtekar was bestowed the award for championing cleaner production in the petrochemical industry. The gala event and the inspiring stories of the Champions were broadcast across the Asia-Pacific and featured in leading publications such as *Time* and *Fortune* magazines. I recall my pride swelling when former Executive Director of UNEP Dr Klaus Toepfer said that, "Singapore is an inspiration for other nations striving to achieve the goal of sustainable development".

There have been other significant partnerships with the UNEP over the years. Singapore hosted the Business for the Environment Summit (B4E), an international platform for businesses and governments that discusses environmental issues, back-to-back with the 2007 and 2008 edition of Champions of the Earth. Led by UNEP and UN Global Compact, B4E continues to enjoy strong support from the business community and governments, and is now commonly held alongside major UN environmental events. The Building Construction Authority established the Centre for Sustainable Building to assist and develop sustainable solutions in the building sector for developing countries in this region, particularly in formulating policies to reduce greenhouse gas emissions in the building sector. The National Environment Agency is also participating in UNEP's Asia Pacific Clean Air Partnership, set up to address air pollution in this region. The National Youth Achievement Award Council serves as the Secretariat for UNEP's South East Asia Youth Environment Network (SEAYEN) to assist UNEP in coordinating youth environment activities and projects in the ASEAN region, which is noteworthy as the programmes aim to develop personal qualities that will serve well when the youths grow up to be responsible adults.

Reflections

The concept of a symbiotic relationship between environmental protection and economic development has gained support over the years, and this has been in no small part due to the efforts of UNEP. In fact, UNEP's motto "environment for development" sums up well what UNEP does. It is a huge field of work covered by UNEP, together with the other UN agencies.

The stakes now are much higher than before as the world population grows and economic activity increases. At the same time, awareness of the role of the environment in human wellbeing has strengthened, and UNEP has likewise steadily gained influence. Singapore sees UNEP as an agency with the ambition and room to play a bigger role in shaping the global agenda and action plan. If UNEP succeeds, we are confident that it will bring about stronger global environmental stewardship.

As Singapore celebrates its 50th birthday this year, given our own national circumstances and development pathway, we will continue to support global efforts towards a sustainable world. Only through an international agency with global influence like UNEP can Singapore's efforts in environmental protection and sustainable development be amplified. As Singapore is a small state vulnerable to global environmental crises, unless we do our part to keep this planet healthy, everything else is for naught.

HAZRI Hassan graduated with a Second Class Honours Degree in Civil Engineering from the National University of Singapore in 1990. He joined the then Ministry of the Environment the same year as an engineer focusing on solid waste management and public health engineering. In 1999, he was posted to the International Environment & Policy Department where he handled regional and global environmental and environment-related issues. At present, as Director of International Policy, his job scope entails formulating strategies and approaches for bilateral, regional and international environmental issues to advance Singapore's environmental diplomacy efforts.

Miak AW Hui Min graduated from the Nanyang Technological University in 2010 with a Second Class Honours degree in Communication Studies. Prior to joining the Ministry of the Environment and Water Resources (MEWR) in 2011, she freelanced as a writer for the Business Times and Eco-Business. She is presently part of MEWR's international policy team that advances Singapore's interests in global environmental diplomacy matters.

More Than a Garden — Singapore's Bid to List the Singapore Botanic Gardens as a UNESCO World Heritage Site

Jean WEE

A World Heritage Site designated by the United Nations Educational, Scientific and Cultural Organization (UNESCO) conjures images of well-known tourist attractions that are described as monumental, if not as stunning wonders of the world. The likes of the manmade Taj Mahal, Great Wall and natural beauty and plant diversity of Mount Fuji and the Amazon respectively. With such lofty comparisons, some Singaporeans were in mild disbelief that our humble, albeit well-loved Botanic Gardens qualified to be assessed for inscription as a UNESCO World Heritage Site. The process of deciding what qualifies as a UNESCO World Heritage Site is not about inscribing a place that has potential touristic and commercial value. Instead, it is about identifying a structure or site that has in some way made significant contribution to World Heritage, as well as to its own community that wants it preserved for the future. As they say, size is relative — Singapore is a city state of 718.3 sq km and the Singapore Botanic Gardens is a green lung of 0.74 sq km.

The journey to nominate the Singapore Botanic Gardens as Singapore's first UNESCO World Heritage Site commenced in 2010. To be awarded UNESCO World Heritage status, sites must be of "Outstanding Universal Value" (OUV). This means that sites must meet at least one out of ten assessment criteria such as exhibiting an important exchange of human values over a span of time, and being an outstanding example of a place that illustrates a significant stage in human history. Beyond the need for the site to be intuitively and recognisably outstanding, UNESCO places tremendous emphasis on how well the site is preserved as well as its evolving changes over time. UNESCO also looks out for the authenticity of the nominated sites and monuments, the presence of a buffer zone that ensures adequate protection of the site, as well as a sustainable site management plan. These work together to protect the integrity of the site especially in the face of future developmental plans and other negative encroachments.

A study was commissioned by the then Ministry of Information, Communications and the Arts (MICA) to identify sites in Singapore that would potentially fulfil UNESCO's criteria. Consultations were also done with members of the Singapore Heritage Society, comprising academics, heritage advocates and heritage experts. It was important for a site to be identified that not only clearly illustrated the OUV, but also a site that was clearly one that Singaporeans would support. The list was eventually whittled down to three potential sites — the Botanic Gardens, the Civic District and the combined historic cultural enclaves of Little India, Chinatown and Kampong Glam. After much deliberation, the Civic District — with nearly eight national monuments in close proximity, as well as the three cultural enclaves soon fell out of the running. Clearly, the requirement to impose a buffer zone would severely limit the amount of development that could take place in these districts. This would not be tenable for Singapore given our land constraints.

The Case for the Gardens

The Gardens are undeniably well-loved and cherished in the social memory of Singaporeans. Many shared stories of childhood walks with families, feeding the swans as well as enjoying the generous shade of the *Tembusu* (featured on the reverse of the five dollar note). Others had performed with their school bands at the bandstand, watched concerts or had romantic picnics and walks with dates. Some others recall that the Gardens was the 'neutral' meeting place for families to introduce partners in arranged marriages. In 1959, an outdoor multi-cultural concert bringing together for the first time, Chinese, Malay and Indian performers took place there.

While personal histories were evident, many Singaporeans were less aware of the significant role that the Gardens played in transforming the landscape of Singapore and her Southeast Asian neighbours with the development of rubber. The 156-year-old Singapore Botanic Gardens was in fact the birthplace of the rubber revolution. Rubber seedlings that were gifted to the Singapore Botanic Gardens by the Kew Gardens in London became the catalyst for the rubber industry's revolution in Southeast Asian and resultant economic boom across the region. Subsequent directors of the Gardens took further the research and development for rubber — which was unabated even during the Japanese Occupation.

The Gardens also presents a humble architectural showcase of 12 historical buildings, some of the "Black and White" genre. These buildings served as residences for the directors of the Gardens, and some were functional or served as laboratories. Well preserved examples include Ridley Hall (1882), Burkill Hall (1867). The Swan Lake Gazebo (1850s) and the Bandstand (1930), are popular markers even till today. The original Potting Yard, where new species were grown, and even the origins of the greening of Singapore took root — are still evident. Today, the original English Landscape, 34 heritage trees — the oldest of which is over 200 years old — and the Palm Valley, present an interesting counterpoint to the urbanised densities of Orchard Road, only a mere five minutes away.

Initially, many Government agencies were either modest in their projections of the outcome, or unfamiliar with the history of the Gardens. There was also the question of "why now?". What would this international accreditation or recognition be for? Did turning 50 present an opportunity for us to profile our heritage preservation efforts, or was it also about recognising sites of social memory for what they really are? Should our inscription be successful, what would future expectations be? Would national pride at securing our first UNESCO World Heritage Site raise stronger awareness of heritage values?

The National Heritage Board (NHB) and National Parks Board (NParks) had to work together to convince everyone that the Gardens was a strong candidate and affirm the historical role that the Singapore Botanic Gardens played. The Ministry of Foreign Affairs (MFA), took care of the international engagement. We relied on MFA's wide network of missions and contacts, to open doors to allow us to promote the idea of the Singapore Botanic Gardens. Non-Resident Ambassador and Permanent Delegate to UNESCO, Mr Andrew Toh dived into the task at hand. It was an important time for all of us, with MFA's help, to understand the international playing field and how things worked functionally as well as by way of protocol. Helpful advice from UNESCO's World Heritage Centre, the International Council on

Monuments and Sites (ICOMOS) as well as from experts in the field allowed us the opportunity to build friendships between diplomats and heritage experts around the world. At some point, we started to think of ourselves as salespersons with a cause. We took full advantage of the subsequent UNESCO World Heritage Committee Meetings to showcase the heritage values of the SBG.

Telling the Story of the Gardens

After we had rallied all relevant government agencies for support the next step was to make the legislative and administrative provisions to submit Singapore's bid. In September 2012, Singapore ratified the 1972 World Heritage Convention, the most universal conservation instrument overseeing the inscription of sites that have cultural and natural importance onto the World Heritage List. Three months later, the Singapore Botanic Gardens was placed on the Tentative List of UNESCO World Heritage Sites, a prerequisite for nominations to the World Heritage List to be considered.

Once a site is on the Tentative List, State Parties have to prepare and submit a nomination dossier that shows how the proposed site has fully met the OUV criteria, demonstrate the unique heritage values of the landscape, authenticity and preservation of the site and lastly, the adequacy of measures in place to protect the site, both now and in the future. There was a need to acquaint ourselves very thoroughly with the specific timelines to meet, as we only had one bite of the cherry if we were to make it as part of the celebrations for Singapore's Jubilee in 2015. This meant that we had a year to put together a comprehensive dossier for submission to UNESCO by 28 February 2014, in order for it to be considered for inscription at the meeting of the World Heritage Committee in 2015.

As we prepared the nomination dossier, a draft was made available online for public feedback and we also invited people to submit their own photographs and fond memories of the Gardens. Throughout this process, we were grateful to receive a tremendous amount of support and encouragement from the public, which affirmed that we had indeed made the right choice in selecting the Gardens to potentially be our first UNESCO World Heritage Site. During this time, an inter-agency steering committee was formed to work out a strategy for local and international engagement in our bid for the Singapore Botanic Gardens to be inscribed as Singapore's first UNESCO World Heritage Site. This steering committee was chaired by the Deputy Secretary of the Ministry of Culture, Community & Youth (MCCY), Chief Executive Officer (CEO) of the National Heritage Board and Secretary-General of the Singapore National Commission for UNESCO Rosa Daniel and the CEO of National Parks Kenneth Er (Poon Hong Yuen served as CEO of NParks until February 2014). The steering committee also comprised representatives from MFA, Urban Redevelopment Authority (URA), MCCY, Ministry of Education, NHB and NParks, reflecting the high level of support and collective effort from the Government to champion this bid.

The committee was really a testament to the diverse nature of capabilities that went into supporting the bid. Our biggest support came in when the land planners at URA ensured that the core and buffer zones were protected in the context of Singapore's development Master Plans. International engagement efforts were in MFA's able hands, as our Non-Resident Ambassador and Permanent Delegate to UNESCO Andrew Toh ensured that we engaged all international partners who were curious about our site. Dr Nigel Taylor, Director of the Singapore Botanic Gardens, and the NParks team were always present with their expertise on the Gardens' heritage and botanical features, and extended great warmth and hospitality to our international guests when they visited the Gardens.

MCCY headed up the Singapore National Commission for UNESCO, with Minister of Culture, Community and Youth Lawrence Wong as Chairman, coordinating our national engagements with UNESCO beyond the areas of culture and heritage, to demonstrate that Singapore is a committed and involved Member State. My team at the Preservations of Sites and Monuments Division in NHB played the role of championing Singapore's heritage preservation efforts as a thought leader and capacity builder for heritage both regionally and internationally.

A Heart-Stopping Moment

Time was never on our side and new material had to be continuously added and edited as we made decisions on how we wanted the nomination dossier to be framed as it was read and evaluated at UNESCO. Finally, the dossier — all

700 pages of it — coupled with numerous annexes, blueprints, photographs, and URA Master Plans, went to print. The best of plans still go wrong, and a heart-stopping moment came when the scheduled pick-up of the dossier from the printer did not happen. With our hearts pounding, we had to make frantic calls to the courier service to explain that this delivery was of utmost national significance and the three 700-page bound coloured copies had to be received at UNESCO's headquarters at the Place de Fontenoy in Paris by 28 February 2014. Our Deputy Chief of Mission at the Singapore Embassy in Paris Koong Pai Ching, who had warned us about bad weather and possible strikes, made doubly sure that the copies were safely delivered to UNESCO — we sighed in relief that we still had our jobs.

What Next?

With the dossier submitted, our local and international engagement efforts continued. The Preservation of Sites and Monuments curated the 'More Than a Garden' exhibition that showcased the history and heritage values of the Singapore Botanic Gardens. This exhibition opened at the National Museum of Singapore in March and will be travelling all over the island to various malls and schools until end 2015.

As an active and committed member of UNESCO, Singapore also continues to contribute to UNESCO's capability building efforts by convening several platforms that facilitate the sharing of best practices on heritage preservation such as a side event on heritage challenges and sustainable solutions at the World Cities Summit 2014 and the Future of Preservation Conference held in collaboration with ASEAN in September 2014. In the long-term, we hope to continue to build up our capacity as a thought leader for heritage preservation issues in the region and strengthen our public education efforts on the Gardens.

To raise awareness of the Gardens at the international level and show our support for UNESCO's important mission, Singapore recently named an orchid — the *Dendrobium* UNESCO — after UNESCO at the 38th Session of the World Heritage Committee (WHC) in Doha, June 2014.

Upon our return from the 38th WHC, the Singapore Botanic Gardens set about preparing itself for the all-important visit by the ICOMOS appointed assessor. The evaluation of any UNESCO World Heritage Site nomination comprises the desk evaluation and the on-site visit to assess the site management plan. Following this evaluation process, the advisory bodies make a recommendation that will then be deliberated by the UNESCO World Heritage Committee members at the subsequent WHC meeting. The on-site visit by the ICOMOS assessor was thus the one and only opportunity to showcase the Singapore Botanic Gardens and demonstrate our capability to ensure the continued protection of the site.

By the time this essay goes to print, the UNESCO World Heritage Committee would have met in Germany in end June 2015, to deliberate on the nominations to the World Heritage List for that year. Based on the advisory bodies' recommendation, the WHC will then vote on each nomination, to approve its inscription as a World Heritage Site, defer it if further information is required from the country, or to reject the nomination.

We hope to have convinced enough State Party representatives that Singapore's site deserves this inscription on its own merit and that it will continue to be a site that future generations will continue to enjoy. One day in the future, when a Singaporean is asked what a UNESCO World Heritage Site means to them, we hope the reply will be "the Singapore Botanic Gardens".

Jean WEE became the first director of the Preservation of Sites and Monuments (PSM), of the National Heritage Board in February 2009. PSM's key function is to research, identify for preservation gazette and promote buildings and sites of national significance. She was formerly Assistant Director at the Singapore Art Museum, and is a firm believer in public outreach and education. She sits on several committees in the field of architectural heritage in Singapore, including the SEAMEO Project in Archaeology in Fine Arts (SPAFA).

Editors' Note: On 4 July 2015, UNESCO approved Singapore's request to list the Singapore Botanical Gardens as a World Heritage Site.

Helping the Refugees of the World

Janet LIM

I joined the UN High Commissioner for Refugees (UNHCR) in 1980, just when Southeast Asia was facing one of its biggest humanitarian crises. At that time thousands of refugees were fleeing from the wars in Vietnam, Laos and Cambodia, crossing overland into neighbouring countries such as Thailand or leaving by boats to Philippines, Indonesia and Malaysia and even Singapore. There were many tragedies and dramatic humanitarian needs faced by refugees which drew world attention. It resulted in one of the biggest mobilisations of humanitarian assistance at the time for refugees in camps dotted all over the receiving countries in Southeast Asia. This was my introduction to the UNHCR and the UN. Since then I have, working both at the frontline and at UNHCR's Headquarters in Geneva, been involved in the humanitarian consequences of most of the major crises of our times. They ranged from the first Gulf War in the 90s to the current crises in the Middle East and Africa, with everything else in between, including the wars in the Balkans, African Great Lakes region, and Afghanistan.

It is my impression that the humanitarian wing of the UN is an area that Singapore, as a member state, has been the least engaged with. Yet, this is probably the fastest developing area of work within the UN, necessitated by the increasing numbers of conflicts in the world. In particular, forced displacement of population has become a global issue, requiring agencies such as UNHCR to grow in size and reach.

UNHCR

UNHCR is one of the major actors in the international humanitarian system which responds to humanitarian crises. It was established by the UN General Assembly in 1951, to protect, assist and find solutions for refugees from the

Second World War. Since then its mandate has been extended in scope and time to cover all refugees in the world (except for the Palestinian refugees for which, another UN agency, UNRWA, has a specific role). While UNHCR's core mandate is responsibility for refugees, i.e. those who are not under the protection of any State (and hence the need for a UN High Commissioner for Refugees and his Office), this responsibility has also been expanded to include those who are Stateless and more recently, also to internally displaced persons. The latter is a responsibility shared with other UN agencies. A particular challenge has been to distinguish refugees from other types of population movements, such as illegal migration or human smuggling and trafficking in what has been called "mixed flow". UNHCR works with governments to put in place mechanisms that can help identify and determine whether those seeking asylum can be recognised as refugees. The determination of refugee status is important as there are international legal frameworks (1951 Refugee Convention and its 1967 Protocol relating to the Status of Refugees) which spell out the obligation and responsibilities of States towards those recognised as refugees. In situations of mass influx, careful review is made of the countries in conflict to determine whether there is generalised violence. In this case, refugees may be recognised on *prime facie* basis, rather than on the basis of individual status determination. Under international law, countries receiving such refugees are obliged to keep their borders open.

UNHCR has 462 offices in 127 countries throughout the world. The offices are served by some 9,400 staff, nearly 90 percent of whom are based in the field where refugees and IDPs are to be found. The causes of refugees, as is true also for most internal displacements, are man-made and political in nature, in contrast to humanitarian crises caused by natural disasters. Yet the principles for managing humanitarian consequences are all the same and are strongly anchored on values based on humanity, neutrality and impartiality.

Current Humanitarian Landscape and Refugees

During the last five years we have seen a quantum leap in the number of major crises which are happening at the same time, and in the scale and the sheer numbers of people forced to flee. Indeed we are currently facing, at the global level, the most dramatic forced displacement of population since the Second World War. More than 51 million have fled from wars, conflict and violence, with more than 17 million leaving their countries and becoming refugees, and the rest internally displaced in their own countries. It would seem that we are entering a new era of forced population displacement. The biggest crises at the present time are in Africa and the Middle East, but there are on-going humanitarian operations relating to forced population displacement in all continents of the world. Why is this the case?

When the Cold War ended in the late 80s, there were hopes that many crises would have been resolved with the decline of inter-state wars. Indeed in the 90s, UNHCR was able to find solutions for refugees displaced by some of these wars to return to their home countries. Unfortunately, the end of the Cold War has also been marked by an increase in intra-state wars, which have their roots in ethnic, tribal or religious divide. More recently conflicts have also been complicated by the multiplication of armed groups of different affiliations that have international criminal or ideological links. The current crisis in Syria and Iraq with multiple and fragmented anti-government groups, and in particular the rise of the ISIL in the Middle East is a good example of the complexity of today's warfare. In the African continent we have seen the resurgence of conflicts in countries where stability has not taken root and peace has broken down, such as in South Sudan and Central African Republic. Elsewhere such as in Somalia and Afghanistan, conflicts have become protracted, sometimes over decades.

Faced with generalised violence or persecution at the individual level, refugees have fled *en masse*, often to neighbouring countries. However, there are often movements further afield to countries far beyond. Hence we can easily find refugees from any crisis in any part of the world, even in Asia. The majority of refugees and displaced population are actually women and children who face particular vulnerabilities. In big humanitarian crises, we face not only the challenge of delivering life-saving assistance, such as food, shelter, water, health etc., but also to meet the immediate protection needs of refugees. The most important protection need of any refugee is to find safety in a country of asylum, and to be protected from being returned to the dangers they had fled from. Refugees often find themselves in environments where they are easily exploited and their rights abused, often even as they flee. Many refugees undertake perilous journeys across deserts and seas, with much loss of life. Given the nature of conflicts today, there are refugees who may be refugees several times over as they are caught up in resurgence of conflicts or find themselves in countries of asylum which have themselves become engulfed in conflicts.

At the same time, humanitarian access to displaced populations in today's conflicts has also become more difficult — refugees and internally displaced populations are often located in the most logistically difficult to reach as well as in the most dangerous places, where unpredictable armed groups operate. Humanitarian workers, who used to enjoy protection by virtue of their neutrality and impartiality, are today often targeted, and like the displaced population, are sometimes used as a weapon of war. It is also common for affected governments to place certain restrictions on humanitarian access to displaced or refugee populations.

The challenges facing humanitarian operations are numerous and complex, and co-ordination and collaboration among humanitarian actors are more important than ever. Hence the UN has established a platform for coordination that brings together not only the UN agencies but also States and Civil Societies, so as to facilitate an international response system aimed at establishing agreed priorities and reducing duplication in the delivering of assistance.

Burden Sharing and International Solidarity

It is recognised that refugees in large numbers represent a huge burden for host countries, be it from the security, political, economic or social points of view. A good case in point today is the situation in Lebanon, a small country of four million with a highly sensitive political environment, hosting more than a million Syrian refugees. In general, more than 85% of the world's refugees are hosted in developing countries, and however generous these countries may be, they cannot be expected to bear this burden by themselves. It is therefore imperative that the international community mobilises resources not only to assist in meeting the humanitarian needs of the refugees in their countries of asylum, but also in finding solutions for the refugees, such as in accepting refugees for resettlement, even if the best solution is for refugees to return home when their countries return to normalcy. It is also increasingly recognised that it is not enough just to provide humanitarian assistance to refugee hosting countries, but given the impact on local economies and social fabrics, there has also to be a concerted effort to target development assistance to these countries, at the same time as providing humanitarian assistance. In fact, it has been found more effective, especially in situations where refugees are living among impoverished local communities, to provide assistance in such a way that both host communities and refugees can benefit.

Refugees are often very resourceful people, by virtue of necessity, and if planned properly there are opportunities to use them to the benefit of local economies. The traditional approach to keep refugees in camps where they are denied means of livelihood and forced to be dependent on hand-outs is not viable in the long run. In Asia where there are growing economies, some countries have found it a sound economic strategy to turn refugees into legal migrants where they can be a source of much needed labour force. This could also address the security concerns that States may attribute to the presence of undocumented foreigners.

The entire international system for the management of forced displacement whether internally within a country or externally to other countries is built upon the notion of solidarity and the sharing of responsibilities. In a world which is increasingly interlinked, no country is immune from the impact of crises anywhere in the world and however far away. The growth in the absolute number of the forcibly displaced we are seeing today is accompanied by the ever increasing complexity of the environment surrounding forced displacement, including by a number of interrelated and mutually reinforcing global trends such as population growth, urbanisation, food and water scarcity, and climate change. Without commitment by the international community to address the root causes of conflict, and to manage their consequences, especially in population displacement, there will never be an end to the vicious cycle of conflict and forced displacement.

The Human Faces of Forced Population Movements

The crises that generate forced displacements may seem overwhelming in their scale; the challenges faced in our responses seem near insurmountable. Yet, I know from my own experience, through the many crisis situations I have been engaged in, that the humanitarian responses of the international community have real impact at the individual level. There have been hundreds of thousands of refugees and displaced persons whose lives have been saved and rebuilt from the ashes. One of the strongest motivations for my work is to see the resilience and strength of individual refugees and families reaffirmed again and again, despite so much personal loss and tragedy.

A few months ago, I met a Vietnamese woman, Carina Hoang, in Australia, who is today an award-winning writer. Some 20 years ago, together with two siblings and 370 other people, she was marooned on Kuku Island after a horrendous journey from Vietnam on a wooden boat, during which they endured violent storms and pirate raids. They were rescued by UNHCR after three months, but not before some had succumbed to disease and malnutrition. Carina was eventually resettled in the United States and moved to Perth five years ago, where she is pursuing her PhD.[1]

Today with the Syria crisis, the same scenario is also being played out. In September this year, a 19-year-old Syrian lady, Doaa, took to the Mediterranean Sea with her fiancé in a desperate attempt to reach Europe to try to join her relatives in Sweden. She was in a smuggler's trawler with more than 500 other people, including many women and children, when they were rammed by an unidentified vessel, causing theirs to sink. Doaa spent three days in the water, during which time she saw many of the initial 100 or so survivors die in the sea. She was handed two babies by desperate people and could eventually keep only one baby alive by the time she was rescued. She also lost her fiancé and was one of only 11 survivors from the 500 on board. This young woman who showed tremendous courage and determination to survive is today on the Greek island of Crete, more determined than ever to join her relatives in Sweden and to begin life anew.

Perhaps, one of the most inspiring messages that we have often received from refugees, especially the young ones, is that they do not want only to survive, but also to thrive.[2] Many times refugees have told me that while daily basic needs such as food, shelter and other necessities are critical, they worry about the disruption in their or their children's education. Many preciously safeguard their school records and certificates when they flee, in the

---

[1] For more information about Carina go to http://stories.unhcr.org/carina-hoang-vietnamese-refugee-award-winning-author-p5831.html

[2] See also the UNHCR Head of Communications, Melissa Fleming's TED Talk at http://www.ted.com/talks/melissa_fleming_let_s_help_refugees_thrive_not_just_survive?language=en

hope that they can still continue their education and through that, their hopes and dreams for the future. We have many individual testimonies of refugees, who, given the chance, have been able to succeed despite their tough environment. This was the case of Chol Yaak Akoi, a South Sudanese refugee from Kakuma Camp in Kenya, who I met recently in Doha, Qatar at the World Innovation Summit for Education (WISE). In 1999, Chol fled from his home in Jonglei State in South Sudan to avoid forced recruitment by one of the warring parties. He pursued his education in the camp and won a scholarship to study at the university in Nairobi. Owing to his leadership skills and exemplary grades, he was honoured at the WISE Conference to benefit from other training.[3]

It is the individual refugees that we help to succeed who may ultimately be able to recreate their broken societies and break the cycle of conflicts. Left to languish, they could become a lost generation who could form the roots of future conflicts.

I have tried in the above to highlight some of the key issues I have confronted in my work in UNHCR. Perhaps the world of conflicts and population displacement with all its humanitarian consequences seems far away for us in Singapore, where we have been able to enjoy economic progress and peace for the past few decades. Yet humanitarian issues, especially those relating to conflicts, have become globalised, and a greater engagement by Singapore would be appropriate. As a country, and despite its size, Singapore has a lot to contribute. In natural disasters where Singapore has been more ready to engage, Singapore has gained a reputation for the quality of its technical expertise and its efficiency and effectiveness. This should also be extended to humanitarian operations relating to conflicts. Today's ever-increasing conflicts have a great impact on international peace and security and no country however big or small will be unaffected.

---

[3] For more information about Chol and WISE go to http://www.wise-qatar.org/learners-voice-chol-yaak-akoi

Janet LIM was recruited into the Administrative Service of the Ministry of Finance (Development Division), but left in 1976 for postgraduate studies in sociology and development studies in Bielefeld, Germany. While in Germany, she became involved with Indochinese refugees resettled there. This experience led to her joining the United Nations High Commissioner for Refugees (UNHCR) in 1980. Since then she has been in assignments in UNHCR Headquarters in Geneva, as well as in the field. She served on long and short missions in Thailand, Malaysia, Syria, Turkey, Western Sahara, Sri Lanka, and Afghanistan. At Headquarters, she was substantively involved in the establishment of UNHCR's emergency response capacity and mechanisms, as well as its security management system. From 2004 to 2009, she served as the Director of the Bureau for Asia and the Pacific, overseeing UNHCR's operations stretching from Iran to the Korean Peninsula. In 2009 she was appointed Assistant High Commissioner for Operations at the Assistant Secretary-General level. In this capacity, she oversaw the work of all five regional bureaux covering UNHCR operations in all parts of the world, as well as HQ Divisions responsible for UNHCR's programme support and management, security, supply, and emergencies. During her UN career, she also worked on a secondment basis in senior roles with UNAIDS and with the peacekeeping mission, UNAMA, in Afghanistan. She retired from UNHCR in January 2015 and is currently a Fellow at the Singapore Management University. Janet graduated from the University of Singapore in 1975 with a Bachelor of Social Sciences (Honours).

Singapore's Rise to Prosperity, and Its Evolving Relationship with the World Bank Group

Janamitra DEVAN

> Singaporeans are an extremely serious people; to engage them, the World Bank Group had to embark on a serious venture for development and growth. I suspect that Singapore's leaders were willing to give me a hearing because of long friendships and earned trust. I believed that Singapore had the foundation of experience and reputation — as well as potential — to contribute to this new intellectual, policy, financial, and business venture. But our effort had to be practical — and ultimately effective!
>
> — Robert B. Zoellick, 11th President of the World Bank

Singapore vaulted towards prosperity in world-record time: In 1966, when Singapore became the 104th member of the World Bank Group (WBG),[1] its real GDP per capita (measured in constant-2005-dollar terms) was around US$3,150. That put the newly independent island economy on the middle rungs among the poor countries of Asia. A generation later, in 2013, Singapore ranked third in the world with a real GDP per capita of almost US$37,000.

Singapore also moved swiftly when, in 1966, its lawmakers considered joining the WBG and the International Monetary Fund (IMF). The then-Finance Minister, Lim Kim San, introduced the Bretton Woods Agreements Bill in Parliament on June 22. The Bretton Woods Agreements Act came into

---

[1] The WBG consists of 5 entities: World Bank (WB); International Finance Corporation (IFC); Multilateral Investment Guarantee Agency (MIGA); International Development Agency (IDA), and International Center for the Settlement of Investment Disputes (ICSID).

effect on July 4. On 3 August 1966, Singapore and the World Bank signed the articles of agreement.[2]

Since the formation of the World Bank (WB) at the end of World War II, many countries have benefitted from working with the organisation. France received the first WB loan ever to help rebuild the war-ravaged country. Deng Xiaoping opened the doors to the WB to help him lay the foundation for China's remarkable growth. South Korea is indebted to the WB for aiding its recovery from the devastation of the 1950s war. Singapore also gained somewhat from its ties with the WB — but not anywhere close to the extent that other countries benefited. Why?

Singapore's relations with the WB pursued a unique course. Between 1959 and 1975,[3] the WB disbursed nine loans (comprising 14 projects) to Singapore.[4] In 1963, with a guarantee from the Federation of Malaysia, Singapore took a small S$45 million loan to finance the construction of the S$65 million Pasir Panjang 'B' Power Station. Additional financing, after 1963, totaling a relatively small US$181.3 million, went toward port expansion, sewage, power, telecoms, water, education and environmental management.

However, after 1975, Singapore's level of interactions with the WB effectively went quiet. Singapore "didn't require loans," recalled J.Y. Pillay, who was the Permanent Secretary of the Ministry of Finance in the 1970s. The context underlying Singapore's ensuing muted relations with the WBG offers a history lesson in development and diplomacy.

Singapore faced unique development challenges, and its first-generation leaders were deeply aware that development needed to, first and foremost, come from within — to be built on sheer hard work and ingenuity and not just from aid money.

Also, during the 1970s and 1980s, many academics began to question the entire concept of aid. Did it really help development, they asked, or did it retard it? Did it force countries into dependency? Singapore's senior leaders then were mostly skeptical of the concept of development aid. After

---

[2] On behalf of the Government of Singapore, Goh Koh Pui, then Chairman and General Manager of the Port of Singapore Authority, signed the articles of Agreement of the IMF and the WBG in Washington, DC.

[3] In 1959, Britain granted internal self-government to Singapore. In 1963, Singapore became independent and joined the Federation of Malaya to form Malaysia. In 1965, Singapore separated from Malaysia and became an independent country.

[4] The data quoted here comes from the archives of the World Bank.

all, the news media were rife with stories of aid gone wrong in many parts of Latin America, Asia and Africa. Economic development stagnated in many an aid-recipient country.

Singapore's leadership chose instead a path toward wealth creation that relied on creating their own sources of funds, such as new savings policies. Complemented by reliable infrastructure, the rule of law and smart commercial regulation, wealth-driven development would be on more stable foundations.

In 1981, I bore witness to one of the first-generation leaders' thinking on the topic of aid. Dr Goh Keng Swee, Singapore's former Deputy Prime Minister, was then also Chairman of the Monetary Authority of Singapore (MAS). As a young economist there, I was privileged to attend a weekly lunch that he hosted for young professionals. There was a discussion on the side between him and a more senior economist about the upcoming payment of dues to the Bretton Woods organization — and, almost in exasperation, he asked, "Why are we even members of the WB and the IMF?" He questioned whether Singapore really benefitted as a member of those institutions, and he suggested that someone should review the country's membership. Singapore, of course, remains a member of these organisations. I suppose that, if a review indeed took place, it concluded wisely that there was no need for Singapore to withdraw from membership.

Nonetheless, Dr Goh did not ask that question out of context. Institutions such as the WBG and the IMF came under attack from various quarters, accused of foisting aid onto developing countries and placing unreasonable conditionalities on them. Many felt that aid recipients became akin to cocaine addicts unable to kick the habit. Singapore was not about to get into that rut. Those institutions were also seen to take unyielding ideological stands, often apparently serving the economic and political interests of developed countries. After all, they took positions that were driven primarily by the so-called "Washington Consensus" that essentially advocated free trade, floating exchange rates, free markets and macroeconomic stability. Singapore's investments in government-led companies, for example, were certainly "frowned upon by WB professionals of that era".[5]

---

[5] Robert Zoellick, my former boss at the WBG, told me that he was aware that WBG officials during the 1970s and 1980s had disagreed with the heavy-handed approach that Singapore had taken in forming various government-controlled companies. He went on to say that Singapore, of course, had proved the skeptics wrong, and rather decisively.

Singapore put up spirited defence of its positions when it mattered. For instance, in the mid-1980s, Singapore together with Israel and Hong Kong mobilised opposition to the idea of being "graduated" into a higher income designation by the WB. Patrick Daniel, then with the Ministry of Trade and Industry, was tasked with defending Singapore's opposition to being graduated. Jean Baneth, the Director of the WB's International Economics Department at the time, was overseeing the development of a new classification system and was in Singapore to meet with Lee Hsien Loong, then Minister for Trade and Industry and Patrick. This new system would give a clearer definition of what constituted "developed" and "developing" countries. Singapore, Israel and Hong Kong would have been defined as "developed" under this proposed classification system, and they opposed it. If Singapore had been graduated, it would lose the so-called Generalized System of Preferences (GSP) trade privileges, which at that time were too important to ignore for Singapore's economic well-being.

Singapore's argument was that its structure was fundamentally different. It benefited from huge foreign investment. "Multinational corporations (MNCs) contributed almost 70 percent of the country's GDP," Patrick explained. "We didn't care who owned the cow as long as it produced milk. But we had to keep the MNCs here. If they upped and left, we would have lost a huge part of our GDP overnight." While Singapore had other arguments (weakness of its social indicators, for example), Jean was swayed by Hsien Loong and Patrick on the MNC argument.

After a year or so, the WB abandoned the "Developed vs. Developing" country classification and went toward a "Low-, Middle-, and Upper-Income" definition. "Singapore certainly played a part to influence this outcome," said Jean. Singapore remained "ungraduated."

By the late 1990s Singapore had indeed entered the ranks of advanced countries. Countless case studies began appearing on its success story. Developing countries all over the world looked toward Singapore for lessons. The truth of the matter is that Singapore pulled itself up by its own bootstraps, Patrick reminded me. In fact, Singapore largely shunned receiving development aid.[6]

---

[6]Only in 21 January 2014 did Singapore raise its contribution to the WB's capital from US$38.6 million to US$672 million, in exchange for increasing its voting power from 0.01 to 0.25 percent.

In the 2000s Singapore's relationship with the WB stepped up. First, in 2006, Singapore hosted the 61st IMF-WB Annual Meetings. Known as "Singapore 2006", the week-long conference was the biggest global event that Singapore had ever organised up until that time. Second, in 2007, Robert Zoellick was appointed as the 11th President of the WBG.

A highly regarded American official who had served in senior capacities in several Republican administrations, Zoellick became an avid admirer and student of the Singapore story. Bob told me that he first visited Singapore in 1989 with then Secretary of State James Baker. Bob developed strong relationships with George Yeo and later with Deputy Prime Minister (DPM) Tharman Shanmugaratnam and PM Lee Hsien Loong. Bob admired Singapore's discipline in "taking an analytical approach on almost everything," he told me. A visionary leader of the WBG, Bob saw a win-win opportunity for the WBG and Singapore.

Bob did not hide his affection for Singapore. I recall my interview with him in 2009 for a senior position at the WBG. He quizzed me on what I knew about Singapore, and it became evident to me that he knew quite a bit, too. At the end of the interview, he quipped, "Well, if you come from Singapore, you've gotta be good." I became the joint WB-IFC Vice President for the WBG's Financial and Private Sector Network.

Bob mentioned to me that he wanted to get more professionals from Singapore to join the WBG's staff. He thought Singaporeans could add weight to the institution's skills and could help counsel clients from emerging markets — and he was right. I met a number of heads of state from Africa and Central Asia in the course of my work at the WBG, and they ceaselessly quizzed me on the development experiences of Singapore. Bob realised that it was not just loans that emerging leaders of the developing world were looking for: They were looking for knowledge, as well.

He recognised that the changing dynamics of a multipolar world order required a change in the way the WB responded to its clients. In a sense, the WB had evolved from being more than just a "Bank": It had become a repository of some of the world's most profound thinking and experience on economic development. Even as it had decentralised over the years to a largely country-based model, the WBG needed to become even less Washington-focused. The WBG needed to be closer to clients — and partners such as Singapore — to be in contact with both the practical challenges and the learning of others who were working to overcome those problems. Expanding its operations in Singapore was an obvious answer.

Bob saw a country that "scrutinised every thing every which way to see what potentials they held; they are seen as reliable allies by many, not only in Southeast Asia but in the globe; and they have experienced economic development within a generation." Singapore had become a knowledge economy and its leaders were keen to develop that even further. On the other side, said Bob, "we in the WB have vast capital and knowledge resources at our disposal that no one else possessed. It just made sense for us to partner with [Singapore]."

Bob also thought that a 'Hub' of sorts could be a plus for Singapore. "I knew that Singapore was competing with other locations to be a financial and knowledge center," Bob recalled. "And a World Bank presence, which could evolve over time, could assist Singapore's 'brand' as a location for cutting edge financial and development work, and boost Singapore as an influential and respected voice on international economic policy issues. I was delighted, for example, to later see DPM Tharman selected as the Chair of the IMFC, which in effect serves as the IMF's board of Ministers. This is a win-win step for Singapore and the world."

In December 2008, just a year and a half after taking the reins of the WBG, Bob signed a Memorandum of Understanding with the Government of Singapore to establish the "Singapore Hub". Peter Ong, the current Permanent Secretary of the Ministry of Finance said, "The Singapore Hub was set up to leverage Singapore's expertise in urban development, as well as the WBG's global development knowledge and operational experience, to develop better urban solutions for developing countries worldwide". The hub, which began operations in 2009, was a major step forward in Singapore's strategic partnership with the WBG.

Moreover, in 2010, Bob put together a team of senior colleagues at the WBG and told them to come up with a plan to scale up the hub, expanding it beyond urban-focused issues.[7] There were skeptics within the WBG, of course, who felt that establishing a hub in yet another developed country would not go down well in the eyes of many other member countries.

---

[7] The team was led by my colleague, former Vice President James Adams. Other senior officials involved in this team included SVP Lars Thunnel of the IFC along with VPs Pamela Cox and myself.

Singapore, after all, was certainly not a "client" of the WBG in the true sense of the word. By this time, it had clearly "graduated" to developed-country status.

I recall conveying to Peter during the Annual Meetings in 2010 that, in my view, we should aspire for much more than just an "urban and infra-structure hub". I saw that Singapore could even house a "microcosm of the WBG", and I asked, "Why not absorb more from the WBG and place them in Singapore?" That would serve the WBG's clients not only in the region but also in the rest of the world. There was no reason why, for instance, African clients could not turn to Singapore to leverage the expertise of the WBG and the city-state.

In September 2011, President Zoellick and DPM Tharman announced the scale-up of the WBG's operations in Singapore. The expanded Singapore Hub co-locates business units of the WB, IFC and MIGA — a first outside of Washington.[8]

Since the hub's formation, Peter and former colleagues at the WBG tell me that it has seen a rapid growth in its engagement with client countries and in multilateral forums. Tapping into expertise in Singapore, the hub has been providing advisory services to client countries regionally and around the world. Projects include working with several East Asian economies on their Public-Private Partnership Financing Framework, organising training programs and policy dialogues with both public- and private-sector players based in Singapore, test-bedding urban solutions, and serving as a knowledge-exchange centre.[9]

For the past year, Singapore has been in intensive discussions with the current WBG President, Jim Yong Kim, and his team on the next phase of the Singapore Hub's operations. Staff members are excited about even better things to come in the future of Singapore's relationship with the WBG.

---

[8] It was one of the two hubs established during Zoellick's presidency, the other being the Fragile and Conflict State Hub in Nairobi, Kenya. The hubs were established to consolidate the WBG's technical skills in logistically convenient locations.

[9] Through the hub, the IFC has built up, through its Asset Management Company (AMC), a Global Infrastructure Fund that reached US$1.2 billion at the end of 2013, surpassing its initial target of US$1 billion. The AMC has begun investment operations. IFC and Government of Singapore Investment Corporation (GIC) are anchor investors of this Fund. In addition, Singapore-based players are also partnering with MIGA to provide loan guarantees for projects in regional countries, such as Vietnam and Indonesia.

There is still untapped potential to promote synergies from the co-location of the three arms — the WB, IFC and MIGA — and to align their work to end extreme poverty by 2030 and promote shared prosperity. Those noble goals, set forth by President Kim, can benefit from the growth experience that underpinned Singapore's remarkable ascent out of poverty.

The continuing collaboration between Singapore and the World Bank Group can lead only to positive results, as the World Bank pursues its twin goals of eradicating extreme poverty and building shared prosperity. Singapore could provide a lesson or two on how smart growth can make them happen faster.[10]

———•◦•———

Janamitra "Dev" DEVAN is currently based in Ankara, Turkey where he is an independent consultant. He was recently appointed as Senior Advisor to the Chair of the B20 and President of the Turkish Chambers of Commerce and Commodity Exchanges. He also is a member of the Atlantic Council, and the World Economic Forum's (WEF) Global Agenda Council on Competitiveness. He was recently inducted into the 'Future Circles' initiative of the Government of the UAE and WEF. Dev was formerly the Vice President and Head of Network of the World Bank Group (WBG), and prior to that, the McKinsey Global Institute's Director for Asia based out of Shanghai. Earlier in Washington DC (1998–2005), he was McKinsey's Director of Operations of its flagship Global Strategy Practice. At the WBG, he oversaw a network of 1,000 professional staff across six global practices and managed a lending portfolio of $10 billion. He was responsible for providing access to a broad range of financial services, and mobilising the private sector towards greater competitiveness. He was the WBG's champion in promoting collaborative public-private dialogue and developing effective regulatory environments conducive

---

[10]This article benefited significantly from interviews with the following: Robert Zoellick, formerly the President of the World Bank Group; Peter Ong, Permanent Secretary of the Ministry of Finance; Patrick Daniel, Editor-in-Chief of Singapore Press Holdings; Jean Baneth, formerly the World Bank's Chief Economist for East Asia and Director of its International Economics Department; Pamela Cox, formerly a World Bank Managing Director; and Parth Tewari, the Head of the World Bank's Competitive Industries Practice.

for job creation. Dev was also responsible for overseeing the WBG's flagship Ease of Doing Business and its Women, Business and the Law annual reports; the latter, effectively called out countries that systematically discriminated against women. He represented the World Bank at the Financial Stability Board in Basel, Switzerland. He was one of the core members of the WBG in shaping the Singapore Hub under the direction of Robert Zoellick, its former President. He is widely published, having authored several influential reports, particularly on topics on competitiveness, SMEs, China's urbanisation and talent and leadership development. Dev obtained his PhD in Business Economics and International Business from Indiana University, Bloomington, USA.

infoDev@World Bank: Alleviating Poverty Through Sustainable Businesses

Valerie D'COSTA

Eight years ago, I left Singapore and moved to Washington D.C. to take up a position leading a programme at the World Bank. The programme I lead, infoDev, supports technology entrepreneurs and start-ups in developing countries. We help them grow sustainable businesses which in turn, creates jobs, economic growth and poverty alleviation. infoDev's work leverages technology's huge disruptive effect in the developing world by creating opportunities to start and scale a business.

I like to say infoDev helps take innovative ideas from mind to market. We are active across the developing world with our largest programmes in Africa and East Asia. Take a look for yourselves at our exciting agenda at www.infodev.org.

It is best to describe the impact of the work infoDev does by talking about the entrepreneurs we serve. Jermaine Henry and Janice McLeod, two young Jamaican mobile application (apps) developers know that Jamaican farmers who cultivate top-quality produce often have a hard time selling their entire crop due to their lack of direct access to the market. They witnessed these farmers face agricultural middlemen who supply the booming hotel and restaurant trade in the Caribbean and who bought produce based on strict standards of colour and size, leaving a lot of the farmers' produce behind to rot.

To solve the problem, Janice and Jermaine created AgroCentral, a mobile app that will be Jamaica's first digital agricultural clearinghouse. Powered by SMS and Web technology, AgroCentral links hotels and restaurants directly with small farmers who previously relied on middlemen.

AgroCentral clients identify and purchase large quantities of produce directly from the farm, allowing for more competitive prices and higher revenues for the farmers. infoDev encountered Jermaine and Janice at the Startup Weekend Jamaica (SWJA) competition, where they won first prize. infoDev gave them feasibility assessments, business models and financial sustainability analyses to help the company grow.

The Keekonyokie slaughterhouse in Kenya is another great example of an enterprise infoDev has assisted. This business has been recycling blood from a community-based Maasai slaughterhouse to create biogas for cooking. The slaughterhouse generates about 10 metric tons of slaughter waste. To manage the waste and turn it into something useful, the abattoir has constructed a biogas digester which channels waste into gas. The firm even stores the fuel in used tires, lessening the environmental impact of the operation. While bio-ethanol fuel and biowaste-based gases are clean and highly efficient energy alternatives, getting Kenyan kitchens to affordably use them was a challenge. infoDev's Kenya Climate Innovation Center (KCIC) in Nairobi has helped Keekonyokie identify target market segments, and develop financial and marketing strategies. The KCIC has worked with Kenyan policymakers to create greater incentives for the adoption of clean fuels.

Keekonyokie is now ready to enter the national market, selling biogas cylinders in Nairobi, Kiserian, Ngong and Ongata Rongai at Ksh 3,700 (US$44) — exactly half the cost of liquid petroleum gas (LPG).

When World Bank Group President Jim Yong Kim visited the KCIC to see innovative energy projects like Keekonyokie, he described these entrepreneurs not just as businesspersons but as change agents to address critical development needs. In Kenya, over 90% of the population uses wood, charcoal, or kerosene for daily cooking needs. These fuels pollute the environment and pose serious health risks such as respiratory infections or even death. The use of clean energy sources like biogas is in its infancy, as less sustainable and cheaper alternatives exist. This is a situation Keekonyokie is working to change.

The KCIC now supports 83 client enterprises working on clean technology innovations. Thanks to these Kenyan entrepreneurs, about 8,300 persons have better access to cleaner water; and 49,000 people are now using low carbon energy sources. infoDev is establishing CICs in seven other countries at this time: Ethiopia, Ghana, India, the Caribbean, Morocco, South Africa, and Vietnam.

My most memorable and defining moments have been meeting and helping clients like AgroCentral and Keekonyokie thrive and grow into market champions. We also work closely with tech parks, innovation clusters, SME support organisations, start-up accelerators, seed funds, and government agencies. Our clients' needs humble and inspire me. I see technology and innovation as great levellers. These forces democratise access to information and opportunity, and they present startling and disruptive prospects for development, growth and prosperity.

infoDev raises funds for the work it does from donor countries. Our major donors are Sweden, the UK, Denmark, Canada, the Netherlands, Australia and Norway. I had never fundraised a day in my life before I came to the World Bank, so a steep learning curve awaited me. It was daunting at first but now, I have become used to the discipline of raising the money I spend, and I really like that it keeps me business-oriented. My donors are my partners. I admire their vision and longstanding commitment to development. infoDev is now a US$115 million programme, thanks to their belief and support.

My clients love that I am from Singapore! They express admiration for Singapore's development journey and they pepper me with questions about the choices we made as a nation over the past 50 years to get to where we are today. I've been delighted to share the experiences I had working from 1992–2006 at the Infocomm Development Authority of Singapore (IDA). It has brought home to me that I contributed to the development of my country during those years.

When I first joined the Bank, there was a lot to get accustomed to. A whole new lexicon of development awaited me. As part of the Bank's commitment to diversity and inclusion, much was made of the fact that I am a woman, that I am Singaporean and that I am from a minority racial group in Singapore. I've come to appreciate efforts to ensure diversity and inclusion, but I also think they just got the best person for the job! As in any large institution, there is bureaucracy to deal with and things take time. I'm not sure I have fully accepted it, but my patience has grown. Decision-making in Singapore is so much faster, more linear and more flexible.

I lead a team of staff from many countries. No two people see things the same way or express themselves the same way. It has made leadership a challenge and I have learned so much about cross-cultural communications. I have assembled a great team who have passion and commitment to our work, and a lot more unites us than separates us.

I've been asked many times why Singapore is not a donor to infoDev. I hope it will happen one day. Singapore has amassed such goodwill in the developing world. Singapore's development path is closely studied and admired. I see a clear "development dividend" for Singapore to exploit in engaging the emerging world.

I feel an enormous passion for the work I do, and I have the World Bank to thank for opening those vistas for me. I'm privileged to do this work, to lead a talented and diverse team, and I have come to deeply appreciate the sense of purpose my work gives me.

I look back on the past eight years and realise I had to leave the relative comfort of Singapore to experience it all, from the big successes to the hard knocks to the profound lessons. I was seeking a new challenge and I wanted to try things I had never done before when I left Singapore to join the Bank. I certainly got what I wished for.

Valerie D'COSTA is infoDev's Program Manager. infoDev is a global partnership programme within the World Bank which works to promote competitiveness, employment and sustainable, inclusive growth by enabling the growth of innovative, technology-enabled new ventures. infoDev catalyses and enables the provision of better access to knowledge, capital and markets for innovative, growth-oriented enterprises by engaging stakeholders across the wide innovation and entrepreneurship eco-system, including business incubators, accelerators, innovation centers, business angel networks, financial institutions, industry, academia and governments. Valerie has led infoDev's evolution from its original founding focus on information and communications technology for development (ICT4D) to current its role as a 'learning lab' and convener for donors, client countries, and public and private sector actors around the innovation, technology and entrepreneurship agendas. The vision Valerie promotes for infoDev's role today is to derive and test new approaches to support the growth of innovative, technology enabled new ventures; provide cutting-edge knowledge, networks and tools to developing countries to navigate these dynamic market and technology evolutions; collate lessons from success and "failure" in the field; and promote the adoption and scaling of interesting and innovative new approaches that work by the World Bank, donors and other development partners. Before joining infoDev, Valerie served as the Director of the International Division at the Infocomm Development Authority of Singapore (IDA), where she formulated the Singapore Government's policies on international ICT issues and oversaw Singapore's bilateral relations with other countries on these issues. She was a member of the Singapore team which negotiated the free trade agreement with the United States. She received a Public Administration Medal from the Singapore Government for her work in building Singapore's international ICT trade and diplomatic ties. Valerie had a distinguished career in private legal practice before joining her country's nation-building efforts in government service at IDA. Valerie holds a Bachelor of Laws degree from the National University of Singapore and a Master of Laws degree from University College, University of London.

Sharing Singapore's Achievements in Education with Africa

TAN Jee Peng[1]

A casual conversation about textbooks was the spark that led eventually to a fruitful collaboration during 2006 and 2009 between Singapore and the World Bank's Africa Region. In the early 2000s, I had just transferred to the Africa Region and a colleague, upon learning that I grew up in Singapore and attended school there, requested help with speakers for a 2003 conference in Dakar, Senegal for African educators and policymakers. Because textbooks were a pervasive problem in most schools on the continent, it was agreed to invite someone to speak about Singapore's transition from dependence on imported books, to having in-house capacity for writing, publishing, and even exporting textbooks.[2] The presentation made a compelling impression and inspired many at the conference to request World Bank facilitation of a study visit to Singapore.

The request incubated for several years and evolved in focus when it became clear that textbooks were only part of what attracted the attention of African policymakers. They were, in fact, interested in a broader question:

[1] This essay draws largely from the author's partnership between 2005 and 2009 with counterparts in the Singapore Ministries of Education, Finance, Foreign Affairs, and Trade and Industry, in her capacity as the World Bank's Education Advisor in the Africa Region at the time. It benefits greatly from the comments of Messrs. Yaw Ansu, Chan Lee Mun, Birger Fredriksen, and G. Jayakrishnan, as well as those of Prof Lee Sing Kong and Dr Law Song Seng. The views are the author's own and should not be attributed to the World Bank, the government of Singapore or those of countries that participated in the Singapore-World Bank cooperation programme or to any of the persons mentioned in the essay.
[2] Eventually, a whole team came, comprising Ho Wai Yin, Alan Ng and Anna Ng, then with IE Singapore; as well as Sim Wee Chee, of Panpac Education, a book publishing company now incorporated into another company.

how did Singapore succeed in aligning investments in education and training with its goals for faster economic growth? As different as African countries are today from Singapore, many of them had per capita GDP levels that were comparable to or even higher than Singapore's in the 1960s. The subsequent divergence in growth paths thus attracts significant attention. Yet the purpose of examining Singapore's experience is not to discover and replicate the specific measures taken by the country to grow its economy (which would be impossible in any event), but to reflect on the lessons and underlying principles that might inform Africans' quest for progress in their own countries.

Because study visits require significant investments of resources, time, and effort, a decision to sponsor them is not taken lightly at the World Bank. A confluence of favourable conditions led eventually to a formal Singapore-World Bank collaboration that produced: (a) a programme of three visits over four years which benefited 115 African policymakers from ten countries, 30 World Bank staff and 30 guests, among them speakers and African journalists; (b) a high-level policy conference in Tunis, Tunisia in 2009 attended by 44 African ministers of finance and of education from 28 countries;[3] and (c) four publications.[4] The collaboration is a good example of the type of sustained, programmatic cross-country exchange that the World Bank convenes to foster and inform dialogue for policy reform in its partner countries.

Many factors contributed to the success of the collaboration, among them the support of key leaders, the substance of the programme, the strength of local partners, and the availability of financial support.

---

[3] The Conference was jointly hosted by the World Bank, the African Development Bank, the Association for Educational Development in Africa, and the Education for All Fast Track Initiative.

[4] The following titles were published by the World Bank, the second listed below in collaboration with the National Institute of Education: (a) Birger Fredriksen and Tan Jee Peng (eds., 2008), "An Exploration of the East Asian Education Experience"; (b) Lee Sing Kong, Goh Chor Boon, Birger Fredriksen and Tan Jee Peng (eds., 2008), "Toward a Better Future: Education and Training for Economic Development in Singapore since 1965"; (c) Birger Fredriksen (2010), "Sustaining Educational and Economic Momentum in Africa," Working Paper 195; and Shahid Yusuf and Kaoru Nabeshima (2012), "Some Small Economies Do It Better: Rapid Growth and Its Causes in Singapore, Finland, and Ireland." The second book listed above has been translated into Spanish under the initiative and supervision of Prof Patrico Felmer Aichele by arrangements with the Chilean Academy of Sciences.

Tangible Commitment by Leaders

When presented with the idea of a Singapore-WB collaboration, Tommy Koh, Ambassador-at-Large at the Ministry of Foreign Affairs, immediately saw an opportunity for Singapore to make a contribution to international cooperation.[5] His facilitation opened doors that enabled the first visit to materialise, in 2006. Another important expression of commitment by Singapore leaders was the participation of then Finance Minister Tharman Shanmugaratnam as keynote speaker at the 2009 Tunis Conference; in his previous capacity as Minister of Education he had also made himself available for substantive dialogue with the first delegation of African policy makers that visited in 2006. That the Conference took place amidst the then unfolding global financial crisis only heightened the relevance of Singapore's story of steadfast and sustained focus on education to build long-term economic resilience.

Equally important was support from leaders on the World Bank side through their personal engagement, notably as speakers and participants in various programme activities; these include Obiageli Ezekwesili, then Africa Region's Vice President; Shanta Deverajan, then the Region's Chief Economist; and John Page, a former Africa Region Chief Economist. Yaw Ansu, then Director of the Africa Region's Human Development Department, saw the strategic significance of enabling African countries to learn from Singapore's experience and gave the Singapore-WB collaboration his full support and also took part in all three visits. Such commitment by the Region's most senior managers signalled the importance attached by the World Bank to the collaboration, thereby elevating its profile among key African policy makers and attracting their participation.

Relevant Programming

The programme of the study visits was at the heart of the Singapore-WB collaboration. Constructed with inputs from the participating countries and World Bank staff, each visit focused on a slightly different, yet connected, agenda: (a) the first sought simply to expose participants to an overview of Singapore's experience in educational development in comparative perspective

---

[5] I thank my friend, Dr Khor Hoe Ee, then at the Monetary Authority of Singapore, for being the first to suggest that I approach Prof Koh with the idea.

(and included a side visit to Vietnam as well as workshop participation and presentations by experts from other Asian countries); (b) the second visit delved into the operational aspects of the education system itself, examining such issues as teacher training, curriculum development, student learning, leadership for school management and so on; and (c) the third visit concentrated on the role of education and skills development in supporting industry and economic growth. This complicated agenda benefited greatly from the guidance of Birger Fredriksen, a former Director at the World Bank and an indefatigable advocate for education in Africa. It was also enhanced by the fact-finding visits made to two of the participating African countries — Ghana and Madagascar — by senior Singapore professionals involved in guiding the preparation and implementation of the programme.[6]

Site visits to schools, the Institute of Technical Education and Nanyang Polytechnic, as well as various industrial complexes (e.g., the Port of Singapore Authority, Jurong Island, and Keppel Offshore and Marine) were a key feature. They offered participants a unique opportunity in experiential learning, and enabled them to share insights with each other as well as engage in direct dialogue with their Singapore counterparts, among them some permanent secretaries who made themselves available to host the visitors over working lunches. Pre-visit preparation and post-visit debriefing by each African delegation, which were typically led by a senior official, such as a minister or a permanent secretary and included officials from outside the education sector, enriched what each team got out of the visits.

Exemplary Partners in Singapore

The World Bank's main counterpart in Singapore was a newly minted unit at International Enterprise Singapore (IE Singapore) which was set up under Alphonsus Chia to deepen ties with multilateral development agencies. The baton was later taken up by G. Jayakrishnan who led a team that expertly managed our connections to others in Singapore. These contacts in turn helped design and deliver the substantive content of the

---

[6] The visitors to one or both of these countries included the following: P.Y. Huang, a former chairman of the Singapore Economic Development Board; Dr Law Song Seng of the Institute of Technical Education; Prof Leo Tan of the National Institute of Education; Ooi Inn Bok of Nanyang Polytechnic; and Anna Ng of IE Singapore.

study visits.[7] Especially critical were the following leaders: Profs Leo Tan and Lee Sing Kong, then Directors at the National Institute of Education (NIE) for the first and last two visits, respectively; Chan Lee Mun, Principal of Nanyang Polytechnic; Dr Law Song Seng, then Director and CEO of the Institute for Technical Education (ITE); and Lionel Yeo, then Dean and CEO of the Singapore Civil Service College, as well as Roger Tan, also of the Civil Service College. We could not have asked for a better cast.[8]

Generous Financial Support

The programme of collaboration benefited from support from two key partners: the Singapore government which defrayed the local costs under the Ministry of Foreign Affairs' Technical Cooperation Programme led at the time by Koh Tin Fook, then the Programme's Director; and the Norwegian government which, through its Norwegian Education Trust Fund at the World Bank initiated by Olav Seim at the Norwegian Ministry of Foreign Affairs, provided resources for the visitors' travel and other expenses. Both governments saw capacity building, in this case through study visits, as an important channel for inspiring and supporting African policymakers in their effort to advance socio-economic development in their own countries. Singapore's experience cannot be copied, but it can serve as source of insights about institutional design and praxis to sustain progress in education and in the economy as a whole.

Impact on Policy Dialogue

Like most capacity building interventions, the full impact of the Singapore-WB collaboration is hard to assess. Some immediate follow-up activities were explored,[9] but the influence of the collaboration on mindsets and capabilities

---

[7] Members of the IE Singapore team comprised the following over the course of the visits: Anna Ng, Alan Ng, Seah Bee Leng, Sabrina Ho, and Anchit Sood.

[8] The involvement of the following staff at the various institutions also greatly benefited the study visits: Ooi Inn Bok (Nanyang Polytechnic) and Goh Chor Boon (NIE); and Sabrina Loi (ITE) and Flynn Ong (Civil Service College).

[9] These include support from the ITE for TVET in Nigeria and from the NIE for teacher development in Madagascar.

for policy development and reform is clearly more consequential. In relation to the main question that motivated the collaboration — how to align investments in education and training to support the agenda for growth — Singapore's experience yields several insights considered relevant by participants of the study visits. These are elaborated in the four publications cited earlier; a few of the key ones are noted briefly below.

First, the cross-cutting nature of the skills for growth agenda made working as one government rather than operating in silos — across economic sectors and also within the education sector itself — a critical precondition for success. Second, when a country has limited resources, it is important to prioritise investing in a strong foundation in basic education in order to sustain and widen successful expansion into higher order skills in tandem with the growth of quality jobs. Third, treating TVET as an integral, yet distinct and genuinely valued, part of a high skills system, is essential to the creation of viable pathways to the job market for all young people, not just the academically inclined.[10] Fourth, paying close attention to implementation is a necessary discipline to ensure that concepts are followed through in practice. Finally, systemic learning by doing is as desirable as it is essential for building domestic capacity for policy reform and implementation. The process can initiate a virtuous cycle of piloting policy ideas and approaches, learning from the experience, deepening capabilities and strengthening system management and performance over time. Such a cycle is crucial for ensuring that good ideas are validated for relevance and impact, amplified as appropriate and institutionalised as efficiently as possible.[11]

That these lessons are not lost in the international discourse on Africa's development is suggested by the changed perspectives among African policy makers and World Bank staff, notably that skills development, broadly

---

[10] As of this writing, Singapore has embarked on new initiatives — notably, ASPIRE, CET2020 and SkillsFuture — which recognise the importance of lifelong learning for all Singaporeans; offer opportunities for every citizen to develop his or her human capital; and encourage the acquisition of skills mastery in every job (see http://www.moe.gov.sg/media/press/2014/11/skillsfuture-council-begins-work.php).

[11] A deeper discussion of these insights may be found in Jee Peng Tan, Kiong Hock Lee, Ryan Flynn, Vivian Gomez and Joy Nam (2015, forthcoming), "Workforce Development in Emerging Economies: Comparative Perspectives on Institutions, Praxis and Policies for Economic Development", Global Education Practice, the World Bank.

defined, is not just about the provision of social services, but is indeed central to a country's strategy for overall economic development. The visits to Singapore helped informed the design of some subsequent World Bank operations in education (e.g., in Ghana, Mozambique and Tanzania) and led managers in the Africa Region to increase attention to skills development in their work with partner countries, along lines inspired by the study visits. More broadly, as a result of the contacts made through the study visits, key lessons from Singapore's experience continue to radiate in other ways. At the 2012 Annual Meetings of the African Development Bank in Arusha, Tanzania, for example, Dr Law Song Seng found himself speaking about Singapore's approach to TVET on a panel organised by Yaw Ansu, now Chief Economist at the Africa Center for Economic Transformation, a leading African think tank. Other speakers on the panel were Mozambique's Minister of Science and Technology, Sweden's Minister of Finance, and a leading Ghanaian businessman; and in the audience were African economic policymakers, international development experts, and the media.

Building on the Collaboration

Singapore's long and rich experience in educational reform fascinates the development community. Its approach demonstrates that aligning education and training to broader goals for economic growth is a concept that can be acted on to produce tangible results. While Singapore's reform journey has not been easy and its education system today is by no means flawless and indeed continues to require adaptation as conditions evolve, there is no doubt that its development experience can inform the efforts of others seeking to improve the situation in their own countries. The success of the Singapore-WB collaboration during 2006–2009 in creating a unique learning opportunity for African policy makers should inspire Singapore to repeat the partnership in future years. Doing so would enable it to continue engaging the international community on ideas and innovations to enhance the role of education and training in building and sustaining vibrant economies and successful communities, not only in Africa but also in Singapore and other countries.

TAN Jee Peng retired from the World Bank in December 2013 following a fulfilling 32-year career. At her last post, as Education Advisor in the Bank's Human Development Network, she led analysis of workforce development under the Systems Approach for Better Education Results initiative, a programme for implementing the World Bank's 10-year education strategy; and she coordinated creation of the multi-country Skills toward Employment and Productivity initiative dedicated to skills measurement. In earlier positions, Jee Peng led teams for a decade in the Africa Region where highlights include: creation of tools for policy analysis; systematic country assessment of and advocacy for education and health under the Highly Indebted Poor Countries Initiative and later under the Education for All Fast Track Initiative; creation of the Africa Program for Education Impact Evaluation to expand use of randomised controlled trials; launch of the New Economy Skills for Africa Program in Information and Communication Technology; and facilitation of policy dialogue between African policymakers and their counterparts in China, India, Singapore and Vietnam. She is a published author and the originator of EdStats, a platform for knowledge and data-sharing. Jee Peng studied at the London School of Economics and Princeton University.

Little Red Specks in the United Nations

Andrew TOH

Question a person on the street about his perception of a United Nations (UN) staffer and you will likely solicit a response that they are a bunch of diplomats engaged in never ending politics by day and debaucherous diplomatic receptions by night. In reality, nothing can be further from the truth. United Nations employees in fact function like any other civil servant but in an international instead of a national setting. This is mainly due to the international mix of staff members recruited from many of the 193 member states that makeup the General Assembly and the likelihood that the staff member would be serving in a foreign location or duty station. As there are no UN agencies based in Singapore, all Singaporeans employed by the UN serve in foreign locations.

Furthermore, UN employees are considered to be international civil servants unaligned to any specific country. The UN passport or *Laissez Passer* does not specify the nationality of the holder. Save for a small coterie of staffers that provide support to the Office of the Secretary-General, most UN personnel do not engage in political issues in their day to day activities. The UN Secretariat in New York provides secretarial support to the political organs of the UN and do not take any positions on political issues.

Most UN organisations and agencies are in fact engaged in highly operational activities such as the provision of humanitarian, emergency and developmental assistance. For example, the UN Office for the Coordination of Humanitarian Affairs (OCHA) within United Nations New York coordinates UN humanitarian and emergency assistance globally; the United Nations World Food Programme (WFP) based in Rome, Italy, provides food aid as emergency and developmental assistance through food-for-work programmes; the United Nations Children's Fund (UNICEF) operates out of New York and is primarily responsible for maternal and child care; the World Health Organisation (WHO) headquartered in Geneva takes the global lead in health matters and the United Nations Development Programme (UNDP) based in New York provides and coordinates developmental assistance worldwide. Some 60 percent of UN employees serve outside the headquarters of their agencies in field offices mainly located in developing and least developed countries.

Despite being one of the smallest member states of the UN, Singaporeans have held key managerial positions within various United Nations entities and fora. Perhaps the most notable Singaporean who gave immense recognition to Singapore was Professor Tommy Koh who served as Singapore's Ambassador to the UN. Professor Koh presided over the historic Third Conference of the Law of the Sea that drafted the United Nations Convention on Law of the Sea (UNCLOS). UNCLOS was formally adopted in 1982. Other Singaporeans held senior positions in full time appointments as Under-Secretary-General and Assistant Secretary-General at United Nations headquarters in New York, as Executive Director of the United Nations Economic and Social Commission for Asia and the Pacific (ESCAP) and as Deputy Director-General of the World Intellectual Property Organisation (WIPO).

The most difficult stage in the metamorphosis to becoming an international civil servant is probably the conditioning required to live and work abroad in a very large and diverse bureaucracy stretched across the globe like no other. As the writer had not hitherto worked or lived outside of Singapore, assignment to a non-English speaking duty station in Rome was both exciting and terrifying. Being the first and only Singaporean employed by the World Food Programme (WFP) headquartered in non-English speaking Rome, Italy did not raise the level of comfort.

However, all fears soon dissipated. In an international working environment, everyone else other than locally recruited staff, are in the same predicament. In reality, this type of situation creates even greater cohesion among colleagues as they have little choice but to learn to accept and adapt to each other very quickly.

The writer spent his first 18 years primarily as Chief of Logistics with WFP, a highly operational organisation tasked with the supply and delivery of food aid to over 100 million people around the world. Within the UN family, WFP is known as "the logistics arm of the UN". For this reason, this essay will only focus on the writer's 18 year journey around the world as a logistics specialist with the WFP. It has indeed been an arduous but most fulfilling journey in the writer's career.

The number of career staff that can be recruited from each UN member states are limited by a quota that is determined through a complex formula. In an average year, there are about 20 Singapore passport holders within the UN system of Organisations, Funds and Programmes. Given that the total staffing in the United Nations system as a whole hovers around 40,000 worldwide, Singapore's representation is miniscule. This raises the question: can Singaporeans make a difference within the UN considering that it is the largest and most international bureaucracy in the world? The short answer is an unequivocal "Yes". A single episode in Ethiopia among many in other parts of the developing world described below provides a sense of how a couple of Singaporeans without any major prior exposure to the African Continent have helped save countless lives and made the world a much better place.

Arguably, one of the most complex humanitarian operations of epic proportions was undertaken in Ethiopia in the 1985 to provide relief to millions of people who were starving in the country ravaged by widespread famine that had already consumed over a million lives. The devastating human misery received worldwide attention following Bob Geldof's Live Aid charity event which raised over $100 million, a great deal of money at the time. WFP dispatched a handful of experts to Ethiopia to establish what was then the largest humanitarian operation ever conducted by the UN. It may surprise many that this small team of five key personnel included two Singaporeans, the writer and a chartered accountant.

The result was the establishment of the WFP Transport Operation Ethiopia (WTOE) to deliver food and other relief items to millions of needy folks in the farthest reaches of the country. WTOE operated some 700 vehicles, the largest truck fleet in Africa at the time, under the most arduous of conditions. The operational headquarters of WTOE was in Assab, then the only operational Ethiopian seaport where ocean vessels with humanitarian cargo could dock. Located in an arid region comparable to the lunar landscape with little infrastructure to speak of, the Singaporeans and their colleagues had to import and build everything that was required in a matter of months to handle the millions of tons of food grain and their subsequent transportation hundreds of miles inland to a starving population. Living conditions in Assab were spartan at best. Accommodation was provided in the form of mobile trailers which constituted the only refuge from the oppressive heat, a far cry from the glitz and glitter of New York, Paris and Rome.

WTOE was originally established as an emergency operation that would last seven weeks. It would be seven years before it was wound down. The success of WTOE set the stage for a similar operation in neighbouring Sudan in 1988 when it too fell victim to famine. There, it was a Singaporean who conceived and organised the first commercial and most massive humanitarian airdrop operation in UN history.

The above single episode among many others illustrates that Singaporeans are a practical and adaptable lot who can adjust and adapt to any situation they face even under unfamiliar and harsh conditions, achieve great heights and in the process raise the profile and reputation of our small island nation.

———•◦•———

Andrew TOH was a staff member of the United Nations for 28 years. He retired as an Assistant Secretary-General in 2008 and is currently serving as Singapore's Non-Resident Ambassador to the United Nations Educational, Scientific and Cultural Organization (UNESCO).

Global Health in Action — from Singapore to Indonesia and Geneva

Vernon LEE

Working in the WHO is a distant dream for most young healthcare workers, a place where senior global health experts walk the hallowed hallways of international health and diplomacy. As a young doctor in the midst of completing my specialist training, working with the WHO was far from my mind. I was, however, deeply interested in evidence-based policymaking and developed a growing local and international expertise in influenza and pandemic preparedness.

My destiny with WHO came one day in 2006, when I received an unannounced call from my mentor, Prof Goh Kee Tai, asking if I would be interested in working for the WHO in Indonesia. This was a request to the WHO from the Indonesian government for technical assistance to tackle H5N1 avian influenza. As Singapore had built a reputation for disease response especially with SARS, we were approached by the WHO to send an expert to their office in Indonesia. I readily agreed to the request, as it was a unique opportunity to represent Singapore and to contribute to regional disease preparedness, although with trepidation as it was a mammoth weight on my shoulders.

It was a task that I rapidly warmed up to, as the work was gratifying and allowed me to engage people from all walks of life. The training and expertise that Singapore had given me provided the tools to succeed in the job, and my time in Indonesia was fulfilling both professionally and personally. I responded to avian influenza outbreaks, and worked with friends in the Indonesian Ministry of Health to develop their national pandemic preparedness plan. In 2008, we conducted the world's first field exercise for the containment of a novel influenza outbreak, performed on the island of Bali.

This involved more than 1,000 participants including officials, healthcare workers, law enforcement, military, community leaders, and villagers. It was held in a Balinese village about two hours' drive from the major tourist areas, and involved the main hospital and airport. The exercise was a resounding success and validated the response plans and a year of preparations including tabletop and functional exercises, and whole-of-society integration. The latter cannot be over-emphasised, as a whole-of-society approach incorporating government agencies, local communities, and other stakeholders is critical to ensuring the effective response to any major threat. Officials from dozens of countries and organisations worldwide attended the exercise, and it showcased Indonesia's capability in dealing with emerging disease threats. Years later in 2014, I was in Jakarta for an international global health security meeting and was pleased to see that a video of the exercise was shown as part of a presentation of Indonesia's contributions to global health.

On a personal level, I made numerous friends in Indonesia, many of whom I still keep in contact with. The WHO office did not provide translators for its international staff, unlike other agencies. While this resulted in a steep learning curve for a non-Bahasa Indonesia speaker like myself, it ultimately proved to be an enlightened decision. Learning the language of my hosts enabled me to forge strong bonds, and to earn the respect and warm welcome of locals in the provinces and villages where I worked. Simple acts of relationship building such as sharing a joke or personal secrets over a cup of tea cannot be achieved through the cold interpretation of a translator. Receiving the warm welcome and hospitality of the locals, including being invited to their homes, made me connect at a personal level with the work I was doing. A year after the end of my secondment, I visited Bali for a WHO meeting. At the airport, I heard someone calling my name and turned around to find that the airport officials whom I closely worked with during the simulation exercise recognised me from the large crowd. We exchanged stories and reminisced about old times. These small incidences are heartfelt payoff to the hard work in the field.

Understandably, some stakeholders had initial concern on accepting a young doctor as an expert advisor, as the perception that age is correlated with experience and expertise is prevalent in professional circles. However, this was quickly resolved soon after I started work and earned the right to be an integral part of the team. Earning mutual respect was a situation I over-came yet again during my next secondment to the WHO headquarters in Geneva. This helps to expose the international community to the capabili-ties that Singapore has, and the educational development and opportunities that we provide to young professionals.

I am grateful to the Ministry of Health for the opportunity to serve in the WHO and the international health arena. These experiences were deeply enriching in my development, both professionally and personally. I have since been constantly on the lookout for young professionals with the potential and passion to fly the Singapore flag at the international stage, and to provide them with the opportunities as my contribution to building the next generation of healthcare leaders.

Flying the Singapore Flag Again

Since my time in Indonesia, I have been participating in various WHO expert working groups, especially during the 2009 influenza pandemic where Singapore made substantial contributions to global health policy and research initiatives. These contributions, together with participation at numerous international health platforms by other Singaporeans, have built Singapore's reputation for excellence in technical ability, policy planning and operational execution.

This close link with WHO led to my secondment to the WHO head-quarters in Geneva as Advisor to the Assistant Director General for Health Security and Environment from 2010 to 2012. It was there that I led initia-tives to strengthen global health security through capability building and whole-of-society participation; pandemic preparedness planning; and anti-microbial resistance. This often involved briefings and negotiations with senior officials, and the enormity of the tasks was made more challenging by the need to bring countries and individuals with different interests and beliefs to the same table, and to reach consensus on world-changing poli-cies. Once again, my training in Singapore's health and military systems have taught me the skills of working with people from diverse backgrounds, of leading teams to achieve objectives under adverse conditions, and of achieving much with little resources.

While some may struggle to collaborate across institutions and incor-porate a whole-of-society approach in their activities, these come naturally to Singapore. One example is the effort it took to bring the health and security (primarily military) sectors across the world to work together, and to remove the reservations that many health professionals have in accepting contributions from the security sector. Suspicions by health professionals of the intelligence and offensive agenda of the security sector were constant underlying currents. Others pointed to the fact that militaries are an integral part of the national healthcare system in many countries, and are one of the first responders to local or international health emergencies. Another example are the suspicions of collaborations by WHO and other public institutions with the private pharmaceutical sector, with many accusations of private sector influence on WHO policy in exchange for political or financial support. However, it is also important that WHO communicates the needs of the global population to the private sector to develop useful medicines and vaccines, and hear the challenges faced by the pharmaceutical sector. To those who have been working with all these stakeholders, the answer is clear — regardless of the agenda of each stakeholder, it is imperative that all sectors and stakeholders work together to pool scarce resources to achieve a common goal. Failing which there will be at best duplication of activities, or worse a clash of purposes resulting in a waste of precious resources. Due to our tireless efforts in educating stakeholders and bringing them together to understand each other's viewpoints, collaboration across sectors at the national and international levels is now more commonplace, especially between the health and agricultural sectors, the health and security sectors, and the public and private sectors.

The core Singaporean competencies of applied knowledge, working in teams, and diligence have also endeared us to the international health community as professionals who can design and execute programmes under pressure. Being a seconded officer was also advantageous because I could provide a fresh and external view of WHO processes, and I felt comfortable in voicing my opinions freely. Similarly, WHO colleagues viewed my contributions as supporting their work and careers, and rarely as competition or threat. This was important as I was working for WHO while it was in the midst of its largest internal reform, when structural reorganisation was taking place and many jobs were on the line, resulting in job uncertainty among staff members.

While Singapore has equipped me with many skills, one that I had to learn from my work in global health is the need to have a certain diplomatic savvy. A WHO colleague who is familiar with Singapore mentioned to me that Singaporeans were generally very direct and open in our approach — laying all our cards on the table. I used to think that it was impossible that nations could disagree on obvious global health issues that save lives — for example childhood vaccination or sharing of information on emerging diseases. However, the truth is that global health diplomacy plays into a broader geopolitical landscape that influences the decisions nations or individuals take. Some of these decisions would appear irrational at first glance, and even callous when the impact on human lives is considered. While honesty and forthrightness are noble traits that endear, obtaining consensus and agreement from seemingly disparate viewpoints requires a higher level of negotiation skill and a diplomatic approach, skill sets that many Singaporeans are generally not imbibed with. This is one example where our positive trait could make us vulnerable in a diversified global setting where there can be many means to reach an end, apart from laying all out on the table at the onset. This is even more apparent in the health sector, where there is less reciprocal recognition of qualifications globally, and where opportunities are less prevalent.

Similarly, I learnt that many of these consensus-building discussions did not take place at the meeting table, but during coffee breaks and lunch where the camaraderie cuts more easily through difficult topics. Likewise, successful outcomes during internal WHO working groups were already determined by the relationships built over time, usually over meals. It does not take much to realise that a warm homely meal on a winter's night was a surefire way of building lasting friendships with colleagues and friends, especially when it is shared with their families. Personal relationships and networks is part of our human nature.

My engagement with key global initiatives enabled me to forge networks with officials and experts across the world. Some have heard about Singapore but have neither visited nor worked with us, and these interactions helped to shape lasting impressions about our country and our people. These friendships have also been important in enabling future collaborations with Singapore, and need to be constantly maintained. Networks take time and effort to build, but can be easily lost without continual investment. It is therefore important for Singapore to continue her engagement with international organisations such as the WHO, and other globally-connected institutions, as an window to networking opportunities.

———•·•·•———

Vernon LEE is a preventive medicine physician and currently Head of the Singapore Armed Forces Biodefence Centre, in charge of preparedness and response to infectious diseases in the Singapore military. He is also an Advisor to the Public Health Group in the Ministry of Health, Singapore, spearheading international collaboration, infectious diseases policy and research; and an adjunct Associate Professor at the Saw Swee Hock School of Public Health, National University of Singapore. He leads translational research to provide evidence to policymaking, and has more than 80 scientific publications in infectious diseases and public health. He was previously Advisor to the Assistant Director General for Health, Security and Environment at the World Health Organization headquarters from 2010 to 2012, leading global health collaborations and pandemic preparedness. He was also a Medical Epidemiologist in the WHO Office in Indonesia from 2007 to 2008, working on avian influenza response and pandemic influenza preparedness. He continues to contribute to WHO advisory and expert working groups on infectious diseases.

A Sojourn in Diplomacy — Working with the WHO in Geneva

David HO

The World Health Organization (WHO) is charged with advancing the health of all peoples across the world — it is a daunting task and challenge taken up by its 7,000 staff operating in 150 countries. As the authority on health within the United Nations (UN) system, it works with 194 member states to achieve this — no mean feat to anyone familiar with global politics.

Health is a unique and important basic human need, but expectations of healthcare differ according to the resources of various countries across the world, and is ever increasing in the face of technological and scientific advances. Global health is therefore important to ensure equitable and sustainable health development across the world. This is made even more urgent due to the emerging and re-emerging crises that the world is faced with, including the spread of infectious diseases, health effects of natural or man-made disasters, and climate change. All of these issues require an international response to bring about effective responses.

Singapore and the WHO

Singapore achieved independence in 1965 and we became a proud member of WHO a year later in 1966. As a fledging country, we were the beneficiaries of WHO's generosity as some of our outstanding young medical officers were awarded WHO Fellowships. This gave them the opportunity to enhance their learning and development overseas. The WHO Fellowship Programme was incidentally among the first programmes created with the founding of WHO in 1948, and is specifically targetted at developing countries such as Singapore in the 1960s, to build their capacities in technical areas.

Singapore is grateful for WHO's key role in accelerating our medical development. Many of these young medical officers have since dedicated their careers to public health and went on to serve on WHO Expert Working Groups. They lend their expertise in a wide spectrum of areas, such as in tackling communicable diseases and non-communicable disease, and give their time freely and with pride. In reciprocation for the early support from WHO, many of Singapore's healthcare institutions now regularly play host and organise training programmes for overseas WHO Fellows to Singapore. In recognition of the institutions' excellence, WHO has designated ten of our institutions as WHO Collaborating Centres (WHO CC), one of the most in the Asia-Pacific region. These are research institutes, belonging to universities or academies designated by the WHO to carry out activities in support of its programmes.

Chairmanship and Member of the WHO Executive Board

The SARS outbreak in 2003 was a defining moment in Singapore's history. The episode highlighted the importance of international cooperation and greater transparency. It also underscored the need for Singapore to foster stronger linkages with the WHO and to be plugged into global decision-making. It was in this context that we ran for and was elected for the first time into the WHO Executive Board (EB) at the 59th World Health Assembly (WHA) in 2006. The EB serves as the executive body of the WHO that determines the decisions and polices that are presented to the WHA. It comprises 34 elected individuals, each designated by a Member State for a three-year term. We were represented on the EB by the late Senior Minister of State (Foreign Affairs) Dr Balaji Sadasivan from 2006 to 2009. Dr Balaji was also chosen by the EB to serve as its Chairman from May 2007 to May 2008. This was the first time a Singaporean had been elected to a leadership role since we became a member of WHO.

Before taking up public office, Dr Balaji was a renowned neurosurgeon. However, not many were aware that Dr Balaji's career was indirectly influenced by WHO. As a young medical student, Dr Balaji had submitted a winning essay on environmental issues for an international contest organised by WHO. This won him a trip to Minamata, Japan, to attend a neurologic seminar and workshop. Minamata was the site of a mercury poisoning disaster, which led to victims suffering from neurological deficits called Minamata disease.

As Chairman and member of the EB, Dr Balaji skilfully guided the WHO to accomplish much in global health development, pandemic preparedness and addressing non-communicable diseases. As this period coincided with the immediate post-SARS period, the landmark accomplishment was the passing of the 2005 revision of the international health regulations (IHR). This was significant as there is now a more robust framework for reporting and responding to epidemics and pandemics, including recommendations for capacity building in member states. As a diplomat and a renowned medical practitioner, Dr Balaji's contributions to the EB won him praise and enhanced Singapore's international standing as an objective and constructive player in global health. Despite his poor health subsequently, it was a testament to Dr Balaji's sense of duty that he continued to lead Singapore's delegation to attend key WHO meetings — doing so for the last time at the 63rd WHA in May 2010. Dr Balaji passed away four months later.

Health Diplomacy in Geneva

As the First Secretary for Health in the Singapore Permanent Mission to the use in Geneva, from 2012 to 2014, I worked closely with WHO and came away with tremendous respect for the organisation. I believe WHO is able to remain relevant because it has the mandate to draw on the best brains in the world to provide their expertise. Not only that, it also has an unparalleled extensive worldwide network. This emanates not just through its headquarters in Geneva and presence in remote parts of the world, but also through its partnership with collaborating centres such as those from Singapore. The global brand of 'WHO' remains a ubiquitous authority in all aspects of public health.

Learning on the Job

What stood out for me when in Geneva were the deliberations and policy-making now taking place through a truly global platform and in a multilateral setting. This was the dynamics that I could not immediately grasp and appreciate. Another important lesson was that global health does not take place in a vacuum but instead is highly inter-related with the macro-political dynamics, most times unrelated to the core subject matter.

As an example, I had participated in a WHO discussion to review the progress towards the prevention and control of non-communicable diseases (NCDs). Whilst an important issue, I voiced in the discussion that WHO should scale down its numerous requests for data from countries. My justification for doing so was the data tracked was not always useful and it was inefficient to continue doing so. Furthermore, such data collection is often tedious and laborious. As a "typical Singaporean", I felt that the time invested could be better used. However, during the meeting's coffee break, a delegate from a developing country came to me and passionately explained the data was of utmost importance to his country. He shared that his Government was unconvinced of the pressing need for them to invest significantly in the strengthening of its healthcare system to prepare itself against the looming NCD threat. As such, he elaborated the data *"from a credible scientific organisation such as WHO"* would demonstrate unequivocally to the Government how far his country was lagging behind international benchmarks. He hoped that this would be the catalyst for the blinkers to be removed and triggering of the urgent actions required for his country. This incident resonated with me the need to look beyond our own interests (and sometimes inconveniences) and to fully understand other stakeholders' interests and concerns. What also struck me was that we were working in partnership with WHO to serve a greater cause. I needed to correspondingly embrace a global view beyond domestic-tinted lens and concerns. I went on to withdraw my objections unconditionally.

On a related point, it was also not surprising that the above informal discussion on a sensitive topic took place during the coffee break. This was not a coincidence and I soon realised there was always generous time set aside for coffee breaks at WHO and UN meetings. This was deliberate. Besides much required caffeine injections that were essential to navigate through tedious negotiations, it also served a useful function where delegates could discuss informally among themselves in a transparent manner on national positions that they may not be able to share openly nor formally. It was thus relatively common that most major breakthroughs take place over coffee breaks and informal consultations. Context is important in this case — WHO is a member state-driven, consensus-based organisation. All major decisions are made by the membership as a whole, usually by the Ministers who convene at the annual WHA in May. Since policy decisions are largely made by consensus, without voting, informal consultations play a vital role in bringing a vastly diverse membership around to an agreement. They are necessary to pave the way and facilitate the making of formal decisions.

At its core, diplomacy is about people relating to people. To push through decisions in a multilateral platform require persuasion and relationships, just as much as logic and facts. The current WHO Director-General (DG) Dr Margaret Chan certainly understood this. A gregarious person by nature, I had witnessed how she had used her charisma and people skills to skilfully forge consensus. For instance, not many outside the health circles are aware that Dr Chan was also known as the "singing DG". This arose from her ability to defuse tensions by bursting into songs when discussions got overly heated as they tended to do since health is after all, an emotive subject. It was a sight to behold when the room of delegates, which moments earlier had been hopelessly divided, also sung along in chorus with Dr Chan! This breaks the tension and facilitates positive atmospherics to continue the forging of consensus. Dr Chan's professed personal favourite song was "Getting to know you" from the musical "Anna and the King". The chorus was particularly poignant and a requisite for international diplomacy — *"Getting to know you, getting to know all about you. Getting to like you, getting to hope you like me."* My key takeaway was there were many different ways of communicating effectively and singing was one of Dr Chan's many ways of doing so.

Looking Back

One achievement which I looked back with pride was to be entrusted by my regional counterparts to serve as their Regional Coordinator for the Western Pacific Region. The WHO is incidentally divided into six regions[1] and Singapore, together with 37 other countries, belonged to the Western Pacific region. As the Regional Coordinator, I worked closely with WHO and the countries under my charge to ensure the information channels were robust. This allowed all stakeholders to be plugged in to the issues and have

---

[1] In WHO, Member States are divided into six geographical regions — African (AFRO), American (AMRO), Eastern Mediterranean (EMRO), European (EURO), South-East Asian (SEARO) and Western-Pacific (WPRO).

a stake in the deliberation processes taking place in WHO. I found my role to be meaningful since good information flows and transparency between WHO and its Member States were critical to promote active participation in policy discussions. I was also their representative to spearhead discussions and ensure the region's position was clearly represented in global health governance, including numerous rounds of intense negotiations for more contentious health issues.

However, there will inevitably be difficulties in coordinating 37 countries. This is where personal engagement and networking were critical. I met regularly with my constituents in person, usually over coffee or a casual meal, to brief them on important issues and to keep networks warm. I found this more productive to impersonal emails since discussions are more fluid and less guarded. It was also important to be proactive and to go the extra mile to build the mutual trust. I am glad that after two years of networking through the different personalities and cultures, many working colleagues have since become friends. Even after most of us have de-posted and returned home, we still keep in touch. Beyond friendships, the continued linkages will come in useful if we require information urgently, we can simply pick up the phone instead of having to navigate through layers of bureaucracy.

I was also glad that I played a role in strengthening ASEAN linkages in WHO. Due to historical circumstances, the ten ASEAN countries, despite our close proximity geographically, were ironically not grouped within a single WHO region. Instead, they were situated across two WHO regions — the Western Pacific region and the Southeast Asia region. As a result of the split, influence of ASEAN as a bloc in platforms such as the WHA was greatly restricted. This was a contrast to the strong linkages regionally taking place in platforms such as the biennial ASEAN Health Ministers Meeting (AHMM).

To address this anomaly, I seeded the idea for ASEAN to deliver a statement at the WHA in 2013. Doing so at the highest platform dedicated to health would raise the profile of ASEAN as a credible bloc in the international health arena. However, we were also cognizant that it may be more appropriate for the then-AHMM Chair (Thailand) to propose this initiative to avoid the perception of us overstepping our jurisdiction. In doing so, I leveraged on the good personal relationships built up with the Thais to seek their buy-in. Thankfully, the Thais agreed that this was a good initiative and a sensible approach. They pushed for and received the endorsement of

ASEAN. It was with pride when I witnessed Thailand taking the floor at the 66th WHA on behalf of ASEAN to deliver its inaugural statement in 2013. This practice continued in 2014 and was subsequently institutionalised in the WHA calendar. In the process, we have gained credibility amongst our ASEAN Health counterparts. As a small country, it is important for us to understand the dynamics, and work quietly behind the scenes, to provide our value-add and relevance. This is the power of "soft diplomacy".

A Community of Practice for the Future

WHO is perhaps the only institution in the world that can bring all countries on the same negotiating table to talk about health issues, and therefore it is of paramount importance for countries to support WHO in its mission. Although Singapore is a small country with relatively few resources compared to the large developed countries, we punch well above our weight when it comes to contributions at the international level. This includes secondments over the years to the WHO Headquarters, the Regional Office for the Western Pacific (which Singapore belongs to), and country offices such as Indonesia. In addition, many Singaporeans have sat on steering committees of global health initiatives such as the Global Outbreak and Alert Response Network (GOARN) and participated in numerous WHO expert working groups, contributing to infectious diseases, non-communicable diseases, and health systems development.

We have come a long way from the 1960s where we were a grateful recipient of WHO's support, to a developed country with one of the best healthcare systems anywhere in the world. The future is fraught with challenges, both in Singapore due to the ageing population, and at the global level. The only way for global health to advance for the better is to build a collective community of practice, where expertise and experience can be shared, and where common goals are forged. Singapore will continue to be a valued member of this global community, and will continue to provide expert support to the WHO and other countries in need, as much as we learn from other countries that have more experience than us. Only through such collaborations can the world be safe from the threat of diseases and poor health.

David HO graduated from the National University of Singapore in 2007 with a Honours (Second Upper) degree in History. He started his career in the Ministry of Health in the same year with the International Cooperation Branch. He took on the Ministry's WHO portfolio in 2010. He was seconded to Singapore's Permanent Mission to the United Nations in Geneva from 2012 to 2014, serving as First Secretary for Health. In Geneva, David was nominated by his international peers to serve as the Regional Coordinator for the Western Pacific Region to represent their interests for a two-year term. The Western Pacific Region consists of 37 Member States and areas.

Intellectual Property and Singapore: A Model of Cooperation with a United Nations Institution

Geoffrey YU

What follows is an account of successful cooperation between Singapore and the World Intellectual Property Organization (WIPO), a United Nations specialised agency. It is an enduring relationship which has lasted some 35 years, from its tentative beginnings in the early 1980s to the present. I was fortunate to be not merely a witness, but an active participant, during the 25 years which I spent in the WIPO secretariat, from 1981 to the end of 2006. This period also saw the transformation of intellectual property (IP) from a pariah in many developing countries, including Singapore, into an indispensable tool in official policymaking.

In this change, WIPO was one among a number of influential change agents. Working in this organisation thus turned out to be a challenging, exciting and gratifying experience. This was largely due to the fact that my first assignment was to promote the use of intellectual property in the development of developing countries of Asia and the Pacific. Over time, my responsibilities expanded to eventually cover all developing countries, as well as transition countries (that is, countries of the former Soviet Union).

How this sea-change came about in Singapore is as much a tale of my years at WIPO as of the relations between Singapore and the organisation. Those relations could be described as that of a productive, mutually beneficial partnership. Because relations were close and fruitful throughout those years, Singapore-WIPO cooperation became a showcase of productive collaboration between a member State and a UN agency. This was certainly how I saw it and tirelessly promoted it to officials of other countries that I worked with.

The Early Years

However, the early years were quite an up-hill slog. In Singapore, as in every other developing country which I visited in the early and mid-1980s, I saw sceptical faces, found ignorance of the subject as well as faced tough questions. One of the toughest barrage of questions came from the then Singapore Institute of Standards and Industrial Research (SISIR), which the government had tasked to investigate whether protecting intellectual property was in Singapore's developmental interests. At that time, widespread commercial-scale counterfeiting and piracy was tolerated in the country, notwithstanding the existence of colonial-era laws prohibiting such activities. Prevailing views then were that since Japan, South Korea and Taiwan thrived on unauthorised copying, Singapore ought to follow. Singapore asked WIPO to do a detailed cost-benefit analysis of why it would be better to protect intellectual property instead of copying. WIPO's answer was straightforward. It was wrong to tolerate copying as the laws then, although already outdated, extended protection to intellectual property owners. Besides, as the country moved up the industrial production value chain as supplier to developed markets, such copying would be unacceptable to the governments of those markets. Equally, a modern IP system was indispensable to any strategy to unleash local innovation, attract foreign high technology as well as foreign high-value investments.

All the same, winning people round to this position took time. People today who read Singapore media accounts of the importance of intellectual property would have some difficulty imagining how different the situation was in the early 1980s. Although officials then received me wherever I went, their positions made it evident that I was in for the long haul, if change was to happen. From the beginning, my WIPO colleagues and I were lucid about our priorities, what was achievable, the time frame and what should best be left alone. Fortunately, my senior colleagues, including the then Director-General Dr Arpad Bogsch, agreed with me that Singapore deserved priority attention.

For many years thereafter, I was in Singapore twice a year, often with various other colleagues and external experts. Nevertheless, it was only nine years later, that WIPO achieved the first treaty breakthrough with Singapore. In September 1990, while I was in Singapore, the authorities handed to me Singapore's instrument of accession to the Convention Establishing the World Intellectual Property Organization. By this act, the country merely became a member State of WIPO, entailing no obligations to provide intellectual property protection. Yet the symbolic importance of the step could not be exaggerated. At last, Singapore formally became a member of the international intellectual property community of nations.

The Take-Off

By the late 1980s, we in Geneva knew that it would be a matter of time before the country would enter into binding treaty obligations. WIPO experts were by then cooperating with the authorities which had embarked on a massive programme of modernising the existing operations and processes of registering patents, trademarks and designs. In addition, the government received some support from the organisation in spreading knowledge of intellectual property within the country's industrial, legal and commercial sectors.

In this respect, the first key policy reference to the role which intellectual property protection could play in Singapore economic development, was found in the 1985 report of the economic restructuring committee headed by Mr Lee Hsien Loong, soon after he joined the Cabinet. Shortly after the report was published, I arranged a meeting of my senior colleagues at WIPO, including the Director General, with Dr Albert Winsemius, then advisor to the giant Dutch electronics firm Philips. Dr Winsemius had been, for some 25 years, an esteemed economic advisor to the Singapore Government. He told us that he was strongly in favour of Singapore adopting modern intellectual property laws, as an instrument of economic and technological policy.

After 1990, the pace of change accelerated. WIPO supported the government in reviewing its intellectual property laws, which were then still those inherited from the British. Government officials debated many questions with WIPO experts. What, if any, should be the changes, what should come first, and why? Whose laws should Singapore follow? Should Singapore evolve its own approach? Many study visits to WIPO and other countries were made. Some WIPO experts spent weeks at a time in the country. The government officials were able and dedicated interlocutors, and working with them, although arduous, was satisfying, as we knew that the outcomes would be substantial and lasting.

And so they were. In 1994, a new patent law was promulgated. To give effect to this new legislation, Singapore became party, in the same year, to a number of important WIPO treaties. In the years which followed, the sceptics in the country were proven wrong. They said that there was no creativity or innovation in the country as few sought protection under the outdated patent law. On the other hand, those, including WIPO, who were persuaded that the new law would provide the crucial missing legal incentive turned out to be right. There was an immediate increase in applications for patent protection, by locals as well as by foreigners, a trend which continues to this day (naturally, there were other contributing factors). Soon, other laws were updated, covering trademarks, copyright, industrial designs and plant varieties. Singapore undertook additional WIPO treaty obligations relating to the new subject matters.

An IP Show-Case

Today, the Singapore Intellectual Property Office (IPOS), a statutory body, enjoys well-deserved recognition as an exceptionally efficient and effective outfit. The latest such recognition conferred on Singapore was in September 2014, when the member States of WIPO formally designated IPOS as an International Search and Examining Authority under the WIPO's Patent Cooperation Treaty, a treaty which underpins the patenting activities of about 150 countries.

Three other significant achievements are worth highlighting here. They happened while I was directly overseeing WIPO's cooperation with developing countries, including Singapore. They were, first the signing, in 1997, of a Memorandum of Understanding (MOU) between WIPO and Singapore on legal and technical training; second, the opening of the WIPO-Singapore Office in 2005; and third, the holding of a WIPO Diplomatic Conference in Singapore in 2006.

Third Country Training

In 1997, although Singapore's new patent law was in force less than three years, it was working well. Together with the upgrading of the national office, we at WIPO felt that the latter was in a position to train officials from other countries in the region, particularly from the other ASEAN countries. As the Singapore side also felt confident, the two parties decided to expand bilateral cooperation to include training and seminars for third country officials and nationals, with sharing of the costs involved. Singapore, through the Ministry of Foreign Affairs' Technical Cooperation Programme, covered the local costs other than accommodation, while WIPO paid all travel and related costs for the participants and foreign trainers. The two sides would agree on the programme, duration and selection of trainees. This arrangement was so successful in its first run of two years that it was renewed many times, and continues to be run today, under an updated MOU. I witnessed the signing of the inaugural MOU between the then WIPO Director-General, Dr Arpad Bogsch and Ambassador K. Kesavapany, Singapore's then Permanent Representative to the UN in Geneva. To date, several thousand people have benefitted from the programme.

WIPO-Singapore Office

The WIPO-Singapore Office (WSO) was inaugurated in 2005. The Guest-of-Honour at the ceremony was then Senior Minister of State for Law, Professor Ho Peng Kee. I represented WIPO. It was the culmination of several years of meticulous work by both WIPO and Singapore. Many discussions took place between the two sides, from the exploratory to planning and strategising. The WIPO side in the discussions was led by me, with as my main Singapore interlocutors, the Singapore Ambassador in Geneva (Ambassador Vanu Gopala Menon and his successor Ambassador Burhan Gafoor), Ms Liew Woon Yin, Director-General of the Singapore Intellectual Property Office, and Chern Siang Jye, Director in the Ministry of Law.

I had initiated discussions in Singapore a few years earlier, with the agreement of Dr Kamil Idris the new Director-General. Once Singapore indicated its willingness to host the office, I fortunately was able to win the support of the WIPO colleagues whose opinions mattered. With the internal hurdle cleared, the next step was for the WIPO and Singapore sides to win over those member States which either felt that they had a stronger claim to be host country as well as those which queried the justification for an overseas office and the attendant cost implications for the organisation. The task of allaying fears and calming competing claims were by no means easy, as there was no precedent for such an office (the two offices in New York and Brussels were liaison points for the UN and the European Commission, respectively). Considerably bigger Asian countries, enjoying much longer association with WIPO, making greater financial contributions and having much bigger intellectual property offices were understandably miffed. Countries in other regions had to be calmed too. They saw no reason why the first overseas office should be sited in Asia and not in their regions instead.

For both WIPO and Singapore, a panoply of diplomatic skills and arguments had to be deployed to win the day. Equally important, nothing was to be rushed, and all the third parties had the time needed for their concerns to be allayed. Lobbying was carried out principally in Geneva and in selected capitals by the two sides. In the end, we did not reach beyond our grasp, and the first overseas WIPO office was established. Today, 10 years later, it continues as the extension arm of WIPO in the ASEAN region, working closely with the Singapore government in supporting the training, advisory and consulting needs of third countries. In addition, it supports the private sector in matters relating to the international registration of patents, trademarks and designs. Recently, the services provided by the office were expanded to include arbitration and mediation support in the event of intellectual property disputes between private parties. The current WIPO Director General, Dr Francis Gurry, visits Singapore every year to attend the well-known Singapore Intellectual Property Week.

First Singapore International Treaty

If the WSO was unprecedented in WIPO's history in more than one way, the WIPO-Singapore Diplomatic Conference on the Law of Trademarks was also a first. It was the first WIPO diplomatic conference on an intellectual property subject to be held in a developing country, and certainly the first in Asia. The conference, ably presided over by Singapore's Ambassador Burhan Gafoor, successfully concluded with the adoption of a new treaty, called the Singapore Treaty on the Law of Trademarks. For Singapore, it was the first time that an international treaty carried its name.

As with the WSO, hosting the conference was far from self-evident. There were people within the WIPO secretariat and among the member States who were astonished that Singapore was bidding (in early 2005) to host the conference so soon after securing itself as the site of WIPO's first overseas office. Moreover, since the member States had decided only a year earlier (in 2004) that the conference should be held in Geneva, Singapore was in effect seeking to overturn that earlier decision. Happily for Singapore, no other country competed with Singapore to host the conference. This allowed both WIPO and Singapore to concentrate their joint diplomatic groundwork on convincing member States that moving the event to Singapore would not be a financial burden for the organisation. To allay their concerns, WIPO and Singapore had to agree between themselves about the budget and cost sharing. Once again, I led the WIPO side in the protracted negotiations with Singapore. The goodwill and confidence of Peter Ho, Permanent Secretary of the Ministry of Foreign Affairs and Ms Chan Lai Fung, Permanent Secretary of the Ministry of Law, enabled the negotiators on both sides to reach a good outcome in the nick of time, barely two months before the conference was due to begin.

Legacy for the Future

The work done and the goodwill generated over three decades have cemented Singapore-WIPO ties. Today, bilateral cooperation is stronger than ever. Indeed, cooperation is now bound to deepen, because in September 2014, as stated earlier, the Intellectual Office of Singapore achieved the distinction of becoming an International Search and Examining Authority under WIPO's Patent Cooperation Treaty, thereby joining the ranks of much bigger and older players such as the American, Chinese, European and Japanese offices.

———•·•———

Geoffrey YU began his professional life in 1969, in the Singapore Administrative Service, during which he worked in the Ministry of Health, the then Ministry of Social Affairs and the Ministry of Foreign Affairs. As a member of the Singapore Foreign Service, he worked in Singapore, Hong Kong, Tokyo and New York. In his overseas postings, he served as the deputy head of mission. He was also a member of the Singapore delegation to the UN Conference on the Law of the Sea. In 1981, he resigned to join the World Intellectual

Property Organization, which is a UN specialized agency based in Geneva, Switzerland. Over the next 25 years, beginning as Senior Programme Officer for Asia and the Pacific, he became in turn Special Assistant to the Director General, Director and then Senior Director in the Office of the Director General, before being appointed Assistant Director General and finishing his career at WIPO as Deputy Director General. In 2007, he returned to Singapore where he held the following posts for four years: Senior Specialist Advisor, Ministry of Foreign Affairs and Ministry of Law; Deputy Chairman, Singapore Intellectual Property Academy; and Senior Fellow and Member of the Academic Panel, Ministry of Foreign Affairs' Diplomatic Academy. He was also Visiting Professor, Intellectual Property Centre, People's (Renmin) University, Beijing; Chairman of the World Economic Forum's Global Agenda Council for Intellectual Property; as well as WIPO Consultant. He continues to be Adjunct Professor at the Lee Kuan Yew School of Public Policy, National University of Singapore as well as Adjunct Senior Fellow, S. Rajaratnam School of International Studies, Nanyang Technological University.

Monitoring and Predicting Weather and Climate: The Singapore–WMO Story

Meteorological Service Singapore*

Every one of Earth's seven billion humans is touched by weather, climate change and natural hazards. Yet relatively few people stop to think about the specialised agency which guides monitoring, sets standards and promotes research of these phenomena: the World Meteorological Organization (WMO). This is all the more true for Singaporeans today, who live in an urban environment shielded from the worst of the elements.

Yet while little-known, the shared history of the Meteorological Service Singapore and the WMO is an eventful one. It is a story about harnessing science and technology to understand our planet and our place in it. Equally importantly, it is a story about the challenges and rewards of collaborating across national boundaries; and about anchoring strategic capabilities for the survival of Singapore.

1966 — Singapore Joins the WMO as a Sovereign State

Singapore has a long meteorological tradition. Our interactions with the global meteorological community precede not only our nation's independence but also the WMO's evolution into a UN specialised agency. It was in 1947 that the International Meteorological Organization (pre-cursor to the WMO), took steps towards integrating with the UN system, and we can take pride that the Singapore-based Malayan Meteorological Service was present at those historic discussions.

---

* A division of the National Environment Agency (NEA).

It was not until 1966, however, that Singapore as a sovereign state would become a full-fledged member of the WMO. The question was not a matter of whether to join, but how soon. The Meteorological Service Singapore at this time came under the direct purview of the Deputy Prime Minister (DPM)'s Office, and the DPM's aides summed it up in a wonderful statement: "The importance of meteorological services to air and sea navigation makes it *necessary* for Singapore, which is at the crossroads of air and sea routes, to be a full Member State of the Organization."

Nature Knows No Boundaries — The World Weather Watch

As a fledgling independent state, membership to the WMO must have seemed a vital support to build Singapore's capabilities. It should not be forgotten however, that our small nation state had something to offer in return.

In the 1960s, a bold new vision was laid out by the WMO that would dramatically enhance the development of meteorology and the atmospheric sciences. This was the World Weather Watch. Its fundamental principle was that weather recognises no geographical boundaries, and therefore every nation should contribute what it could to the global effort of making meteorological observations. In turn, all Meteorological Services, large or small, could draw on a comprehensive global pool of observations made on land, sea, in the atmosphere, and from space. The World Weather Watch is today considered as one of the most outstanding examples of international cooperation: without it, countries would have to negotiate bilateral agreements to facilitate the exchange of data.

The World Weather Watch does not simply enable weather forecasting operations, but has made contributions to scientific understanding. An oft-told story is that a certain phenomenon had confounded scientists for decades, now known as the "Quasi-Biennial Oscillation". It was data from Singapore and a handful of other locations, shared under this programme, which unlocked some of its secrets. For although the Quasi-Biennial Oscillation originates in the tropics, its effects are far-reaching. Some studies suggest that it even affects the strength of hurricanes in the Atlantic Ocean. More than a curious scientific footnote, this illustrates how the whole system is greater than the mere sum of its parts.

Serving the Region — The ASEAN Specialised Meteorological Centre (ASMC)

The WMO's mission to promote cooperation is global in scope, but often regional in implementation. A sterling example of this is the ASEAN Specialised Meteorological Centre (ASMC), which had its origins in a WMO initiative.

In 1985, proposals were made under the WMO for ASEAN to be served by a "Regional Specialised Meteorological Centre". The Centre was meant to help foster cooperation and develop technical capacity in the region. This was particularly important since modern meteorology was moving away from manual methods alone and incorporating greater degrees of computing-intensive numerical weather modelling. The WMO commissioned a study into the possibilities for ASEAN, and the concept for the ASMC was born.

It took several more years of discussion and careful groundwork within the ASEAN community before the ASMC was established in Singapore in 1993. The ASMC's portfolio was initially more research-based and focused on weather modelling. Following severe transboundary haze episodes in 1994 and 1997, however, the ASMC took on the role for which it is now best known: to monitor and assess the occurrence of transboundary smoke haze from land and forest fires in the region.

While not as well-publicised as its work in haze, the ASMC has never lost its objective to promote regional capacity-building and continues its scientific mission today in partnership with the Meteorological Services in the region.

Our Shared Future — Understanding Climate Change and Extreme Weather

Climate change is one of the foremost challenges facing humankind, and early on, experts in the WMO realised that Earth's climate was taking an unprecedented and potentially dangerous trajectory. The WMO's World Climate Conference in 1979 set the stage. After discussions jointly organised with the UN Environment Programme (UNEP), and the International Council for Scientific Unions in 1987, the WMO decided in 1988 upon establishment of the Intergovernmental Panel on Climate Change (IPCC). UNEP gave added endorsement and the IPCC's work began.

Where climate science (and controversy) are concerned, the IPCC is now at the forefront of international debate. Its achievements are undeniable: in assessing the science of climate change, in communicating research findings to policymakers, and in making a complex topic accessible and actionable. Nevertheless, it is not within the IPCC's mandate to generate research, only to review what already exists.

Southeast Asia therefore faces a multi-faceted challenge. Our tropical weather is surprisingly complex — we are positioned at the confluence of multiple weather and climate phenomena, many of which are not well understood. This region's geography is varied, encompassing deep and shallow seas, deltas, mountains, islands; all of which influence the weather in subtle ways. Furthermore Southeast Asia's climate research capability is at a comparatively early stage of development. All this means that research literature on our home region is sparse, and we cannot look to the IPCC or scientists from outside Southeast Asia to fill it.

Singapore's First National Climate Change Study, commissioned by the National Environment Agency in 2007, brought several learning points. Chief among these was the fact that to adequately prepare for the future, Singapore would need a stronger grasp of the physical science underpinning climate change and extreme weather. In achieving this, Singapore would also make a valuable contribution to our region's well-being and the international scientific community.

Therefore in 2013, the Meteorological Service Singapore, with support from the Ministry of the Environment and Water Resources and the National Environment Agency, established the Centre for Climate Research Singapore. As of today, the Centre is responsible for producing national climate projections, tailored for Singapore's needs, and has spearheaded the Second National Climate Change Study. The Centre's research on weather and climate science also anchors a vibrant community spanning both local and overseas institutions.

A Safer Sky and Sea, Everyday

Considering the number of flights worldwide, the relative infrequency of weather-related accidents is a testament to the strong collaboration between National Meteorological Services and the aviation sector. This is in no small part due to the International Civil Aviation Organization (ICAO) and WMO working in close harmony in the specialist area of aeronautical meteorology. Whether it is developing quality standards for new services, encouraging the uptake of new technology, or designating regional centres to watch for volcanic eruptions that might disrupt air traffic, Singapore both benefits from and contributes to their efforts.

What underpins all these capabilities is the exchange of meteorological data. Here, the Meteorological Service Singapore has a critical role to play. We act as a hub, managing regional data and transmitting these to Europe for dissemination; as one of five special databanks in the Asia-Pacific, we also maintain up-to-date meteorological data for aviation and provide automatic responses to *over a million* online queries every year.

Another element of WMO's mission is the provision of forecast and warning services in support of the safety of life and property at sea, as recognised in the International Convention for the Safety of Life at Sea (SOLAS). More than two-thirds of the Earth's surface is covered by water, and yet meteorological observations over the oceans are sparse. The WMO has an ingenious approach to filling this gap: leveraging instrumentation on ships. The Voluntary Observing Ship (VOS) scheme, jointly run with the International Oceanographic Commission of UNESCO, trains merchant ships in taking weather observations while at sea and in calibration of weather sensors when in port. The datasets are not only used for operational forecasting, but also to deepen understanding of how the oceans affect the climate system.

Singapore has lent its support to the VOS scheme for decades. Whenever ships that have signed up to the scheme enter our waters, a Port Meteorological Officer is on hand to liaise with them on their needs. Whether it is supplementing their suite of instruments with new sensors or providing training, Singapore is part of a specialist and highly valued community that contributes to safer seas.

Looking Upward and Forward

While Singapore has progressed by leaps and bounds in 50 years, we are reminded of this: the world we live in is as dynamic as the weather and we need to constantly improve ourselves and reach higher. In doing so, we can act as a beacon to other countries who are on their own journey of development.

There are myriad ways in which we work with WMO and the global community. Even as we write this, the Meteorological Service Singapore is aiming to play a greater role in WMO's regional programmes and initiatives. Simultaneously, we are putting in place improvements to our data infrastructure to provide better and larger volumes of information. Our journey with the WMO has been a mutually enriching one, and one we hope to traverse together for many more decades into the future.

———•—•———

Meteorological Service Singapore (MSS) is a division of the National Environment Agency, which is a Statutory Board of the Ministry of the Environment and Water Resources (MEWR). The main functions of MSS are: to make, collect, process and exchange weather observations; provide weather forecasts and data for aviation, shipping and the public; conduct research and development to enhance its services; compile and archive climatological records of Singapore; and promote and participate in international cooperation programmes in meteorology. For more information on the service, please visit www.weather.gov.sg.

UNITED NATIONS
Peacekeeping

The SAF and UN Peace Operation

Singapore Armed Forces

As a concerned and responsible member of the international community, Singapore fully supports the efforts of the UN in facilitating international peace and security, and upholding the international rule of law. In particular, the SAF's support for UN peace operations — which includes peacekeeping, peacemaking and peacebuilding missions — underscores our belief that the UN is an important institution in maintaining the stability of international order, and providing humanitarian assistance to those in need.

SAF's Philosophy for Contributing to Peace Operations

We take our international responsibilities and commitments seriously. As a small armed forces with limited resources, we try to participate where we can make a useful and meaningful contribution. We develop niche areas of expertise, and are selective about the missions that we contribute to. We participate in missions where our contributions would have the most effect and where they are most valued. Participating in peace operations also benefits our soldiers operationally as they are exposed to the realities of war and its consequences, and required to put their skills into practice. Our soldiers also get the opportunity to work and interact with soldiers from other countries with different operational procedures and cultures.

The SAF first donned the "blue helmet" in 1989, a distinguishing feature of UN military personnel, when it participated in the UN Transition Assistance Group (UNTAG) in Namibia. Since then, we have participated in UN peace operations in various countries, including Angola, Afghanistan, South Africa and Guatemala. Our personnel have assumed a variety of roles in these missions, such as election supervisors, military observers and medical officers. More than 1,500 SAF personnel have participated in 15 UN peace operations to date.

"It's indescribable. Frightening. Earth-shattering." Then-CPT David Tay, a nursing officer, describing the war front in a nutshell.

Remembering Operation Nightingale — The SAF's First Peace Operation in a Foreign War

It was in the thick of the Gulf War in January 1991 that the British Government requested that Singapore provide medical manpower enhancement to a 600-bed hospital in support of UN efforts against Iraq's invasion of Kuwait. The SAF was quickly activated on 7 January 1991, and a medical mission codenamed *Operation Nightingale* was born.

The medical team comprising 30 men left Singapore on 18 January 1991, the start of their 54 days in the Gulf. The team was nervous. It was the first time the SAF was sent to help in a foreign war. Little did the team know that being part of a medical mission did not mean that they were safe from the risks of operating in a zone of conflict.

2300 hrs, 20 January 1991. The team had barely started their work at the 205th General Hospital located inside the uncompleted Terminal 4 of King Khalid International Airport, alongside the British Royal Air Force detachment. They were about 400 kilometres behind the battle frontlines. DING! The missile alert went off, drowning out all ambient sounds. Quickly donning their gas masks and chemical suits, the team rushed for cover. They lay in wait. There was a long pause. *Silence.* The team heaved a sigh of relief. It was a false alarm.

0100 hrs, 21 January 1991. BOOM! The sonic boom of missiles launched from the battery near the camp shook the entire building. The real attack had come a few hours later. The explosions were soon followed by thuds of *SCUD* and *Patriot* fragments littering the ground. The team watched in fear as the warnings over the tannoy went from "red alert" to "black". *Chemical contamination.* It then hit home that there was a very real danger of being killed on this peacekeeping mission.

Air raid sirens were frequent, and the risk of exposure to chemical agents meant that nerve agent pre-treatment tablets had to be consumed.

Subsequent rumours of Iraqi arsenal containing *Anthrax* and *Plague* organisms resulted in the team having to take vaccinations against these two biological agents as well.

Although the team was mentally and physically exhausted, they remained disciplined and focused. They knew what they were there for, and they were determined to get their job done well. Whenever the daily work began, thoughts of their safety and danger became a secondary consideration. Treating patients was their top priority.

One of the high points during *Operation Nightingale* was when the SAF surgical team comprising then-CPT (NS) Pang Ah San and anaesthetist then-MAJ (Dr) Edwin Low performed the first surgery in the operating theatre suite since the hospital's deployment. The event attracted the attention of the whole hospital, and was even recorded on video.

The team's flight surgeon, then-MAJ (Dr) Richard Tan, also proved to be a valuable asset as he was the only qualified flight surgeon at the 205th General Hospital. He developed aeromedical evacuation policies for the hospital, and also personally flew forward to accompany casualties back to the hospital in C-130 aeromedical flights.

The medical team left Saudi Arabia on 13 March 1991, six days after the 205th General Hospital was closed. Over the span of 54 days, they had treated 210 casualties, including Iraqi prisoners of war. It was unanimously agreed that the experience was invaluable. The team had benefitted professionally — from their peers from countries like the US, UK, France, Canada and Sweden, and from circumstances, as frequent shortages in supplies demanded innovative improvising.

"There was an underlying fear in our minds as we faced the spectre of chemical attacks daily." Then-MAJ (Dr) Tan Chi Chiu, mission team leader.

Most importantly, the team was now operationally ready for war.

A Tribute to Timor-Leste — The SAF's Largest Contribution to UN Peace Operations

Medical support is one niche area that the SAF has built up considerable expertise in. Apart from *Operation Nightingale*, the SAF also sent 10 medical teams to Timor-Leste over the period of 1999 to 2002. To date, Timor-Leste remains the country where the SAF had made its largest contributions to UN peace operations — first from 1999 to 2003, and later from 2008 to 2012. This was also the first SAF peace operation with SAF female personnel.

31 August 1999 — the day the Timorese people voted for their freedom. However, the price for freedom had to be paid. An angry and violent response from the Indonesians and anti-independence Timorese militias soon ensued. Over the next three weeks, approximately 1,400 Timorese were killed. Homes, irrigation systems, water supply systems, schools and nearly 100 percent of the country's electrical grid were destroyed. The UN peacekeepers that had arrived earlier in June that year, following the establishment of the UN Mission in East Timor (UNAMET), were not spared either. Nine UN peacekeepers died in the violence.

The UN Security Council quickly sanctioned multinational missions to provide humanitarian aid and peacekeeping support for the Timorese people. Singapore swiftly responded to the call to protect the fragile peace of Timor-Leste, and we were one of the first countries to arrive in September 1999. The SAF sent a 370-strong contingent, which included two Landing Ship Tanks, as well as logistics and medical teams.

> "Like most Singaporeans, the closest I had seen our troops in action was when they were in training ... However, after spending some time with these SAF men and women, following them throughout their missions and patrols, and living with them in their platoon operating bases, I have come to respect and admire their commitment and professionalism, the focus and confidence they show, in spite of the harsh, unfamiliar and often dangerous environment they have to work in." Ken Seet, photographer behind photographic exhibition titled "Mission Ready — SAF Peacekeepers in Timor-Leste".

In May 2001, the first platoon of SAF combat peacekeepers — also the SAF's first deployment of combat peacekeepers — arrived in Timor-Leste. The team soon realised that no amount of realistic training could replicate the actual operations on the ground, the bewildering range of climatic conditions in Timor-Leste being one of them. The sweltering 40 degree Celsius heat enveloped the team upon arrival in Suai, where the RSAF's heli-detachment was based. About 50 kilometres away — roughly the width of Singapore — the winds at Belulik Leten were, in contrast, bone-chilling.

The SAF men and women took turns doing seven to 10-day shifts keeping watch at Observation Post Castle at a hill near Belulik Leten, which overlooked the Indonesian-Timor-Leste border. Peace was both precious and costly.

Each batch of SAF peacekeepers was expected to leave behind their loved ones and the comfort that Singaporeans take for granted, for up to six months at a stretch. There was no mobile phone network coverage. Letter-writing returned to fashion, a cheaper alternative to expensive satellite phone calls. And yet, the SAF peacekeepers never regretted volunteering to be part of the team. It was all worth it.

In return, special bonds were formed between the peacekeepers and the villagers. Language barriers were broken with smiles. The locals were thankful that there were troops protecting the peace in the independent country that they had fought for.

After 10 years, the last platoon of SAF peacekeepers finally left Timor-Leste at the end of December 2012, when the UN Mission in Timor-Leste (UNMIT) completed its mandate.

We had kept the peace.

> "I volunteered for it, and got selected. I'm very proud and happy. This has been the most memorable and significant experience I've ever had in the Army." Then-SSG Adenan Mohammad Eskan, on keeping the peace in Timor-Leste at a time when the country, like his daughter, was less than a year old.

The UN Special Mission in Afghanistan (UNSMA) — The SAF's First Peacemaking Mission

Unlike peacekeeping, peacemaking involves the use of diplomatic means to persuade parties in a conflict to cease hostilities and negotiate a peaceful settlement of their dispute. At the invitation of the UN, Singapore sent a Military Adviser — then LTC Lo Yong Poo — to participate in UNSMA from May 1997 to 1998. UNSMA was the first peacemaking mission the SAF participated in.

The UNSMA was set up to help lay the groundwork for peace after civil war broke out in Afghanistan in the early 1990s. Military Advisers deployed in UNSMA were expected to provide timely and accurate information and assessments on military situations at the frontlines and around the country.

Visits to the frontlines meant being caught in exchanges of rocket and artillery fire, and occasionally stumbling upon dead, mutilated or decomposing bodies. Military Advisers were also tasked to talk to local militia commanders and faction leaders, as well as negotiate ceasefires and peace settlements between the local warring factions. The catch — peacemakers could *not carry* any weapon or military equipment, even for self-defence.

In September 1997, the military situation worsened in the north of Afghanistan. Lo was one of the two peacemakers assigned to travel to Mazar-I-Sharif, a major city in the north, to assist in the evacuation of UN personnel and provide a professional assessment on the situation. However, the trouble started even before the team arrived at Mazar. The usual half-day journey dragged out into a lengthy four-day affair because of two attempted robberies by gunmen and a detainment by local militia for several hours. An intervening party of militia fighters eventually had to negotiate with the local militia for the team's release.

When the team finally arrived at Mazar, the conflict had escalated to the point where it was no longer safe to remain in the city. 15 UN and two non-governmental organisation personnel were moved to the neighbouring province of Shiberghan on the very next day. Two peacemakers, however, chose to remain behind. Lo was one of them. The two men felt that maintaining the UN presence despite the worsening situation would, at the very least, give the locals some hope that the UN *did not desert those in need.*

"The relative peace and harmony enjoyed by our own multi-racial, multi-cultural society in Singapore is a sobering contrast to the violent racial and religious upheavals in Afghanistan and is something for which we can be truly thankful." Then-LTC Lo Yong Poo reflecting on his experience in Afghanistan.

Unfortunately, things only got more chaotic as all attempted efforts to negotiate with the local authorities and restore some semblance of peace were in vain. However, the team was determined to uphold the UN peacemaking mandate. It was only when the duo received a death threat issued by one of the warring factions that they knew — it was time to let go.

Even though the first three heli-evacuation attempts ended up being aborted due to bad timing and weather, the team did not give up hope and continued to explore escape options. Finally, after more than three weeks after their arrival in Mazar, a friendly chopper passing by managed to successfully pick the two men up and send them to Shiberghan. It was then that the duo were able to bid Mazar farewell — *relief.*

Upon Lo's return to Singapore in May 1998, Lo was awarded the SAF Medal for Distinguished Act, an award given to personnel who have displayed bravery in adversity. Lo was one of only two SAF personnel who have participated in UN peace operations to be conferred this award.

Other Contributions to UN Peace Operations

The SAF's contributions to UN peace operations go beyond participating in such missions. We also contribute expertise. At a time when the UN was faced with downsizing and fiscal stringency in 1995, Singapore acceded to the UN's request to second qualified personnel to serve in management positions in the UN Department of Peacekeeping Operations (DPKO) and the Department of Field Support (DFS) to support the UN's peacekeeping efforts. This practice continues today.

Most recently, the SAF participated in the UN Military Units Manual (UNMUM) Initiative driven by the UN DPKO and DFS to improve peace-keeping standards and the safety of peacekeepers in the field. We chaired the Maritime Working Group and participated in the Aviation and Engineer Working Groups. The manuals were presented at the UNMUM Final Conference in December 2014.

The Way Ahead

The SAF remains committed to do its part for UN peace operations. We continue to be ready to offer our assistance and expertise where we can make a useful contribution.

The **Singapore Armed Forces** (SAF) has contributed to UN peace operations since 1989. To date, more than 1,500 SAF personnel have participated in 15 such missions, namely, UNTAG, Operation Nightingale, UNIKOM, UNAVEM, UNTAC, UNOMSA, UNSCOM, MINUGUA, UNSMA, INTERFET, UNTAET, UNMEE, UNMISET, UNMIT and UNMIN. The SAF personnel have assumed a variety of roles in these missions, including that of military observers, medical officers and election supervisors. The SAF also regularly seconds qualified personnel to serve in management positions in the UN Department of Peacekeeping Operations and the Department of Field Support to support the UN's peacekeeping efforts.

List of UN peace operations the SAF has participated in to date

- UN Transitional Assistance Group (UNTAG), to supervise elections in Namibia [October to November 1989]
- *Operation Nightingale*, to provide medical support for the Allied Forces during *Operation Desert Storm* [January to March 1991]
- UN Iraq-Kuwait Observation Mission (UNIKOM), to serve as military observers [April 1991 to March 2003]
- UN Angola Verification Mission (UNAVEM) II, to serve as military observers [July 1991 to December 1992]
- UN Transitional Authority in Cambodia (UNTAC), to provide transport services and aerial support [May to June 1993]
- UN Observer Mission to South Africa (UNOMSA), to supervise elections [April to May 1994]
- UN Special Commission (UNSCOM), to serve as a member of the UN Special Inspection Commission Team in Iraq and verify Iraq's compliance with UN Security Council resolutions [June 1996]
- UN Verification Mission in Guatemala (MINUGUA), to provide medical support [February 1997 to May 1997]
- UN Special Mission to Afghanistan (UNSMA), to serve as a military adviser and facilitate national conciliation and reconstruction [May 1997 to May 1998]
- UN-Sanctioned International Force in East Timor (INTERFET), to provide medical, logistics and aerial support [September 1999 to February 2000]
- UN Transitional Administration in East Timor (UNTAET), to provide medical support and serve as armed peacekeepers [February 2000 to May 2002]

- UN Mission in Ethiopia and Eritrea (UNMEE), to serve as military observers [January 2001 to July 2003]
- UN Mission in Support of East Timor (UNMISET), to provide aerial support and serve as armed peacekeepers [May 2002 to July 2004]
- UN Integrated Mission in Timor-Leste (UNMIT), to serve as operations officers and military information analysts [September 2006 to December 2012]
- UN Mission in Nepal (UNMIN), to serve as military observers [May 2007 to July 2008]

References

"The Operation Nightingale Experience", LTC (NS) (Dr) Tan Chi Chiu, United Nations Peacekeeping — a Decade of SAF's Participation, *POINTER Supplement*, July 1999.
http://www.mindef.gov.sg/safti/pointer/back/suppleme/1999/Jul/5.htm

"1991 — Operation Nightingale", Elaine Lim, *This Month in History*, Vol 4 Issue 1, January 2000.
http://www.mindef.gov.sg/content/dam/imindef_media_library/imindef2012/about_us/history/maturing_saf/v04n01_history/TMIHJan2000.pdf

"The SAF's Experiences in Peace Support Operations", LTC (Ret) Deep Singh, *POINTER*, Vol. 30 No. 4, 2004.
http://www.mindef.gov.sg/imindef/publications/pointer/journals/2004.html

"Beyond our shores", Ong Hong Tat, Cyberpioneer, November 2011.
http://www.mindef.gov.sg/imindef/resourcelibrary/cyberpioneer/topics/articles/features/2011/nov11_fs3.html

"Factsheet — SAF Participation in Peacekeeping Operations in Timor-Leste", May 2005.
http://www.mindef.gov.sg/imindef/press_room/official_releases/nr/2003/jul/11jul03_nr/11jul03_fs2.print.img.html

"Mission Ready — SAF Peacekeepers in Timor-Leste", Ken Seet, A Photographic Exhibition.
http://www.mindef.gov.sg/dam/publications/eBooks/Featured/missionready.pdf

"In the company of peacekeepers", David Yeo, *Cyberpioneer*, July 2003.
http://www.mindef.gov.sg/imindef/resourcelibrary/cyberpioneer/topics/articles/features/2003/jul03_cs.print.img.html

"A triumphant return", Kairen Chan, *Cyberpioneer*, October 2002.

http://www.mindef.gov.sg/imindef/resourcelibrary/cyberpioneer/topics/articles/
news/2002/October/14oct02_news.html

Chronicle of Singapore, 1959–2009: Fifty Years of Headline News, Peter H.L. Lim,
page 235.

https://books.google.com.sg/books?id=CbY062uN1MoC&pg=PA235&lpg=PA235&dq=
operation+nightingale+the+saf&source=bl&ots=4VYPbJ-y_g&sig=pKAQIDoptF
SoLz2j2gg3DOgbpXQ&hl=en&sa=X&ei=BYQOVffHEcyOuASq14LwBQ&ved=
0CEYQ6AEwBw#v=onepage&q=operation%20nightingale%20the%20saf&f=false

Write-up on Timor-Leste, CIA.

https://www.cia.gov/library/publications/the-world-factbook/geos/countrytemplate_
tt.html

"East Timor: militia member sentenced in murder of local UN worker", UN
Department of Public Information, July 2001.

http://reliefweb.int/report/timor-leste/east-timor-militia-member-sentenced-murder-
local-un-worker

"The UN Experience", *Medlink — Chronicle of the SAF Medical Corps*, Dec. 2006,
page 6.

http://www.mindef.gov.sg/content/dam/imindef_media_library/pdf/hqmc/0009.res

"Tough road home for refugees from Timor bloodshed", Philip English, *The New
Zealand Herald*, 10 Dec. 2000.

http://www.nzherald.co.nz/world/news/article.cfm?c_id=2&objectid=163786

"My Experiences in Afghanistan as Military Adviser", LTC Lo Yong Poo, United
Nations Peacekeeping — a Decade of SAF's Participation, *POINTER Supplement*,
July 1999.

http://www.mindef.gov.sg/safti/pointer/back/suppleme/1999/Jul/3.htm

"Flashback Friday: SAF officers honoured for brave acts on May 30, 1998", Amanda
See, *The Straits Times*, 30 May 2014.

http://www.straitstimes.com/news/singapore/more-singapore-stories/story/
flashback-friday-saf-officers-honoured-brave-acts-may-30

Policing in a Foreign Land

Singapore Police Force

Since 1989, the Singapore Police Force (SPF) has participated in UN peacekeeping missions collectively with other member States of the UN as part of Singapore Government's contributions when called upon.

The UN usually only intervenes in countries that have undergone severe internal strife. The SPF officers deployed in such missions play a key role in maintaining peace and security and also where safety and security issues quickly move from being conflict-related to organised crime. Under these circumstances, the SPF officers deployed would perform executive policing duties including patrolling and responding to incidents of fights, riots, demonstrations, and other criminal cases and social disturbances to restore peace and reinforce the rule of law. Sometimes, the officers are also involved in election monitoring and as observers.

In May 1989, the SPF participated in its first peacekeeping mission with a 40-strong contingent as part of the civilian component in the United Nations Transitional Assistance Group (UNTAG) in Namibia. Since then, SPF has contributed **484** personnel (inclusive of repeated deployments) in **9** other UN missions, spanning across the globe in distant countries such as South Africa and closer to home like Cambodia, East Timor/Timor-Leste, and Nepal. See Annex A for details.

Maintaining Peace and Security Through Executive Policing

During the United Nations Transitional Administration in East Timor (UNTAET) in March 2000, 40 SPF officers were vested with executive powers to provide security, maintain law and order and establish a system of governance in East Timor as she moved towards independence, led by veteran peacekeeper, Acting Superintendent (Ag Supt) Heng Sou Kaw. The officers served as UN Civilian Police Officers (CIVPOL) and were also called upon to set up the East Timor Police Service.

For the first time, female officers were also deployed in this mission. Whether veterans or first-timers, men or women; the SPF officers were highly regarded for their discipline, professionalism, and competencies in a variety of policing work, including command and control, investigations, operations, training, frontline policing and staff work.

Sergeant Steven Tay was then attached to an investigation team that was probing killings that had taken place during a particularly violent period between April and September 1999. It was a grisly duty, as he accompanied the team to exhume bodies of victims killed by the militias. Indeed, it requires passion in the work, perseverance in carrying on and ensuring that it is done to the best of our abilities. As time passed, he won the trust and confidence of the Timorese and the respect, friendship and confidence of officers from other countries.

Whatever their experiences, they learnt a great deal not only about professionalism but also compassion, and not being judgemental.

Building Law Enforcement Capacity and Capabilities by Imparting Policing Knowledge and Skills

The local national police in most host countries of UN missions would be newly set up and may not be properly trained. Through supervision, training and mentoring programmes, the SPF officers serve to impart professional policing knowledge and skills in general areas such as patrolling, operations, investigation and intelligence as well as specialised areas such as maritime, traffic, community policing and more. Establishing a good foundation in these core policing skills are fundamental to building credibility and improving the performance and morale of the local police and community at large.

In October 2007, Ag Supt Sng May Yen was the first woman SPF Contingent Commander to lead the 2nd contingent of 21 officers to the United Nations Integrated Mission in Timor-Leste (UNMIT). Then 36, Ag Supt Sng was no stranger to peacekeeping missions, having participated in the 2001 United Nations Transitional Administration in East Timor (UNTAET). During her one-year stint in UNMIT, she was deployed as the officer in charge of training the officers and planning the traffic arrangements for East Timor's Independence Day Celebrations. She recalled fondly how the newly formed local police, which she had a hand in training, progressed from amateurs to professionals in performing VIP escort for the week-long celebrations. It was heartening for her, knowing that the hard work she and her teammates put in had paid off. What motivated her as a Contingent Commander was the thought that they would be able to make a difference to as many individuals as they could, and through the police officers trained, they would be able to change the lives of the masses in Timor-Leste.

Building Community Confidence Through Engaging the People

To perform their duties, the SPF officers also go beyond their law enforcement roles to reach out to the local communities. By showing a sincere desire to help them, the officers, working hand in hand with the local police, strive to earn the trust and respect of the local communities. This would also lead to better cooperation and increased willingness on the part of the community to assist the police in the fight against crime.

Senior Staff Sergeant Tan Buck Song was grateful to be able to witness and be personally involved in the return of the internally displaced persons (IDPs) from Dili to Mauk Sub-village of Maleuwana in UNMIT (2nd batch). With the assistance of the International Organisation of Migration and Ministry of Social Solidarity as well as various UN and Non-Governmental Organisation agencies, the teething issues of electricity and water were resolved so that the IDPs could resettle and reintegrate into the society peacefully. Indeed, the multiracial and multi-cultural composition of the Singapore Contingent had served as a welcome example for a strife-torn country.

Learning from the Experiences

The challenges faced by the SPF officers deployed in these missions are multifold, some of which are hostile surroundings, differing values and cultures, non-acceptance of police authority in countries with ineffective criminal justice systems, lack of government support in infrastructure and logistics, and the officers' anxiety of separation from their families. More often than not, the officers' commitment as a peacekeeper and perseverance, coupled with adequate training, preparations and strong teamwork, helped them to overcome these challenges.

At the Force-wide level, the SPF has benefited tremendously from participation in peacekeeping missions. The experiences of working in a very different and unfamiliar environment, interactions with international police officers from various countries, and proactive engagements with the local communities, have established good relationships with our foreign counterparts and enhanced the SPF's professionalism, credibility and standing in the international policing arena.

The SPF recognises the important role of police in international peace operations which serves to ensure that countries in conflict receive the support and assistance they require, particularly in a post conflict attaches. In such environments, establishing a stable national police force which can effectively combat insurgent criminal activity is necessary to foster sustainable peace and the rule of law. The SPF is proud to play a part in international policing to build sustainable security in the countries we have operated in.

———•◦•———

The **Singapore Police Force** (SPF) has contributed to peacekeeping missions since 1989. Since then, the SPF has participated in ten missions, namely, UNTAG, UNTAC, IPSO, UNOMSA, JIOG, UNTAET, UNMISET, PNAM, UNMIN and UNMIT. The duties that SPF officers undertake ranges from frontline policing, investigations, operations, training and staff work. To provide the SPF with the capability to deploy specially trained officers to perform policing duties in overseas peacekeeping missions at short notice, the SPF United Nations Peacekeeping Force (UNPKF) was set up under the Special Operations Command to centrally manage its recruitment, selection and training. To date, the SPF UNPKF has a total of 79 officers, including 17 female officers who hold concurrent appointment as a member of UNPKF.

List of SPF Peacekeeping Missions

	Overseas Missions	Duration	Country	No. of Personnel Deployed[1]
1.	UN Transition Assistance Group in **Namibia** (UNTAG)	May 1989–Apr 1990	Namibia	49
2.	UN Transitional Authority in **Cambodia** (UNTAC)	Apr 1992–Sep 1993	Cambodia	150
3.	UNTAC International Polling Station Officers in **Cambodia** (IPSO)	May 1993–Aug 1993	Cambodia	20
4.	UN Observers Mission in **South Africa** (UNOMSA)	Apr 1994–May 1994	South Africa	3
5.	UN Joint International Observers' Group to **Cambodia** (JIOG)	Jul 1998	Cambodia	8
6.	UN Transitional Administration in **East Timor** (UNTAET)	Mar 2000–May 2002	East Timor	120
7.	UN Mission of Support in **East Timor** (UNMISET)	May 2002–Jul 2003	East Timor	25
8.	UN Police Needs Assessment Mission in **East Timor** (PNAM)	Nov 2002–Nov 2002	East Timor	1
9.	UN Mission in **Nepal** (UNMIN)	Aug 2007–May 2008	Nepal	1
10.	UN Integrated Mission in **Timor-Leste** (UNMIT)	Nov 2006–Oct 2012	Timor-Leste	107

[1] Including repeat deployment.

UNITED NATIONS
Secretariat

Advancing Global Statistical and Geospatial Information: Contributions of the United Nations and Singapore

Paul CHEUNG

On 10 October 2010, some 140 countries and 50 international entities celebrated the first-ever World Statistics Day. Ceremonies, conferences, and press interviews were organized to highlight the many achievements of official statistics and to reaffirm the core values of official statistics: Integrity, Professionalism, and Service to the Nation. On this day, the global statistical community, under the leadership of the United Nations Statistical Commission, stepped up to showcase its work and its impact on the world. Their efforts and achievements in quantifying the world have indeed been impressive.

Official Statistics and the United Nations

Recognising the importance of high quality and comparable statistics in tracking national and global development, the United Nations convened the first meeting of national statistical experts in May 1946 to build a system of statistical indicators for the post-war era. This inter-governmental mechanism was supported by the United Nations Statistical Office (later re-named Statistical Division). What the United Nations has accomplished in this 70-year span is described by many observers as "an unsung success". It manages, quietly but effectively, global statistical activities: setting methodological standards, raising statistical capacity and evolving a community of practice of lasting impact. Official statistics are used every day in this globalised world for comparisons and analyses, by the media, businesses, the governments and the general public. International availability and comparability of data would not have been possible if the United Nations had not exercised its leadership role through its convening power.

Each year in March, chief statisticians around the world attend the UN Statistical Commission in New York, where they debate measurement issues that require global attention. The Commission has often been characterised as the most effective "functional commission" in the UN system, serving its role as an expert body with minimal political influence. As the apex entity of the global statistical community, the Commission approves statistical standards and coordinates global projects. As an example, the recently completed 2010 round of the global census programme witnessed the successful completion of population and housing censuses in 216 countries and areas, representing 93% of the global population. A global comparison of prices was completed in 2014 which produced new figures on purchasing power parities. The System of National Accounts was successfully updated in 2008, and the new re-based GDP estimates are beginning to be released around the world.

Over the past 70 years, the statistical community confronted new user demands and challenges surfaced by global crises. The changing structures and flows of the global economy necessitate the updating of the methodology for measuring the GDP of an economy. Our trade statistics must now reflect unique value-added contributions in a distributed global production system. The 2008 financial crisis called for quicker surveillance of fluctuations in the production and financial sectors. This has led to more decisive action in the global compilation of short-term economic and financial indicators. The widespread use of internet and social media as data collection and dissemination tools has also called for revisions in methodological standards on surveys and censuses. The concept of "Open Data", now widely adopted as the paradigm for data access, was initiated in 2006 through the introduction of "UNdata", a free, accessible data service that makes UN data readily accessible to everyone in the world.

The Commission's work goes beyond just technical matters. History has documented many instances whereby official statistics were deliberately manipulated for political gain. The Commission has been forceful in articulating and advancing the core values of global statistics: Integrity, Professionalism, and Service. In 1994, the Commission enshrined these core values by adopting the "Fundamental Principles of Official Statistics".

Countries around the world have embraced these principles; many have written them into their national legislations or incorporated them in their codes of conduct. But while statements on values could help guide behaviors, they cannot prevent abuse. The European Commission has recently empowered Eurostat to take on auditing powers to prevent any potential manipulation of statistical information by member countries. Could the Statistical Commission one day be given the authority to hold countries accountable to the Fundamental Principles? This debate is still continuing.

Towards a New Information Architecture: Integrating Geospatial Information, Big Data, and Official Statistics

There is a growing recognition in recent years that new technologies and transformed administrative practices are leading to a rapid rise in the volume and variety of data. The Secretary-General of the UN coined this process a "data revolution" and has appointed advisory groups to study the issues. The UN Statistics Division has responded quickly to the rise of geospatial information and the lack of an inter-governmental mechanism to address technical and management issues. It initiated a process in 2009 to form an inter-governmental body and in 2011, the Economic and Social Council endorsed this proposal and established the Expert Committee on Global Geospatial Information Management. At a time of great reluctance for the UN to establish any new inter-governmental bodies, the ECOSOC decision signified the recognition that the world was heading towards a new information era in which the UN has to play an active role. A full programme of work has now been established.

In 2014, both the Statistical Commission and the Geospatial Information Committee officially endorsed a programme of work to develop "global standards" for the integration of statistical and geospatial information. In many countries, the necessity of working together across disciplines and organisations to integrate multiple sources of information has gained significant momentum and recognition. The introduction of global standards on definitions, processes, and aggregation methodology will add impetus to this process.

The integration of official statistics, geospatial information, and unstructured "big data" as an information platform at national and global level will be the next challenge for the United Nations. This new initiative may in due course give the Statistical Commission a new expanded mandate. The UN, just like it did in 1945, will once again be expected to play a critical role in an era of rapid information.

Contributions from Singapore

I served as Singapore's Chief Statistician for 14 years from 1991 to 2004, before joining the United Nations in 2004 as the Director of UN Statistics Division. I am honoured to have been the first person from the developing world to take this leadership position. Having followed UN standards and methodologies for many years, including serving as the resident of the International Association of Official Statistics (2001–2003), I was familiar with the work of UN Statistics Division. But New York is far from Singapore, and I could not have imagined that I would be given the opportunity to lead the global statistical community.

My experience in the UN was heavily influenced by my tenure in Singapore's statistical office and by my professional peers around the world. Singapore is a small country, a city-state. We do not have the political weight or economic significance of large countries. Like other developing countries, we do not have adequate expertise in all aspects of statistical measurement. Nonetheless, as a country, Singapore has to produce the full range of official statistics, and meet the demands of national and internationally users. We have to follow UN standards, adopt global best practices, and make unique contributions of our own. It is a demanding task to keep a national statistical system running smoothly. I am glad that steady progress has been made in Singapore. This experience of building a national system led me to place capacity building and helping other UN member states to build their statistical system as the highest priority.

In my opinion, Singapore has made contributions to the global system through the years in the following aspects:

First, Singapore often plays an important role as "thought leader". For while we may lack resources, we do not lack in ideas. Because we are a small city-state, we face measurement problems arising from rapid socio-economic changes much faster. Solutions have to be quickly found. When this happens, we bring these issues and proposed solutions to the ASEAN community and discuss them with our neighbours. Any regional solutions are eventually brought to the UN to be considered at the global level. For example, Singapore's comprehensive and systematic reporting of its economic performance grew out of the need to inform investors and business planners. The reporting schedule and the manner in which economic data are being released have influenced global statistical dissemination standards.

Second, experimentation and innovations in Singapore's statistical system have contributed to the evolution of global practices. We have gained respect with our willingness to try new ideas. In 2000, Singapore was the first country in the world to use the Internet as the primary means of multi-modal data collection methodology in its population census. The Internet has since become an emerging method across the world; some 33 countries have since deployed multi-modal data methodology in the 2010 round of population censuses. Singapore was also the first Asian country to adopt a register-based population census. Singapore's experience in the integration of geospatial information and official statistics is well-recognised as a global best practice. The "One-Map" platform, as an integrative framework for statistical and geospatial information, has been discussed and showcased in many UN meetings. As host of the International Monetary Fund's Training Center and other UN training initiatives, Singapore continues to play a critical role in developing innovations and facilitating knowledge transfer.

Third, Singapore takes Integrity and Professionalism as core values of official statistics very seriously, with appropriate safeguards built into legislations and institutional arrangements. Credibility and confidence is high among the users of Singapore statistics. There have been many debates on the quality of Singapore's official statistics. But the adherence to global standards, the transparency of compilation methodology, and the dedication of professional staff have reassured the users. There is no doubt that a constant, transparent flow of high quality statistical information facilitates Singapore's development as a major financial and manufacturing hub in Asia.

A new information age is upon us. Countries will no doubt take advantage of the rapid and abundant information for decision-making support in every aspect of our life. As we move forward with a new information architecture combining official statistics, geospatial information, and "big data", there will be a new role for the United Nations to bring countries together to work out new standards and protocols. Singapore, along with others, is moving aggressively to develop an integrated data platform in its Smart Nation development agenda. As a "thought leader" in the professional community and as a member of the UN, Singapore will undoubtedly help shape the global information of the future.

———•—•——

Paul CHEUNG is currently a Professor of Social Policy and Analytics at the National University of Singapore (NUS). He joined NUS in 2013 after serving as the Director of the United Nations Statistics Division (UNSD) and the Secretariat of the UN Committee on Global Geospatial Information Management (UN-GGIM) for 9 years (2004–2012). At the UN, he facilitated the development of the global statistical system and coordinated the work of the United Nations Statistical Commission. He also managed a diverse programme of work implementing UN mandates on global geospatial information, cartography, and geographic names. His initiative to establish the UN-GGIM was endorsed by ECOSOC in 2011. Prior to joining the UN, he was the Chief Statistician of Singapore from 1991 to 2004, managing and coordinating the national statistical system of Singapore. He was awarded in 2001 the Public Administration Gold Medal by the Government of Singapore for his leadership in modernising Singapore's census and statistical systems. He has received awards and medals from governments, universities and international organisations. He is now senior advisor to a number of countries on national planning and statistical systems. He is also the Chair of the International Steering Committee on Global Mapping. His current research project focuses on evolving the next generation of global information infrastructure, integrating "big data", official statistics and geospatial information for decision support.

"Saving Humanity from Hell": A Personal Perspective from UNHQ

CHEW Beng Yong

I joined the UN Secretariat from 1980 to 2006, following my posting to the Permanent Mission of Singapore to the UN from 1975 to 1979. It was indeed gratifying to have witnessed up close and to have participated in the work of the UN in its effort to make our world a better and safer place for all.

My years of service in the Organization started out first in the Department of Political and Security Council Affairs, then in the Department of Disarmament Affairs, and lastly, in the Department of Political Affairs. During the early 1980s, the UN was practically paralysed by the vetoes cast by one or more of the Permanent Members of the Security Council. There was more "action" in the General Assembly where the non-aligned Member States and the Group of 77 usually had the votes to pass any resolution they wanted. It was only with the end of the Cold War that the workload of the Security Council increased dramatically. Agreements were reached, bringing an end to several of the proxy wars in Latin America, Africa and elsewhere. The number of peacekeeping operations mushroomed and various new peace-making, peace-building and political missions have since been established.

In our part of the world, the intensive work done by the original five ASEAN countries, together with UN officials and other interested Member States, paved the way for the signing of the Comprehensive Agreements on Cambodia in 1991. The Security Council had, in 1975, called on "all States" to respect East Timor's right to self-determination, but this was achieved only in 1999 when agreement was finally reached by Indonesia and Portugal to request the UN to conduct a referendum there.

It was an unforgettable experience for me to have led the first inter-departmental needs assessment to East Timor and to head UNAMET's political affairs unit. Other interesting assignments I had during my years with the UN included planning, organising and coordinating the UN system-wide participation in activities for the 1986 International Year of Peace; assisting in implementing the Secretary-General's (SG) good offices role in Myanmar, the Korean peninsula; and working closely through the UN Political Office in Bougainville to help the Bougainvilleans and the National Government of Papua New Guinea reach a peace agreement on 30 August 2001, thus bringing an end to a ten-year conflict in Bougainville.

As Special Assistant to the Under-Secretary General for Disarmament Affairs, I had the opportunity of assisting in a wide range of the Department's activities. I also provided substantive support to the UN Regional Centre for Peace and Disarmament in Asia and the Pacific located in Kathmandu, Nepal. In the early 1980s, I was assigned to serve as Secretary to the group of experts who, as requested by the General Assembly, were appointed to study the consequences of the 1981 "armed Israeli aggression against the Iraqi nuclear installations", an attack which both the Security Council and the General Assembly condemned. The next attack to destroy Iraq's nuclear and other weapons of mass destruction (WMD) came March 2003 with the invasion of Iraq. Five months later, we were terribly shocked and saddened by the tragic bombing of the UN headquarters in Baghdad which took the lives of 22 people including the SG's Special Representative.

This unilateral military action against a Member State, without authorisation, has serious implications for the Security Council, the UN organ charged with the maintenance of international peace and security. The disastrous consequences of this attack are still unfolding. The unleashing of a "global war on terror" has led to a growing threat of non-actors seeking WMDs to commit nuclear terrorism in retaliation. Any conflict involving nuclear weapons will be catastrophic for humanity. Curbing the proliferation of WMDs is vital. Hence, is it unreasonable to insist that the Permanent Members themselves begin to implement Article VI of the 35-year old Non-Proliferation Treaty without further delay?

The UN is a convenient whipping-boy for Member States and, unfortunately, many of the criticisms of its shortcomings, double standards, flaws and failures, e.g. in Kosovo, Bosnia, Rwanda and elsewhere, are justified. However, to be fair, some factors are beyond the Secretariat's control e.g.

when some parties reject certain parts of the agreement, but more frequently it is because of inadequate resources and unrealistic time frames for implementing complex and difficult mandates. Nevertheless, it has to be recognised that, over the past seven decades, the UN has done a fairly impressive job "to promote social progress and better standards of life in larger freedom" as its founders had pledged in the preamble of the UN Charter.

Today we live in a globalised and digitised world. Billions of dollars can be moved in matter of seconds. Pandemics, natural and man-made disasters can affect our safety and security overnight. The need for collective action to address current and future threats facing us in this new millennium cannot be overstated. The sovereign equality of Member States is a valuable democratic principle, especially for the smaller and less powerful States, along with the cardinal principles of respect for the territorial integrity and the non-interference in the internal affairs of Member States.

Singapore's active and constructive role in bridging differences, harmonising the positions of the diverse groups among developing as well as small island States and helping to ensure that their interests are taken into account, is widely appreciated.

Building consensus among 193 member States is a time-consuming and arduous task, but the legitimacy of resolutions and decisions arrived at by consensus make their compliance more likely than those rubber-stamped because of pressure from the powerful States or adopted because of the "tyranny of the majority". The International laws that have been developed, and the new norms that are emerging as a result of these efforts, are essential if we are to have a stable environment for growth and for the orderly conduct of international affairs.

Singapore's relations with the UN have broadened and deepened over the years. It is highly regarded as a reliable and responsible partner by fellow Member States. Its track record of paying its membership dues on time and in full is exemplary. Singapore-UN relations have been mutually beneficial. Its active participation in vanguard movements like the 3G (Global Governance Group) so as to enable the UN "to save humanity from hell", to quote Dag Hammarskjold, is in Singapore's interest as well in the interests of all member States.

CHEW Beng Yong joined the United Nations in March 1980 as a Political Affairs Officer in the International Security and Regional Affairs Section of the Political Affairs Division of the Department of Political and Security Council Affairs. Since then, she had served in various capacities in the UN, including as Chief of Section for Inter-Agency Cooperation of the Secretariat for the International Year of Peace (1983–1986); Secretary of the Expert Group to study the consequences of the Israeli attack against the Iraqi nuclear installations (1983–1984); Special Assistant to the Under-Secretary-General for Disarmament Affairs (1988–1992); and Senior Political Affairs Officer in the East Asia and the Pacific Division of the Department of Political Affairs (1992–1995). She represented the Secretary-General at the 32nd Pacific Islands Forum summit held in Nauru (August 2001). She was Deputy Director of the Asia and the Pacific Division of the Department of Political Affairs from 1996 to October 2006. Prior to joining the United Nations, Beng Yong served in the Ministry of Foreign Affairs of Singapore from 1969 to February 1980. Her positions in the Ministry included that of Research Officer for Mainland South-East Asia (1969–1972); Desk Officer for Malaysia (1972–1975); Second Secretary, Permanent Mission of Singapore to the United Nations (1975–Jan 1979); and Deputy Director, Protocol and Consular Division (Feb 1979–Jan 1980). Beng Yong is currently a member of several non-governmental organisations, including the Academy of Senior Professionals at Eckerd College, St. Petersburg, Florida, and the Academic Council of the United Nations System (ACUNS). She holds a BA (Hons) from the University of Singapore and a MA from the New York University.

Financial Administration at the UN: An Insight into the United Nations Secretariat (1972–2005)

Cecil K.Y. EE

The vision for the United Nations embodied in its Charter covers a wide range of activities. As it is very ambitious, it would be easy to conclude that the Organization has not lived up to the purposes for which it was created. Over the length of my UN career, I have come to see it as a "work-in-progress". Viewed from the perspective of a staff member, I am happy for what it has achieved and recognise that much more remains to be done.

My appointment in the Secretariat began in September 1972 with the International Narcotics Control Board (INCB). I was assigned to review the confidential reports that INCB received from Governments on illicit drug activities in Asia. Together with a small team of colleagues who covered other regions, we developed a comprehensive picture of drug abuse and trafficking around the world. The annual report of INCB continues to be an authoritative publication on this subject and identifies areas where countries cooperate to reduce the availability of drugs to those who would abuse them.

A year after I joined the Secretariat, the United Nations introduced the "planning, programming and budgeting system (PPBS)" to replace its "line-item budget" approach to budgeting. The UN Secretary-General's proposed biennial budget for 1974–1975 would be his first budget under PPBS. Having studied PPBS at university, I readily volunteered to be the focal point for drafting the 1974–1975 budget proposals of INCB. This turned out to be a career-changing decision as I would spend the rest of my years at the UN working on finance.

In 1977, I transferred from INCB to the Budget Division of the UN Office in Geneva (UNOG) to work as a Budget Officer on conference services. The UN plays an important institutional role in multinational co-operation by convening meetings and conferences on various subjects. While meetings do not always translate into improvement of the human condition, the UN is available to nations as a venue whenever they wish to meet. The effectiveness of the framework for dialogue and cooperation set up by the UN depended on the ability of Member States to agree on the related activities, the commitment of Member States to these activities and their willingness to fund them.

As a major conference venue, a large part of the UNOG expenditures was on conference services. My work included preparing cost estimates for these meetings and ensuring that the actual expenditures were accurately apportioned to the relevant programmes or billed to participating Governments in the case of special conferences. At first, I was surprised at the high cost of holding UN meetings. This was mainly because they were usually conducted in at least four, and often six, of its official languages. Providing simultaneous interpretation required the assignment of two or three interpreters to each language booth. The high cost of providing dele-gates with documents in the official languages used at UN meetings was also a surprise to me. Millions of pages of documents are produced every year. UNOG employs hundreds of conference typists, translators, revisers (these were senior translators who revise the work of translators) and editors who convert original drafts into the other official languages.

The budget experience in Geneva led to my next career move in 1980 to the Budget Division at UN Headquarters in New York. Over the next four years, I would be responsible for the budgets of the UN Conference on Trade and Development (UNCTAD), the United Nations Industrial Development Organization (UNIDO), the Economic Commission for Africa (ECA), the International Trade Centre (ITC) which was jointly financed by UNCTAD and GATT (the predecessor of the World Trade Organization), and the Office of the UN Disaster Relief Co-ordinator which later became part of the UN Department for Humanitarian Affairs. In addi-tion to budget formulation and budget performance monitoring, I also pre-pared statements of programme budget implications whenever Governments were considering draft decisions (that include resolutions) involving activi-ties that were not foreseen in the approved budget. The three months of each year when the General Assembly was in session were especially busy for the

Budget Division because several draft decisions would be submitted by Member States to the General Assembly. The informal consultations on draft decisions often took place after office hours and frequently extended late into the night and over weekends. I worked with delegates from around the world, including those from Singapore, on many such draft decisions and developed close professional ties with a number of them.

After eight years working on the UN's budget in Geneva and in New York, I witnessed the Organization go through several financial crises. Rich nations balked at the ever increasing size of its budgets and have even withheld their contributions because of disagreement with activities voted by the majority of nations. Of course, much of the increases in the budget were due to the gradual decline in the value of the US dollar which began in the early 1970s. There was also the impact of the oil embargo that saw economies around the world struggle to contain inflation. Real growth was modest at best but the UN's regular budget, which is paid from assessments on all Member States, had reached approximately US$2 billion per biennium.

In 1985, I was appointed as Chief of the Salaries and Allowances Section at Headquarters. The Section was responsible for approving the salary scales of locally-recruited staff at all UN duty stations of which there were more than 150 worldwide. These scales were based on the best prevailing local salaries for the various job groups. Most scales were revised annually to account for inflation. They were also subject to salary surveys conducted every three or four years to ensure that UN salaries matched the best local salaries. The results of these surveys were often contentious with staff representatives sometimes threatening industrial action.

Apart from deciding on salary scales for locally-recruited staff, I also participated as a representative of the UN Secretariat at meetings of the International Civil Service Commission which reviewed and approved the salaries and allowances of the UN's staff in the Professional and higher categories. In addition, I participated at the meetings of inter-secretariat bodies in the effort to maintain a common system of salaries and allowances for the UN and the Specialised Agencies.

So far, most of my work at the UN involved interacting with other staff and with Government representatives accredited to the UN. This would change with my next career move in 1988 to join the Investment Management Service of the UN Joint Staff Pension Fund as the Senior Investment Officer responsible for the Fund's cash and fixed-income portfolios. Unlike my previous assignments, I would now work closely with investment banks in New York and around the world.

The UN Pension Fund pays the pensions of its retirees either in US dollars or in the currency of the countries where they reside. A conscious effort is made to match the Fund's multi-currency liabilities with investments in multiple currencies. My work on the Fund's cash portfolio involved foreign exchange and short-term interest rates. The Fund had cash reserves in more than a dozen currencies and adjusted its currency exposure periodically through foreign exchange transactions to bring the exposure in line with its medium-term currency targets. For its fixed-income portfolio, the Fund invested the equivalent of a few billion US dollars in the highest quality bonds also in several currencies. The investment performance of the UN Pension Fund was regularly in the top ten percentile among institutional investors in the US. The record of its average annual returns since its establishment in 1949 was around 3 percent above inflation. This strong performance was achieved through the close collaboration among its investment staff, the advice they received from an investment bank that the Fund engaged as its investment advisors and the strategic decisions on asset allocation and currency exposure determined every quarter with members of the UN Investments Committee which is made up of a small group of experts selected from different countries. The experience of working on the investments of the UN Pension Fund continues to have an impact on my personal life. It has made me more aware of developments and trends in the financial markets and the opportunities that they present.

My next and final career move occurred in early 1992 and took me back to Geneva to be Chief of Claims Payments at the UN Compensation Commission (UNCC). The Commission had been established in 1991 following Iraq's invasion of Kuwait. After it was forced from Kuwait, the UN Security Council decided that Iraq should compensate individuals, corporations and governments for the losses they suffered as a result of the invasion. The Compensation Commission was established as a subsidiary of the Security Council to process compensation claims and payments. A Compensation Fund was also established where a percentage of the proceeds from the sale of Iraqi oil would be deposited to pay for the compensation programme. This was an unprecedented exercise undertaken by the UN and the mechanisms for the exercise had to be developed from scratch.

During the first few years after UNCC was established, Iraq did not accept the terms for the sale of its oil. This period saw widespread hardship for its citizens until 1995 when the "oil-for-food" programme was agreed. Thirty percent of the proceeds from the sale of Iraqi oil under the programme went to the Compensation Fund. This allowed the secretariat of UNCC to accelerate the processing of the 2.7 million compensation claims that were received. Although the total amount claimed exceeded US$350 billion, just over US$52.4 billion was awarded to more than 1.5 million successful claims. The majority of these claims were from individuals who received relatively small awards of under US$10,000 each. The rest went to a few large individual claims and those of corporations and Governments some of which were awarded billions of US dollars. A payments management system was developed in my office to process payments to the successful claimants. The system had to achieve accuracy and the highest standards for accountability and transparency. Awards exceeding US$2,500 were paid in instalments with claims of more than US$100,000 being paid in multiple instalments.

Since the establishment of UNCC in 1991, several governments, including Singapore, participated as members of its Governing Council which is made up of the same Governments that are members of the UN Security Council. Decisions of the Council needed 9 votes from its 15 members. Unlike the UN Security Council, no Government had the right of veto. To date, however, all of the Governing Council's decisions numbering over 270 have been adopted by consensus. There were several meetings where it seemed like consensus could not be reached putting at risk the Council's decision-making record. Credit for the unbroken record belongs to the tireless work of its members helped by suggestions from the secretariat to arrive at compromise if not agreement. This record has enhanced the credibility of the Commission and its work.

By the end of 2005, all claims received had been reviewed. Over $20 billion in compensation payments had been made to nearly 100 governments for distribution to their successful claimants. All but a handful of individual claims had been paid and only 85, mostly corporate and Government claims, remained to be paid in full. These were the largest claims with combined outstanding balances totaling US$32.4 billion. Accordingly, UNCC undertook to downsize its secretariat. I saw this as an opportunity to take early retirement and to bring my career at the UN to a close on a high note.

I am happy to have been part of UNCC in my last UN assignment. Only a small number of UN programmes, (for example refugee protection and emergency food aid) directly touch the lives of individual victims. I visited several countries and witnessed claimants arriving to receive their payments. Many were from poor countries who received modest pay for their work which they sent home to support their families. Their lives and livelihoods were significantly disrupted when Iraq invaded Kuwait in 1990. Meeting with them and their representatives assured me that the Commission's work had helped them to recover at least a part of what they lost in the invasion.

———•◦•———

Cecil K.Y. EE retired from the UN as the Chief of Claims Payment, UN Compensation Commission (UNCC), Geneva in December 2005. He began his career as an Administrative Assistant at the Port of Singapore Authority in 1971. In 1972, Cecil took up his first post in the UN was Assistant Social Affairs Officer, International Narcotics Control Board, Geneva. This was followed by a stint as Budget Officer in Geneva, and then New York. From 1985, he was Chief, Salaries and Allowances Section, New York. In 1988, he was Senior Investment Officer for the UN Joint Staff Pension Fund, New York. He took up his UNCC appointment in 1992. After leaving the UN, Cecil had financial management consultancies at the World Intellectual Property Organization (WIPO), Geneva; Bureau of the Ramsar Convention on Wetlands, Gland, Switzerland; and the International Renewable Energy Agency (IRENA), Abu Dhabi. Cecil graduated with a Bachelor of Economics (Honours) from the University of Malaysia, Kuala Lumpur, in 1971.

My UNDP Story

Shirin HAMID

The United Nations Development Programme (UNDP) is one of the largest field-based UN entities in the UN system committed to the reduction poverty worldwide. Since 1966, UNDP has partnered with people and organisations at all levels of society to help empower lives and build resilient nations that benefit from sustainable development, democratic governance and peace building, and climate and disaster resilience, improving the quality of life around the globe. The UNDP is integral in the overall UN efforts to attain the Millennium Development Goals (MDGs) and a new development agenda starting later this year.

As the MDGs deadline draws near, it is gratifying to know that so many people across the globe have risen out of poverty and are now better fed, better educated, with improved chances for healthier and longer lives than in 1990. UNDP monitors its milestones for progress every year: in 2013, for example, UNDP programmes supported the creation of 6.5 million jobs, over half for women, in 109 countries, broadening access to justice in 117 countries, and helping to build resilience in 14 crisis-affected regions.

On the ground in more than 170 countries, UNDP offers an inclusive approach with local insights and expertise to help empower lives and build resilient nations. From the earthquake in Haiti in 2010, the first democratic elections in Tunisia in 2011, Hurricane Haiyan in the Philippines in 2013, and the Ebola outbreak in 2014, UNDP has been there to help millions of people benefit each year from UNDP programmes that fight poverty, build democratic societies, prevent crisis, enable recovery, protect the environment, halt and reverse HIV/AIDS, grow national capacity, and empower women.

Singapore and UNDP

50 years ago, UNDP was a central partner in the economic planning for Singapore's independence, as Craig Murphy notes[1] in that Singapore then received the highest per capita UNDP support of any country, and Prime Minister Lee Kuan Yew's government used it wisely, "focusing heavily on education, industrial development, and urban planning, on every aspect of the now successful industries." UNDP had the technical knowledge, contacts, overseas training, and information resources worldwide to rapidly assist in developing an economic framework aligned to the World Bank and the IMF. Then, as now, UNDP has been a trusted knowledge broker in Singapore with an outstanding global reputation.

The government of Singapore and UNDP jointly established a Global Centre for Public Service Excellence in Singapore in 2012, as just another example of their close and enduring relationship. The Centre is dedicated to policy research and the global exchange of knowledge and information on public service policies, strategies, and institutions. UNDP's Administrator Helen Clark recently spoke at the Centre[2] about women's equal participation and leadership in decision-making as a global development priority.

My own story is simple: I grew up in Singapore, a racially diverse society, where education is universally available, and where meritocracy prevails regardless of gender, race or religion. After years of management consulting and leading teams of information and communications technology (ICT) professionals, including several in the traditionally male-dominated maritime industry in Singapore, an opportunity opened up in 2005 to join UNDP. Having dedicated my life to and benefited from the principles of diversity, meritocracy, and women's empowerment, joining UNDP was an opportunity for me to give back so that others, especially in developing nations and among women worldwide, can benefit from these same principles.

I joined UNDP in 2005 as its Chief Technology Officer and Director of the Office of Information Systems and Technology. The appointment of a relatively young professional from the private sector, especially a woman

---

[1] Craig Murphy, *The United Nations Development Programme: A Better Way?* (Cambridge, 2006).
[2] See speech here — http://www.undp.org/content/undp/en/home/presscenter/speeches/2014/06/03/helen-clark-inaugural-address-at-the-undp-global-centre-for-public-service-excellence-in-singapore-on-women-s-equal-participation-and-leadership-in-decision-making-a-global-development-priority-/

from the South, to its director level was testimony to the international community's recognition of the professionalism and values that a Singapore upbringing and experience brings. Indeed, in the years that I have been with UNDP, I have bridged my passion and interest for technology with the desire to see change and improvements in the lives of individuals and communities. This means driving innovation within the organisation and with our strategic partners for effective UNDP programme delivery. In many ways, innovation in technology directly reflects how Singaporeans of my generation have grown up with progressive models of leadership, economic development, and cultural diversity.

As the point person for ICT in UNDP, my responsibility extends beyond assuring that technology is available, efficient, and productive across the organisation and its staff in 177 offices around the world. An integral part of this responsibility is for ICT to strategically support UNDP's programmes to benefit the people and societies that they serve.

Indeed, the job has taken me to countries and places where I have witnessed first-hand a lot of hardship and distress. These places include Bangladesh with its rapidly urbanising population, Sudan and South Sudan with their ongoing struggles; conflict-ridden Gaza and the West Bank; Niger, one of the poorest nations in the world, Guatemala with its civil strife, and Sierra Leone, where Ebola and an 11-year civil war have made their mark. It is humbling to see the anguish, the extreme poverty, and the challenging conditions that people are living in. Still, these are the very reasons why we at UNDP are committed to make a difference in their lives.

Sustainable development can be hard to measure and report on, and it takes years to create an impact. Nevertheless, concrete outcomes where the strategic use of ICT in development have been demonstrated include the impact on citizen security using sophisticated, geo-spatial systems in Guatemala; the use of solar power in Somalia and Eritrea; a pilot "Delivering As One" Pakistan programme; videoconferencing solutions for the government of Afghanistan; mobile systems to assist farmers in Bangladesh and Macedonia, and several more.

The Value of Technology for Institutional Effectiveness

UNDP has pursued several technology strategies to streamline its internal operations and support staff delivering innovative development programmes. For example, the organisation undertook a bold strategy to consolidate its hundreds of disparate and independent transactional systems into one global Enterprise Resource Planning (ERP) system, thus simplifying business processes and increasing the organisation's resilience. This was the first of UNDP's journey into the "cloud," allowing for self-service, automation, ease of adoption of international public sector accounting standards (IPSAS), and harmonised business practices not only with UNDP, but also across UN Agencies.

In recognition of its efforts and successes, the 2014 Publish What You Fund Aid Transparency Index placed UNDP first in the world out of 68 major agencies worldwide, with "commendable performance" in publishing information beyond international standards. Indeed, Administrator Helen Clark noted that "we are working in the open to spark innovation, to ensure the best possible use of funds entrusted to UNDP, and to accelerate the development of a sustainable future for all."[3]

This was one of several accolades received by UNDP under my leadership. In 2014, and for the third year in a row, we demonstrated UNDP's ICT professionalism with an International Data Group's (IDG) CSO50 Award for 2015, an Information Security CS040 Award in 2014, and an Information Security Computer World Good Award in 2013. The ICT industry also recognised my role as Chief Technology Officer in these successes by awarding me the Computerworld Premier 100 IT Leaders 2014 Award. These successes led to many keynote speaking roles in far-flung places like Los Angeles, Copenhagen, Kuala Lumpur, and Dhaka, Bangladesh.

UNDP's ICT programme includes reinventing the role of ICT in our 177 offices, while reducing the ICT footprint through lean and green initiatives. The primary objective is to enhance business productivity through ICT services and for development projects that have a direct impact on our results on the ground. Helen Clark also noted that "these awards underscore the value of our Information and Communications Technology programme on development results," including rallying for in-kind contribution support for the Ebola outbreak in western Africa, mobile libraries in Egypt, and gaming solutions for youth unemployment in Bhutan.

---

[3] http://www.undp.org/content/undp/en/home/presscenter/pressreleases/2014/10/08/undp-global-leader-in-transparency/

Concrete Results and Customised Solutions

Some concrete examples of our innovative ICT delivery include the impact of cloud computing on natural disasters and political disruptions worldwide, where UNDP offices have benefitted from having information stored and available safely in the cloud. Specific events where these have proven to be critical were the Arab Spring in Egypt, Libya, Tunisia, and Syria, as well as flash floods in Bangladesh and the Solomon Islands.

The Democratic Republic of Congo (DRC) has also benefitted from innovative ICT solutions, with solar power and lean, green infrastructure kits replacing cumbersome and unsafe data centers. The DRC office also introduced innovative services like mobile money, an atlas for renewable energies for its vast expanses of natural preserves, and robust videoconferencing solutions that have led to reduced need for travel.

Our ICT programmes have also delivered mobile police stations (laptops in police cars) and facial recognition software in Guatemala for effective rule of law, SMS texting capabilities in Pakistan affording 120 million voters a way to find voting locations, and crisis prevention and recovery in Syria, the Central African Republic, Iraq, Somalia, Ukraine, and Yemen.

The Way Forward

UNDP champions leadership, engagement, and trust. We've led an effort for UN Agencies to adopt cloud computing, marshaled a global initiative on cyber security, and have established a well-grounded, agile ICT foundation. Working in the UN system is complex, fickle, and driven by change. It is a dynamic economic and political landscape within the organisation and in communities that are beneficiary to its services. It is meaningful to know that the things we do, through the strategic deployment of ICT, have direct and profound impact on people's lives —from urbanising centres in Vietnam, wind-blown villages of Mali, town cooperatives in Ecuador, farmers' collectives in Kyrgyzstan, to sun-drenched Palestinian olive orchards where people's livelihoods are at stake.

With the MDGs concluding at the end of 2015, efforts to achieve a world of equity, freedom, dignity, and peace will continue unabated. The post-2015 development agenda will keep tackling many of these issues, including the eradication of extreme poverty, rolling back inequalities and exclusion, with a global agenda for the ICT sector to foster growth, inclusiveness, sustainability, innovation, and partnership to bridge the world's digital divide.

While UNDP has many successful examples of female leadership in its top ranks, including its Administrator Helen Clark and Associate Administrator Gina Casar, it still has a long way to go to meet the promise of gender parity in leadership within the organisation, just as we work day in and day out to advocate this for women worldwide. When I visited the UNDP/DFID Urban Partnerships for Poverty Reduction Project in Dhaka, Bangladesh last September, it was so inspirational to see women from the margins of society stepping up to lead Community Development Committees in health, education, environment, and employment issues. Today I'm very proud that my own UNDP story can be central to this promise.

———•·•———

Shirin HAMID is Chief Technology Officer and Director of the Office of Information Systems and Technology, United Nations Development Programme. She was appointed in November 2005. Shirin was honoured as a Computerworld Premier 100 ICT Leader for 2014. She has been instrumental in driving ICT governance and delivering innovative enterprise ICT systems and services, managing the largest UN inter-agency Oracle/PeopleSoft Enterprise Resource Planning (ERP) system. Before UNDP, she ran the technology units of Singapore-based Keppel Corporation and Keppel Offshore and Marine. Prior to that, she was a consultant in the Boston office of Deloitte Consulting as well as the Singapore offices of Deloitte and Accenture. Shirin holds a Masters of Business Systems Analysis and Design from City University, London, and a Bachelors of Science in Computer Science. She was a student at the National Junior College and Methodist Girls School in Singapore. One of her first international humanitarian experiences, Shirin was selected to represent Singapore in Operation Raleigh, Kenya expedition.

A United Nations–Singapore Story: The Courage to Transform

Noeleen HEYZER

> Unless we aim for the seemingly unattainable, we risk settling for mediocrity.
>
> — Sérgio Vieira de Mello, 2007

It was the 21st of September 1965. The Singapore flag was raised for the first time at the United Nations. With it Singapore became the 117th member of the community of nations. Like other newly independent countries coming out of colonialism, Singapore was at the threshold of a new era, at the edge of a new time. With the raising of its flag, Singapore was recognised as a legitimate member State of the international community with rights and responsibilities as defined by the United Nations Charter. In turn, Singapore pledged to uphold the values and principles of the United Nations which form the foundation of how member States should engage with one another, with its citizens and with humanity at large.

It is now 50 years since that day and Singapore has transformed itself from a "Third World country" to a prosperous nation. It is a journey of courage, withstanding the pressures and drama of transition from a colonial entrepôt to a rich thriving city-state. As a colonial entrepôt, migrants from China, India and the Malay world flocked to Singapore, creating a diverse population. Most were poor and uneducated, living in overcrowded working-class areas with no access to public health services. They aspired for a better life and provided the political force that brought about independence. The process of nation building was not simple or linear. Forging a sense of common purpose, and creating institutions to manage a common future were fraught with difficulties. In 1964, there were a series of racial riots on issues of special rights, religion, and privileges. There were political and ideological struggles over the appropriate path to development. It was a jagged period made difficult by the Cold War and bomb threats during the climate of "Konfrontasi" with Indonesia.

With independence, Singapore quickly decided on the building blocks of its transformation towards a prosperous and stable future, reducing poverty and inequality through job-led growth, public housing, and investing in all its people based on meritocracy. It created an expanding middle class by focusing on education, health care, and infrastructure. This was the Singapore I was born into. I benefitted from the nation's emphasis on quality education irrespective of race, religion and gender.

Singapore at Fifty; United Nations at Seventy

As Singapore turns 50, the United Nations turns 70 with a powerful story to tell. The world in 1945 was a very different place. The Charter of the United Nations was written while the world was engulfed in the horrors of the Second World War. Faced with untold sorrow and the potential of human self-destruction, world leaders were determined that never again should our world be destroyed by injustice, hatred and violence. These leaders had the courage to try to transform our world by creating global legitimacy and laying the strong foundations of shared values, and common responsibilities, affirming their faith in the dignity and worth of every human person. Their purpose was to use collective power, working together to secure a better world "free from want, from fear, and all forms of discrimination" for present and future generations.

On 24 October 1945, the United Nations Charter entered into force, established in the name of "We, the Peoples" with the endorsement of all 51 member States. The United Nations was born. The Nobel Laureate, Ralph Bunche, who was closely involved in drafting the Charter, wrote: "The United Nations exists not merely to preserve the peace but also to *make change* — even radical change — possible without violent upheaval... It seeks a more secure world, a better world, a world of progress for all peoples." The collective power of people to shape a shared destiny of peace and security, development, and human rights is greater now than ever before and the need to exercise it more compelling.

Security Council Resolution 1325: Women, Peace and Security

When I was appointed as the Executive Director of the United Nations Development Fund for Women (UNIFEM) in 1994, I was determined to make the world a better place for all women, supporting the progress of member States and their people, using the United Nations' principles and values.

On the first UN Day of this millennium, 24 October 2000, a major opportunity arose for me to address the issues that go the heart of our Charter. For the first time my team and I succeeded in putting the issue of women, peace and security before the Security Council. Since my appointment, UNIFEM had provided assistance to women in conflict-affected countries and supported their participation in peace processes. But women continued to be targeted in times of conflict, and rape and other forms of sexual violence continued to be used as weapons of war. I asked the Security Council for a full-scale assessment of the impact of armed conflict on women. In conflict after conflict, I met women choked with painful memories of their own humiliation and those of their loved ones. In response, I demanded that the protection for women and girls in conflict be addressed at the highest level of the United Nations, the Security Council.

At the invitation of former President Nelson Mandela, the facilitator of the Burundi process, UNIFEM had succeeded in bringing Burundi's 19 negotiating parties to accept the need for women involvement in the peace process. 23 of the women's recommendations, including provisions for education, health, employment, and inheritance rights, were included in the final peace accord and became critical components of the country's reconstruction efforts. We brought women from similar conflict-affected countries to share their stories with the Security Council of how they have the most to gain from new opportunities and also the most to lose if fragile communities break down. These women knew the cost of exclusion and failed states, and now wanted to be key players in shaping a stable new future for their children and for their country. Through UNIFEM's support for these women, I convinced the Security Council of the importance of supporting women's leadership in peace building and post-conflict reconstruction.

The Security Council passed the historic landmark resolution 1325 on Women, Peace and Security (SCR 1325). For the women who have organised for peace and security on the ground, it represented a long overdue recognition of their accomplishments and challenges. SCR 1325 became the resolution that inspired substantive and widespread action in the whole UN system, in the security sector of our member States, and among advocates for women human rights. It is regarded as one of the UN's most transformative and legally binding frameworks that we have created together with women living in conflict-affected countries.

Afghanistan: A Test Case for SCR 1325

I tested the implementation of SCR 1325 in a very difficult political context — Afghanistan after the fall of the Taliban. Images and stories of all forms of violence against women dominated our television screens and media after the September 11 terrorist attack in New York, 2001. The suffering and exclusion of Afghan women — from public execution, to their complete removal from social, economic and political life — provoked international outrage. For me, the world finally got it. The condition of women in a country is the barometer of peace and security and is associated with better governance and functioning states. This was the message of SCR 1325.

I was thrilled when the United Nations Secretary-General Kofi Anan invited me to be part of his delegation to the International Conference on Reconstruction Assistance to Afghanistan in Tokyo, January 2002. Ambassador Lakhdar Brahimi had overall authority for the political, human rights, recovery and reconstruction activities of the United Nations in the post Taliban transition of Afghanistan. He was in the midst of solidifying the 2001 Bonn process that created the current Afghan Government. With all the difficulties of bringing stability, self-rule and security to the country that he had to handle, he advised me to postpone the issue of gender equality and women's empowerment to some future date in the hope that it would be easier to handle. He felt that I had not even visited the country, and did not fully understand the complexity of the local situation or even what local women really wanted. On my side, with UNIFEM's experience in supporting women in Rwanda, Liberia, Burundi, Kosovo, Guatemala and Timor-Leste, I knew that support to women affected by conflict and in countries undergoing transition could not wait. Ensuring gender equality in Afghanistan's legislative, judicial and policy frameworks was an essential starting point for building the new future. I immediately prepared to visit

Afghanistan to identify and work with women on the ground who wanted change. I held intensive consultations with the government, and with a wide range of women from doctors, teachers and lawyers, to displaced women and girls in the refugee camps.

By the time the first International Women's Day was celebrated in the country on 8 March 2002, UNIFEM, in partnership with the Ministry of Women's Affairs headed by Minister Simar Samar, was able to mobilise over 1,000 Afghan women from seven districts to make their voices and demands heard. In the ruins of a cinema burnt down by the Taliban, Chairman Karzai, Ambassador Brahimi and the whole cabinet listened to the aspirations of women from rural and urban areas, from all ethnic groups. Their message was united and clear: The women of Afghanistan wanted to help build a government accountable to all Afghans, at peace with itself and with its neighbours. They knew the cost of accumulated conflicts, what it meant to have sons, brothers, and husbands who were forced to fight, and daughters who were forced to hide. They knew what it meant to be displaced, to have one the highest rates of maternal and child mortality, one of the lowest rates of access to education and healthcare and total exclusion from public life. These women were now the highest stakeholders of peace, stability and development.

From that day, SRSG Brahimi became our champion and helped with UNIFEM's work to support 100 women leaders to engage with the 500-member Constitutional Loya Jirga (Grand Assembly for major decisions) in December 2003. Eventually, after difficult negotiations, women were recognised as equal citizens for the first time in the constitution of Afghanistan. The inclusion of women's equal rights in the constitution was a huge historic victory, although challenges remain in implementation.

Our work on rebuilding conflict-affected countries through the empowerment of women, using the legitimacy of SCR 1325, continued to deliver results. By educating women voters and supporting peer networking, women elected Ellen Johnson Sirleaf as the first women President of Liberia and of Africa. By supporting women to become elected leaders, Rwanda has the highest percentage of women in parliament in the whole world, with women playing a bigger role to shape the new direction of their conflict affected country. These experiences are testimony to the fact that people are the most powerful agents of change and when supported and empowered in the direction envisioned by the UN Charter can shape their destiny towards a future of greater freedom and dignity.

Myanmar

It is commendable of the United Nations Secretary-General Ban Ki-moon that he has made women's leadership a priority in leading different parts of the UN system. He appointed me to the rank of Under-Secretary-General and to serve as the first woman Executive Secretary of the Economic and Social Commission for Asia and the Pacific (ESCAP) since its founding in 1947.

In 2007, at the time of my appointment, Myanmar hit the headlines because of the protests led by Burmese monks, triggered by the military government's removal of fuel subsidies. In the first week in office, I realised that this was one member state in a very difficult situation and that this political situation would make it almost impossible to engage with Myanmar on the economic and social agenda. But then, on the 2 May 2008, Cyclone Nargis hit Myanmar. More than 100,000 people were missing or dead — with up to 2 million people affected. Even more problematic were the severe restrictions on getting humanitarian aid and aid workers into the country. I accompanied the Secretary-General into the country at the time of the donor conference at the end of May. The Secretary-General was able to get full humanitarian access for the international community after his meeting with President Than Shwe, and a tripartite aid coordination mechanism was established, between ASEAN, the UN and the Government of Myanmar.

For me, it was the first of several visits which by December 2009 led to an unprecedented dialogue with Myanmar leaders on development and poverty reduction. The Government requested me to form a development partnership with them at a very tense time. It was a difficult tight rope to walk because Myanmar was politically isolated. The West was strongly opposed to the country's human rights record. The Secretary-General's good offices were rightly focused on securing the release of political prisoners — especially Aung San Suu Kyi — and the overall human rights and governance situation. The UN Resident Coordinator had been asked to leave the country for raising concerns about poverty conditions following the monks' uprising. Yet the ESCAP mandate of supporting economic and social development in all our member States gave us reason to stay engaged and to find new areas of building trust and cooperation. I decided to push as hard as I could on the development front, even when the politics left much to be desired, opening the new chapter for engagement and using the newly forged economic and social space to further the dialogue that put people and poverty reduction at the centre of the development agenda.

The result was the Second Development Partnership Forum that allowed practitioners and eminent international scholars such as Economic Sciences Nobel Laureate, Professor Joseph Stiglitz and local researchers to exchanges experiences and ideas with government agencies and civil society. This engagement has been regarded by many, especially current President Thein Sein, as helping to provide the initial direction and substance to the country's economic reform agenda when it was most needed.

As I reflect on my UN experience and look beyond 2015 when Singapore turns 50 and the UN turns 70, one thing is certain — no country or people can hope to navigate the turbulence and uncertainty of the future alone. We need moral courage and authority in our interdependent but divided world to address new dangers and major challenges of conflicts, disasters, climate change, rising extremism and economic turmoil. It is only through shared values, common purpose and collective responsibility that we can forge a future of progress, peace and sustainability for all. Our destiny now rests in our own hands.

Noleen HEYZER is an Under-Secretary-General of the United Nations (UN) and the highest-ranking Singaporean in the UN system. She is the United Nations Secretary-General's Special Adviser for Timor-Leste, working to support peace-building, state-building, and sustainable development in fragile states. She was the first woman to serve as the Executive Secretary of the UN Economic and Social Commission for Asia and the Pacific since its founding in 1947. Under her leadership from August 2007 to January 2014, the commission focused on regional cooperation for a more resilient Asia Pacific, founded on shared prosperity, social equity, and sustainable development. She was at the forefront of many innovations including those for regional disaster preparedness, inclusive socio-economic policies, sustainable agriculture and urbanisation, energy security and regional connectivity. As the previous Executive Director of the UN Development Fund for Women, she was widely recognised for the formulation and implementation of Security Council Resolution 1325 on Women, Peace, and Security. She holds a BA (Upper Hons) and a MSc from Singapore University, a PhD from Cambridge University, and has received numerous awards for leadership.

The United Nations and Social Development

Thelma KAY

The United Nations (UN), established to "save succeeding generations from the scourge of war" is better known to the world for its political role. However, from its inception, the UN has also provided a platform beyond peace and security. The Economic and Social Council (ECOSOC) is one of six principle organs established under the Charter of the UN, tasked to cover "international, social, cultural, educational, health and related matters". Under ECOSOC, the main bodies dealing with social development include the key Commission on Population and Development, Commission for Social Development, and Commission on the Status of Women. The UN also has programmes, funds and specialised agencies dealing with social development among which, some key ones are United Nations Human Settlements Programme (UN-HABITAT), UN Women, International Labour Organization (ILO), United Nations Educational, Scientific and Cultural Organization (UNESCO), World Health Organization (WHO), and others. Geographically, economic and social issues are covered by the Regional Commissions. Singapore is a member of the Economic and Social Commission for Asia and the Pacific (UNESCAP), where I worked as the Director of the Social Development Division.

2015 marks the 20th anniversary of the World Summit for Social Development convened by the UN in Copenhagen in 1995. The Programme of Action adopted at the Copenhagen summit covered 10 commitments focused on the interrelated core issues of poverty eradication, full employment and social integration. The Programme of Action also advocated the processes to achieve the objectives — through fairer distribution of resources and opportunities, and through increased participation and inclusion.

Today, this inclusive and holistic vision of social development remains important and relevant, although the context and priorities have shifted.

The UN advocates a comprehensive framework for development, grounded in the understanding that progress is not an exclusive issue of economics and the role of social policy was not a residual category of 'safety nets' that merely counteract policy failures or development disasters. Today the discourse has evolved to ensure that social and economic policies work together to achieve socially, economically and environmentally sustainable goals.

Over the last 50 years, Singapore's impressive transformation from a small city state to a economically developed country has been attained through prudent and forward-looking economic and social policies. In education, the country now has a high performing school system and reputable institutes of higher learning. Singapore's direct dealing with the UN system on education is through UNESCO. I was on the Governing Board of the Paris-based UNESCO International Institute for Education Planning and during my tenure, high ranking UNESCO officials would inevitably broach the possibility of Singapore's return to the UNESCO "fold" after withdrawing in 1985. I was very pleased when Singapore rejoined UNESCO in 2007 and there is now a Singapore National Commission for UNESCO, supplemented by subcommittees on education, science, and culture and information.

In health, the quality of healthcare in Singapore is of international standard, coupled with affordability and accessibility. Constant improvements are being made, bearing in mind the needs of an ageing population. Singapore works closely with WHO especially on issues of importance to the country such as strengthening healthcare systems, promoting universal health coverage and combating non-communicable diseases. I have worked closely with the WHO Global Network of Age-Friendly Cities and Communities, key dimensions of which have been incorporated in Singapore's successful City for All Ages initiative. Singapore has been actively involved in the governance of WHO. When I attended the 2007 World Health Assembly in Geneva, I was proud to meet up with the late Dr Balaji Sadasivan who was then Chairman of the WHO Executive Board.

In Singapore, social security is currently provided by four pillars — home ownership, the Central Provident Fund (CPF), healthcare assurance, and workfare. The measures which have progressively evolved to meet the changing needs of the population, especially an ageing one are gradually becoming congruent with guidance and advice provided by relevant UN entities. The International Labour Organization (ILO) of which Singapore served on the Governing Body from 2002–2011 has advocated basic income security and access to essential social services for all. Singapore, through the provision of a myriad of programmes such as Medishield Life, CPF Life, Silver Support, Pioneer Generation Package, Comcare, has enhanced and strengthened social protection especially for lower income groups and the elderly. Singapore's policies are to some extent in line with ILO Recommendation 202 on a Social Protection Floor. Singapore is also involved with the United Nation's activities on urbanisation and housing, with Singapore entities such as the Centre for Liveable Cities initiating joint activities with UN -HABITAT.

The UN addresses inclusion and social justice through promoting global commitments to agreed actions. These would include those emanating from global mandates and conferences on children, women, ageing, youth, disability, human settlements, etc. Of particular significance is a body of rights-based binding instruments. Singapore is a state party to the Convention on the Rights of the Child. Singapore acceded to the Convention on the Elimination of all Forms of Discrimination against Women (CEDAW) in 1995 and has since submitted four comprehensive periodic reports to the review Committee covering progress on action taken to comply with the Convention. Implementing and reporting on the Convention has engendered cooperation among all entities dealing with gender issues such as the Inter-Ministry Committee (IMC) to oversee implementation of CEDAW, the Singapore National Committee for UN Women and many related NGOs. My UN colleagues servicing CEDAW reviews have been very impressed by Singapore's meticulous and inclusive preparations for the CEDAW reports.

In 2013, Singapore acceded to the Convention on the Rights of Persons with Disability, and Singapore's Enabling Masterplan lays the foundation to progressively implement and realise the vision of the Convention. Singapore has actively participated in UN programmes on disability. I remember in particular a meeting at Sanya in Hainan, China on accessible tourism at which Ms Judy Wee from the Disabled People's Association ably represented Singapore. When Judy, who is a wheel-chair user, subsequently came to attend a meeting in Bangkok, I arranged for her to point out to my building management colleagues from the United Nations Conference Centre modifications which would make the building more barrier-free and in line with universal design.

Social development in the UN also entails incorporating the social dimension and perspective into key issues such as natural disasters. Shortly after the Indian Ocean tsunami in 2004 I was on an UN mission to Aceh where I learned that sanitary conditions in the temporary housing ("barracks") were very unsatisfactory and dangerous, especially for women and girls. I subsequently communicated this to the relevant UN officials for remedial action. I am glad that Singapore is now actively championing global efforts to improve sanitation and toilets in the developing world.

Conceptually, the past 50 years of Singapore's social compact have gradually and progressively evolved from a philosophy of individual, self-help and family responsibility to one of greater involvement of other entities (especially community-based organisations) under the "many helping hands" approach to the current one of inclusion with greater collective responsibility and social solidarity.

As Singapore enters its next 50 years, changing economic and demographic trends will necessitate an expanded social security system to meet the needs of economic restructuring and reform and the impact of population ageing and longevity. Of particular importance will be the fault lines of rising inequality and migration. The forthcoming social agenda would have to include issues of citizenry voice and participation, and of the trade-off between social spending and fiscal sustainability.

These and other pressing issues will also have to be addressed in the UN post-2015 agendas and the forthcoming Sustainable Development Goals. Singapore's current multi-pillared and holistic social security system has its commendable features but will also need to be adpated and refined to meet evolving challenges.

Thelma KAY is the former Chief of the Social Development Division, United Nations Economic and Social Commission for Asia and the Pacific (UNESCAP) and also the former Senior Advisor on Ageing Issues, Ministry of Social and Family Development, Singapore. She serves as advisor and consultant to governments and international organisations on social development issues. Thelma was educated at the National University of Singapore and the London School of Economics and Political Science. Before joining the UN, she was a faculty member at the Department of Sociology, National University of Singapore. She directed UNESCAP's work on social development including population (demographic structures, ageing, migration), social protection and social inclusion including disability. She was in charge of the UN's implementation and monitoring of global and regional mandates on population and development, gender equality, ageing, and disability. She has spoken at numerous national, regional and global events organised by entities such as the Asian Development Bank, ASEAN, AARP, International Federation on Ageing, and HelpAge International. She has also addressed private sector events such as the Asia Business Advisory Council, Asia Pacific Business Forum, Conference on Diversity and Inclusion in Asia Pacific, and Conferences on Corporate Social Responsibility. She served on the board of the UNESCO International Institute of Education Planning, and was a council member of the United Nations International Institute for Ageing, Programme for Asia. She is a board member of the Active Ageing Consortium for Asia Pacific, and the School of Energy, Resources and Development, Asian Institute of Technology.

My Experiences with the United Nations Sanctions System

Christine LEE

When Singapore was elected to the United Nations Security Council for the 2001/2002 term, I had assumed that we would, in the usual tradition, take on the sanctions committee[1] that had been chaired by our regional predecessor, which was the Rwanda Sanctions Committee. I had assumed wrongly. The Rwanda Sanctions Committee had been basically dormant for some time and it usually only met once a year to adopt the Committee's annual report. The powers behind the scene apparently thought that it would be an under-use of the skills that we could bring to the work of the Security Council. Since a new resolution was in the works to transform the Liberia Sanctions Committee from a simple one-sanctions (arms embargo) monitoring committee, into a sanctions committee with teeth (secondary sanctions were being imposed on Liberia for its role in the deteriorating situation in the Sierra Leone conflict), the idea was mooted that Singapore would take over that sanctions committee.

---

[1] Under Chapter VII of the UN Charter, the Security Council can take enforcement measures to maintain or restore international peace and security. Such measures range from economic and/or other sanctions not involving the use of armed force to international military action. The use of mandatory sanctions is intended to apply pressure on a State or entity to comply with the objectives set by the Security Council without resorting to the use of force. Sanctions thus offer the Security Council an important instrument to enforce its decisions. The universal character of the United Nations makes it an especially appropriate body to establish and monitor such measures. The Council has resorted to mandatory sanctions as an enforcement tool when peace has been threatened and diplomatic efforts have failed. The range of sanctions has included comprehensive economic and trade sanctions and/or more targeted measures such as arms embargoes, travel bans, financial or diplomatic restrictions. Source: http://www.un.org/sc/committees/

Serving on the Liberia Sanctions Committee

My then boss, the Permanent Representative of Singapore to the UN at the time, Ambassador Kishore Mahbubani, jumped at the chance, much to my trepidation, as he saw it as a great learning opportunity for Singapore. I was worried because we would be breaking new ground and it would be a sharp learning curve. It turned out that we were both right. It was a tremendous and wonderful learning opportunity for Singapore and for me personally.

As the Chairman's delegation, in the first few months of our taking on the committee, we made a trip to the region and had the opportunity to meet with the great villain of the piece, President Charles Taylor, as well as the other leaders of the region, President Olusegun Obasanjo of Nigeria; President Alpha Oumar Konare of Mali, President Ahmad Tejan Kabbah of Sierra Leone and some members of the UN Mission in Sierra Leone (UNAMSIL) based in Freetown.

I remember most vividly, when we were in Monrovia, being driven past bullet-ridden buildings as we made our way to the meeting with then President Taylor. We arrived in the middle of a "smear campaign against the UN" that Charles Taylor had engineered and so we had to endure hourly radio broadcasts of how the UN was targeting the people of Liberia, and soldiers with machine guns were patrolling everywhere, even the roof top of our hotel. I remember not being able to sleep that one night we spent in Monrovia.

I also remember the bomb-blasted buildings in Freetown, where we also spent one night. It was in Freetown too, that I saw the listlessness and hope-lessness in the eyes of a young population that was just standing around the street corners as our UN convoy drove past. It was then that I realised the impact that the Security Council could have on countries in conflict zones. The conflict was real. The people were real. The devastation was upfront and in-your-face real. It was a very sobering experience for me.

In terms of what we learnt as part of the Chairman's delegation leading an evolving sanctions committee, I would say that more countries should be so fortunate as to have that chance. Firstly, we learnt how the UN Secretariat really works behind the scenes. Basically, working with a Committee Secretary who is experienced in the UN's sanctions committee's procedures and has the institutional memory and know-how to make things happen, helps the Chair's delegation to be effective.

The tradition is that only elected members of the Council take on the Chairmanship of the sanctions committees and we were only there for two years. Often, it seemed that unless it was an issue or sanctions committee in which one of the permanent members (P5) of the Council was vested, the Secretariat was rather less than effective. I have seen other Chairs' delegations fumble and become increasingly frustrated at the Secretariat's bureaucratic approach. Thankfully, Liberia and the conflict in Sierra Leone was an issue that key members of the P5 were vested in. We were also very fortunate to work with one of the most experienced Secretaries in the sanctions branch, one who truly believed in what she was doing and a professional on the issue of sanctions. I learnt most of what I now know on sanctions because of her.

Secondly, we learnt how to deal with other members of the Council and countries that were directly involved in a specific country-conflict issue. The informal sanctions committee meetings were often verbal matches which we learnt to referee and still get the job done. We gained a reputation for standard-setting and effective leadership.

Thirdly, we learnt that the sanctions committees had developed many archaic procedures on the monitoring of sanctions implementation which some of the P5 were loath to let go or even consider changing. For instance, it took a lot of time and effort to get the other members of the Liberia Sanctions Committee to adopt the Chair's redraft of the Committee's Guidelines. The Guidelines, which dictate how the sanctions committee conducts its work, are posted on the individual sanctions committees' website and accessible to other UN Member States and the general public. However, once adopted, our draft became the basis for changes in other sanctions committees.

As an Expert on the Al-Qaida and Taliban Sanctions Committee

I was in New York on 11 September 2001. It was a Tuesday and I was in the office when some of my colleagues in the Singapore Mission to the UN, starting shouting for the rest of us to come to see something that was on the news. It was not yet 9.00 am (the first plane struck the North Tower at 8.46 am). Thus began my connection to the day now known as "9/11". One of the consequences of the events of "9/11" was the empowerment of the

1267 Sanctions Committee, named after UNSC Resolution 1267 by which it was created in October 1999. At that time, the focus was on the Taliban's assistance to Osama bin Laden and the use of Taliban-controlled territory in Afghanistan for terrorist training and other terrorist purposes. Following the events of 9/11, the focus shifted to al-Qaida and it became the al-Qaida and Taliban (AQT) Sanctions Committee until it was split into two separate sanctions committees in 2011.

In February 2004, following the adoption of UNSC Resolution 1526 on 30 January 2004, I was approached by the UN to become the legal and sanctions expert in the Panel of Experts assisting in the work of the AQT Sanctions Committee. There were to be 8 experts from various fields relevant to the work of the committee (now 1267/1989 Sanctions Committee) in monitoring the effectiveness of the implementation of the three sanctions measures imposed by the Security Council against AQT and associates. I was appointed to the AQT Monitoring Team from March 2004 until December 2012, a period of over eight years.

On what I have learnt from those eight or so years, well, three things come to mind. The first is that the relationship between the Secretariat and the Panels of Experts (or POEs) can be somewhat conflicted. The establishment of POEs was to provide expertise to the sanctions committees in practical and operational areas which the Secretariat and Sanctions Committees' did not have. At the same time, the POEs were often called the "eyes and ears" of the Sanctions Committees, being the main resource that the Sanctions Committees could send out to the field to gather information and interact with Member States and relevant organisations. It was inevitable that some Sanctions Committees began to rely on the POEs for advice and direction. This was sometimes to the consternation of the Secretariat, which considers itself the guardian of such things and on committee procedures.

The second, it was a novel experience for me to work with experts from other countries. It is a huge difference working with nationalities of other countries as a Singapore delegate at the UN and working with them as a colleague at the UN. We, the eight experts of the AQT Monitoring Team were both "stateless" in the sense that we were all colleagues in the same team, but at the same time each of us was considered to be the expert representative of our respective regions. I had never thought of myself as a stereotype, but as the expert from Asia, I was considered to be the "Asian standard".

Luckily for me, it was generally thought that Asians were hardworking and effective. I did my best not to let that standard fall. However, no matter how much I tried to resist it, I found myself also stereotyping other experts according to their region. It was with great amusement that I came to realise that some experts really did emulate their regional stereotypes and I had to learn how to work with and around this.

The third is that the POEs became political tools rather than simply resource tools. Before the usual UN politics got in the way, the first POEs were comprised of experts that enabled some of the sanctions committees to perform more effectively. The selection of these experts was based on criteria such as practical expertise and qualifications in the required fields and equitable geographical distribution. For example, in the AQT Monitoring Team, there was always a position for a financial expert, to help analyse the financial flows of terrorists funding and suggest ways to deal with it. The experts that filled this position therefore had financial investigative backgrounds. However, the Monitoring Team was also the first POE that had an expert from each of the P5 countries. In later POEs, it became apparent that key POEs were always comprised of an expert from each P5 country. It was also apparent that experts from currently elected members of the Security Council, somehow found their way into the POEs as well. On the one hand, having real expertise in the required fields is important. On the other hand, I found that having expert colleagues who were nationals of each of the P5 countries and other key Security Council members, was also an asset. The challenge for the UN is to find a balance between the two.

———•◦•———

Christine LEE is currently employed as a Special Consultant with the Ministry of Home Affairs. Prior to this, she worked as a project-based Consultant with a number of international think-tanks and security policy groups. She also served as the Legal and Sanctions expert of the United Nations Analytical Support and Sanctions Monitoring Team for the al-Qaida and Taliban Sanctions Committee from 2004 to 2012. Before joining the UN, she served the Singapore Government in a number of positions, including the Public Utilities

Board, Ministry of Foreign Affairs and Attorney-General's Chambers. Whilst with the MFA, she served as the Senior Deputy Director in the Southeast Asian Directorate, then as the Director of the International Organisations Directorate before being posted to the New York Mission from 1999 to 2003. During Singapore's term on the Security Council from 2001 to 2002, she was the Deputy Permanent Representative of the Security Council team. Christine also worked for eight years in the Attorney-General's Chambers as a Deputy Public Prosecutor. As a senior DPP, she also served as mentor to a team of junior professionals and advised the law agencies of the Singapore Government on national and international legal issues. Christine also worked for three years in the private sector as a civil lawyer. She is a graduate of the National University of Singapore Law Faculty and holds a Masters Degree from University College London.

Navigating the (Un)United Nations

Dileep NAIR

"Be careful. You'll be entering a cesspit of vipers." So advised a former senior UN diplomat who I went to see before taking on my job as Under-Secretary General of Internal Oversight in the United Nations.

Being thus forewarned, I entered the UN in April 2000. I soon realised the Office of Internal Oversight Services (OIOS), the Department I headed, suffered from a lacklustre reputation. The US and the other European countries, that had actually been the main sponsors behind the formation of OIOS, felt that the Department had no "bite" in doing its job. Madeline Albright, the then US Representative to the UN, once described my predecessor, Karl Paschke, as a "junkyard puppy rather than a watchdog". On the other hand, the G77 bloc led by countries such as Cuba and India, accused OIOS of being a lackey of the Western Bloc, particulary of the US.

My major task, therefore, was to re-establish the credibility of OIOS. It was clear to me that unless I gained the confidence of my stakeholders, I would not be able to contribute to effective oversight of the UN.

Two avenues of doing this presented themselves to me. *First*, was to build an effective, high performing organisation, with the right people "on the bus". While many of the staff in the Department were experienced and industrious, there were quite a few whose track record and reputation suggested strongly otherwise — they simply would not meet the standards of both competence and personal conviction needed to deliver the right outcomes for the UN. In particular, the Auditing and Evaluation Divisions of OIOS had been treated as "dumping grounds" for under-performers from other departments in the UN.

I was determined to change the ethos in OIOS as the existing management practices were actually demotivating the more engaged staff members.

How would we attract and keep the best and brightest people if we maintained cushy conditions for those unable to meet the standard? Indeed, a Department in charge of Oversight had to demonstrate its seriousness about performance standards to the rest of the UN. While being fair to people, we had to be exemplars of robust management practices. I therefore focussed on improving the quality of staff within OIOS, making it a key leadership priority.

One of the hiring principles the UN prides itself for, is ensuring equitable representation from all Member States. With the preponderance of Indians and Filipinos already in the UN's employment, I was careful to look for good staff from under-represented countries. I was fortunate to recruit a number of promising Auditors and Investigators from countries such as Kazakhstan, Finland and Romania. Doing so, I certainly earned kudos from the Member States concerned.

However, there was one "stakeholder" I failed to consult sufficiently with. This was the UN Staff Union. The UN was, and remains, a heavily unionised employee-relations environment, with the Staff Union displaying a degree of militancy at the time that I had not encountered before in my career in the Singapore public service. In my experience, management-union relations in Singapore had generally been collaborative, open and constructive. When I joined the UN, I was focused on a certain outcome. I was intent on performing a task that I felt was critical in order to serve the UN. I had no real desire to play games, as I saw it. However, I realised the depth of my own naivety about the quagmire I had entered when it came to identifying and then removing those people who were chronic under-performers and unable to effectively contribute to the work of IOIS. By no coincidence, I found that many in this category were also precisely the people who take on positions in the Staff Union or, at least, have strong ties with the Staff Union officials. As a result, there were howls of protest when I stopped the automatic renewal of the employment contracts of these non-performers. I persevered because I believed what I was doing was the right thing, and that it was in the best interest of the UN, and in particular our stakeholders.

To be fair, in the early years of my tenure, Secretary-General Kofi Annan clearly supported me and dismissed all the spurious complaints against me. Towards the end of my term, though, the Secretary-General himself came under attack from the Staff Union. Then, he started prevaricating and even succumbed to having a complaint from the Staff Union against me investigated. This was despite the fact that the underlying complaint was actually anonymous and that I had been earlier cleared of any impropriety. In the event, though, I was cleared yet again, and the Secretary-General sent me an apology for putting me through the ordeal.

The *second* thing I did to gain the confidence of my stakeholders, was to generate a consensus for the important tasks within OIOS' workplan. With an enormous "oversight universe", it was imperative to focus on things that really mattered. I therefore initiated very early on, a risk assessment exercise of the various activities of the UN, which OIOS had a mandate to oversee.

From the preliminary risk assessment exercise, it was apparent that the Iraq Oil-for-Food Programme was an area of very high risk. Iraq was then subject to Security Council sanctions and under the Programme, the UN was responsible for ensuring that the millions of barrels of oil being produced in Iraq were being sold strictly for food, medicines and other humanitarian supplies. However, I was aghast at the poor controls that were in place to ensure this was being done. Compliance with the mandate of the Programme was far from effective.

I therefore wrote to the Secretary-General about my discomfort with how the Programme was being managed and stated my intention to increase OIOS' oversight of it. More importantly, as the Programme had been instituted under Resolutions of the Security Council, I said I wanted to submit my Report eventually to the Security Council. There was an immediate reaction from the Programme Manager, Benon Sevan. He called up my Audit Director and rudely told her off that it was none of the business of OIOS to report to the Security Council. I told my Audit Director to ignore him. The next thing I knew I received a call from the Deputy Secretary-General, Louis Frechette, telling me that it was not within OIOS' purview to report to the Security Council.

In retrospect, I should have persevered. I dare say had OIOS' Audit Reports of the Programme been tabled at, and debated by, the Security Council, the so-called Oil-for-Food scandal that rocked the UN later on, could have been defused. However, at that time the protocol was for all reports from the UN Secretariat to the Security Council, to be submitted through the Secretary-General. Without the Secretary-General's agreement,

I had no access to the Security Council. From the reactions of the Deputy Secretary-General and the Programme Manager, I reckoned that the Secretary-General, too, was also not on my side. Hence, it may have been futile to have even tried.

The risk assessment exercise I initiated also highlighted topics for Programme Evaluation, another activity undertaken by OIOS. One area that appeared to be of critical importance in terms of assessing the impact and effectiveness of UN programmes, was that of water management and conservation. This was particularly critical for the many arid parts of the world, such as the MENA region. My Programme Evaluation Director, therefore, proposed to do a cross-cutting assessment of the UN's programmes in this area undertaken by various UN agencies.

However, here, too, I faced stiff resistance. A number of Member State representatives called me to say that OIOS should drop the proposal. I recall the then Egyptian Permanent Representative, Ambassador Aboul Gheit, paying me a visit in my office and saying categorically that Egypt would strongly oppose any attempt to launch such an evaluation exercise. It was clear that some countries were afraid an evaluation exercise might uncover various attempts to "sabotage" effective water management across borders between affected countries.

I countered these attempts to block me by making my intentions known to Member States, particularly those that were supportive of OIOS. Without question, I sought Singapore's support, particularly from our 5th Committee representatives such as Gerard Ho and Raziff Aljuneid. However, as Kishore Mahbubani, who was our Permanent Representative then, advised me, it might backfire if it became too obvious that Singapore was championing OIOS simply because of my nationality.

I also developed a strong relationship with the US Permanent Representative who clearly was an advocate of strong oversight. In fact, towards the end of my term when I was publicly attacked by the Staff Union, it was the then US Permanent Representative, John Negroponte, who wrote a forceful letter of support to the Secretary-General, for the work done by OIOS under my leadership.

I tried to ensure that OIOS received bipartisan support from Member States. Historically, Cuba had adopted a strong anti-OIOS position, primarily because it sought to oppose practically every US-led initiative. In fact,

I understand my predecessor, Karl Paschke, never got his final OIOS Report accepted by the General Assembly because of opposition by Cuba and others in the G77 bloc. Being aware of this background, I made a conscious attempt to engage and cultivate the Cuban delegation. I tried hard to convince them of my independence and of my intentions to do what I felt was right for the UN. I think I succeeded in developing a good relationship, particularly with the Cuban 5th Committee Representative, Norma Estenoz. In fact, my friendship with her extended to me taking my family for a holiday to Cuba and visiting her home.

My credibility, and that of OIOS, was also burnished by getting the support of a respected "elder" in the UN fraternity. When I was in the UN earlier in 1996 as a short-term consultant, I was introduced by Bilahari Kausikan, our then Permanent Representative, to Conrad Mselle, the Chairman of the Advisory Committee on Administrative & Budgetary Questions (ACABQ). This powerful Committee handles all the requests for resources from the UN's various Departments. Mselle had been Chairman of ACABQ for over 20 years and was a veritable institution in the UN. I kept my ties with Mselle all through the years and made it a point to keep him apprised of all my initiatives for OIOS. I believe this went a long way in my getting adequate resources, both people and money, to do my work more effectively.

All said and done, I believe I did my best to re-establish the credibility of OIOS and, that with the help of some very good people, significant progress was made in this regard. The General Assembly Resolution acknowledging my final OIOS Report was generous in its appreciation for what OIOS had achieved during my tenure. I share this not in order to win praise now or to seek any kind of validation. It is far too late for that and much water has passed under the bridge since my time in the UN. My intent is to share something of the leadership style that we have been exposed to in Singapore as exemplified by our leaders. In particular, it is the courage that is essential to do what is right in the Public Service. The UN certainly needs more people with conviction and commitment, and who are prepared to take on the weight of its bureaucracy, to strip out the inefficiency that dogs the Organisation and its people, as well as its various internal and external vested interests.

A number of people have asked me if, in retrospect, I would have turned down the UN job, given the scurrilous anonymous accusations I had to endure and the lack of top management support I received. I tend to look at the matter somewhat philosophically. I think there are very few organisations that can match the experiences one gets in the UN. The sheer diversity, breadth and topical nature of the issues dealt with by the UN, are without parallel. No doubt the UN suffers from a lot of bad press and many units within the UN are indeed dysfunctional. Then again, the UN is about the only organisation that is so widely respected and has the moral authority to act on behalf of the world. For all its faults and shortcomings, the UN is still the only true global organisation with universal membership. I do feel proud to have served it and been a part of it and in so doing, flying the Singapore flag high.

Dileep NAIR has a total of over 40 years of senior-level management experience in the United Nations, banking industry, diplomacy and the Singapore Government. Currently Singapore's Non-Resident High Commissioner to Ghana, Dileep is also a Board Member of the Agri-Food and Veterinary Authority of Singapore, and two public-listed companies. In addition, he lectures on an *ad hoc* basis at the Singapore Management University and the Civil Service College.

Dileep completed his two-year term as Singapore's Ambassador to Laos in January 2013. Prior to that, he was Singapore's Consul-General in Dubai for six years. Before moving into the diplomatic service, Dileep was the Under-Secretary-General for Internal Oversight Services at the United Nations for five years, from 2000 to 2005. As de facto Inspector General of the United Nations, he reported directly to Secretary-General Kofi Annan as well as the General Assembly.

Before going to the UN, Dileep was a Managing Director of the DBS Bank in Singapore. He came to DBS Bank in 1998, when it acquired POSBank, Singapore's national savings bank, where he served for two years as Chief Executive Officer. Dileep came to banking after 20 years in Singapore's Administrative Service, and served in Ministries of Defence, Trade and Industry, and Finance. He started his working career in 1974 as a Mechanical Engineer at Singapore's Housing and Development Board.

Dileep attended the Advanced Management Program at Harvard Business School in 1994. He also obtained a Master's in Public Administration from Harvard University's Kennedy School of Government in 1982. His first degree was a Bachelor's in Mechanical Engineering from McGill University, Canada, on a Colombo Plan scholarship.

The United Nations — A Personal Experience

YEO Bock Cheng

This is the story of one Singaporean's journey from callow youth to maturity in the service of the United Nations. Yes, the UN can be a huge, faceless bureaucracy, prone to occasional inertia and bickering. But it is a calling for those of us who were privileged to perform meaningful and personally satisfying assignments for the Organization.

I believe I am the first Singaporean to have made a complete career at the UN Secretariat.[1] I served for 32 years, from 1969 to 2001, and rose from the junior-most internationally recruited professional career level ranks to the highest Director level, without hindrance or help from the government.

This is not to suggest disinterest on the part of the Singapore government as to the whereabouts and doings of its citizens abroad. The staff at its Bangkok Embassy and at the Permanent Mission of Singapore to the UN in New York were always aware of my presence and assignments (and of other Singaporeans that followed) at those and other locations. Professionally, when they had need for information or assistance on a UN matter I was involved in, they would contact me. Socially, we crossed paths like ships passing in the night.

Being Singaporean stood me in good stead. From early days Singapore's reputation for good governance was respected. By association, this translated into a lot of goodwill for Singaporeans working in the Secretariat who were perceived as hardworking and honest, which was helpful to my career.

After graduating from the University of Singapore with a BA in Political Science in 1968, I immediately joined the Singapore Civil Service in May. In

---

[1] My recollection is that there was a first Singaporean by the name of John C.C. Chew who was recruited by the UN ECAFE Secretariat a year or two before I was, but he apparently resigned a few years after I joined.

January 1969, I was part of a Singapore delegation from the Finance Ministry's Trade Division attending a session of the then United Nations Economic Commission for Asia and the Far East's (ECAFE)[2] Committee on Trade in Bangkok, Thailand. We were also tasked with meeting ECAFE Secretariat staff to discuss logistic requirements in connection with Singapore's prospective hosting of the Commission's 25th annual session in April 1969 at the old Singapore Conference Hall by Shenton Way. This was one of the first, if not the first major UN conference that Singapore successfully hosted as a sovereign nation following its split from Malaysia in 1965.

During preparations for the Conference, ECAFE's Chief of Administration had asked me whether I would be interested in joining the UN Secretariat. Not taking it too seriously, I said yes; filled out the application he handed me and thought nothing more of it. Shortly after the Conference ended, a Finance Ministry representative called and informed me that the UN was requesting for my release to its ECAFE Secretariat, initially on a two-year secondment. He told me that the Ministry could not agree to my release, with its attendant obligation to keep my post for me if I returned, and that I would have to resign if I wanted to join the UN.

When opportunity knocks, one either grabs it or loses it. I resigned from the Singapore Civil Service and joined the UN Secretariat, initially as a staff member of ECAFE in Bangkok, on 17 August 1969. My decision was made easier by my then fiancé, Lee Kim Eng (now my wife of 45 years), who despite her own career prospects in Singapore, encouraged me to pursue my dream of working and living abroad.[3] Our parents, though not happy about it, did not oppose our leaving Singapore. My brother, Yeo Bock Chuan, who was a teenager then, ended up by default with the responsibility of looking after my parents until their passing some years ago.

During my nine years in ECAFE's Division of Administration I performed functions ranging from running a printing shop, buildings management,

---

[2] Later renamed United Nations Economic and Social Commission for Asia and the Pacific (ESCAP).

[3] After joining me in Bangkok, my wife, Kim, re-invented herself as an artist (art always having been her first love). She studied with Sawat Tantisuk, one of Thailand's foremost artists, as one of his few private foreign students. She went on to hold several successful solo and group shows in Bangkok and later in the United States, and to this day continues working in the watercolor medium and exhibiting. Kim has her own website: www.kimengyeo.com

travel, contracting, managing a duty-free programme for staff and the logistics of organising meetings and conferences to being an Emergency Officer during times of crises. I recall being an observer in the crowds of workers and students milling around Bangkok's Democracy Monument in October 1972, when the Thai military attacked the demonstrators. The UN premises were shut down, with all the staff sent home for a couple of days, except for the UN security personnel, my boss and myself to look after the UN property. When rioters attacked the police headquarters located nearby, the police fled into the UN premises. We had some anxious moments while persuading the rioters not to enter and attack the UN premises and at the same time, convincing the police who had changed into civilian clothes to leave by a side exit. I was also involved in the evacuation of UN civilian staff out of Saigon when South Vietnam fell, and later on, the evacuation of civilian staff out of Dacca during the civil strife that led to the creation of Bangladesh.

In early 1978 something unexpected and traumatic happened. In the course of my work, I had been instrumental in nipping in the bud a number of dubious schemes with potential for malfeasance. This apparently annoyed certain parties who schemed to get rid of me. One morning, I was abducted at gunpoint while on my way to work by a disgruntled ex-local staff member (instigated by unknown others) accompanied by an accomplice. He was supposed to kill me. Instead, to my good fortune, after first making me drive home and threatening physical harm to my wife and two young daughters, he robbed me and then abandoned me in a paddy field far out of town. Ironically, those who wanted me out of the way were unaware that I was already scheduled to leave Thailand later that year to a new assignment at UN Headquarters in New York! The incident made the local newspapers and my family and I were the uncomfortable subjects of local police protection for the last months of our stay.[4]

I transferred to UN Headquarters, New York, on 16 August 1978, and joined the Secretariat of the Advisory Committee on Administrative and Budgetary Questions (ACABQ) where I spent 13 years. The ACABQ, an expert committee of 16 members appointed in their individual capacities by the General Assembly (GA), is tasked by the GA to consider and submit

---

[4] For the record, the Thai police did apprehend the perpetrator a couple of years after I transferred to New York. The UN paid for my return to Thailand to testify at his trial: he was found guilty and sentenced to seven years in jail.

recommendations to it on all administrative and budgetary proposals of the Secretary-General (SG) for the Organization. It works largely by convention, unencumbered by rules of procedure, and in closed session. As a Committee scribe my job was to draft reports for the Committee, following its hearings with representatives of the SG and private executive sessions. It was somewhat surreal being part of the main UN Secretariat and yet not a part of it since I was working for the GA! I got to learn first-hand how Secretariat officials interacted with representatives of Member States and how the latter group negotiated and reached compromises among themselves. Sometimes it wasn't pretty! But the experience was invaluable. I ended up being one of those few Secretariat staff who had experience working "both sides of the street". By the time I left the ACABQ Secretariat I had become its Deputy Secretary.

Sometime in September 1991, the then UN Controller approached me and told me that he had asked for my release back to the main UN Secretariat. He wanted me to immediately replace the incumbent Executive Officer of the Department of Public Information (DPI). The recently appointed Under-Secretary-General (USG) for DPI who had been recruited from the corporate world was having difficulty adjusting to the UN bureaucracy. The incumbent Executive Officer's performance as her interlocutor and interface within the department and with other Secretariat units as well his day to day management of the department's administration on her behalf was an issue. The Controller thought that she might find me an improvement. Would I accept this challenge? I agreed and spent four years in DPI. As it turned out, I enjoyed working for this USG whose confidence and trust I earned over time. She was mercurial, but a breath of fresh air compared to some of the other department heads. I was sorry to see her leave. After she left, I worked for three other USGs who replaced her in quick succession.

During these intervening years at UN Headquarters I was acquainted with Kofi Annan who was then a senior Secretariat official (he later became Under-Secretary-General for Peacekeeping Operations, and subsequently, the UN Secretary-General). In addition to his official duties, Kofi was also Chairman of the Board of Trustees for the United Nations International School in New York at a critical moment in the school's history when its management, finances and financing were in need of improvement. He asked me to join him on the Board as its Treasurer. Over the next 10 years, we succeeded in putting the school on a sound financial and managerial footing. After he became Secretary-General he would still ask me occasionally to perform *ad hoc* assignments for him. In my opinion he is the best Secretary-General the UN has had in recent times.

In September 1993, I serendipitously ran into a former member of the ACABQ who had recently been appointed as UN Controller. He remembered me and inquired as to what I was doing. I told him I was working in DPI, whereupon he asked me whether I would be willing to assist him on a temporary basis during his transition into his new job. I said yes; DPI released me and I ended up on loan in his office for several months.

This led to my selection, in 1995 as Deputy Director of the Peacekeeping Financing Division (PFD), and later, as Director, PFD in May 1998, reporting directly to the Controller. The Division reviews all administrative and budgetary proposals for the individual UN peacekeeping operations managed by the Department of Peacekeeping Operations (DPKO), and then revises and re-casts them into reports of the SG to the General Assembly. Among other things, the Division also manages peacekeeping cash flow and reimbursements to troop-contributing countries. As Director, PFD, I was usually lead representative of the SG among the Secretariat representatives charged with explaining and defending the SG's administrative and budgetary requests to the GA (via ACABQ and the Fifth Committee).

It was the most interesting and challenging time to be involved with UN peacekeeping which was undergoing a traumatic transition period.

Prior to 1990, few peacekeeping missions were authorised by the Security Council. The missions in Cyprus (UNFICYP), Lebanon (UNIFIL) and the Golan Heights (UNDOF) for example, tended to be modest, stable and fairly low-risk affairs. Historically, the "Blue Helmets" were interposed between two states which, following hostilities, wanted a face-saving pause or way out. Backstopping was performed by a small group of civilian staff at Headquarters.

From 1990 to 1994, following the end of the Cold War era, amid renewed optimism and enthusiasm for multilateral action, the UN was suddenly thrown into the deep end of the pool and called upon to operate and manage significantly larger missions with complex mandates such as in Somalia (UNOSOM) and Yugoslavia (UNPROFOR). Neither the Secretariat nor the GA were equipped to cope with these new Security Council mandates, and things got messy for a while. With even more peacekeeping missions on the horizon, both the GA and the Secretariat had to act quickly to address the new reality. A new Department of Peacekeeping Operations was set up to establish policy and manage all peacekeeping operations. A new Peacekeeping Financing Division was also set up in the Controller's office to deal with the consequential administrative and budgetary requirements that DPKO and the field missions would need to request from the GA. There were the usual turf battles and initially well-founded suspicions on the part of the GA regarding the capacity and ability of the Secretariat to fully use the enormous resources being sought, and therefore, the credibility of the SG's budget requests! At the same time, the Security Council and the GA didn't help themselves or the Secretariat by insisting on authorising short mission mandate extensions and corresponding budget financing periods of three to six months at a time! By the time such short-term financing was approved and assessed contributions began to trickle in from Member States, the corresponding mandates and financial periods would be almost over; the Secretariat would consequently under-use the approved resources and end up being criticised for under-performing!

Another seminal change had to be addressed. UN peacekeeping operations were now more dangerous. The combatants involved were no longer just Member States, but included failed states, civil wars and ethnic conflicts. The "Blue Helmets" were no longer always welcomed and viewed by the combatants as neutral parties — they were now fair game to sometimes be shot at and attacked. Death and disability cases began to mount. The traditional troop contributing countries from the West became skittish about the participation of their military and police personnel and began encouraging other countries to more actively participate and contribute their military and police personnel. As a consequence existing troop reimbursement rates and death and disability benefits (as well as corresponding new rates for police personnel) had to be rationalised and revised, involving difficult negotiations.

I was involved in all these negotiations among the Member States which finally led to pragmatic, workable arrangements that allowed the Secretariat to carry out its peacekeeping responsibilities more efficiently and effectively, including the agreement to consider annualised budgeting and financing for each peacekeeping mission, subject to their mandates being extended. As part of Secretariat confidence building and transparency efforts also, fellow DPKO colleagues and I devoted considerable time regularly meeting with defence, police, finance and audit officials from the capitals of the major contributor countries, to brief them and to respond to their questions about the peacekeeping budget and finance process.

I made one other contribution to this transition period. Given the complex history and evolution of administrative, budgetary and financing policy and practice regarding UN peacekeeping from its inception through the latest tumultuous transition period, as well as the tendency of Secretariat and Member States' representatives to reinvent the wheel, I decided, on my own initiative and time to prepare a comprehensive compilation of the accumulated collective institutional memory on the subject that I had acquired. The Secretariat colleagues and interested Member State representatives to whom I later gave copies of this informal handbook found it a useful resource.

The payoff from all these efforts was threefold. With improved Member States' confidence in the new peacekeeping support structures at Headquarters and in the field, as well as in the new budgeting and financing process for peacekeeping, the major and other contributors to the assessed budgets of the missions were persuaded to be more timely in paying their dues in full and on time. This in turn made the troop contributing countries happier about their participation as the Secretariat was able to reimburse them their costs in a more timely fashion. Finally, the United States, the major contributor, was persuaded to pay off most of its accumulated peacekeeping assessments withholding arrears in late 2001. It was with great satisfaction that I, in turn, was able to arrange for the immediate reimbursement to all the troop contributing countries of much of the long outstanding payments due to them.

Recognising how unlikely it would be that I could top that exhilarating moment, I decided it was as good a time as any to bow out gracefully and I took early retirement at age 55 in December 2001.[5]

---

[5] In the interest of full disclosure: my wife and I retired in the United States and we became American citizens recently.

YEO Bock Cheng was born in Singapore and is a Peranakan. He was educated in Singapore: first at St. Andrew's School (1953 to 1964), and then at the University of Singapore where he graduated in 1968 with a BA in Political Science. After graduation he worked briefly in Singapore in the Ministry of Finance. On 17 August 1969 he left Singapore to join the United Nations Secretariat where he worked for 32 years, rising to the top career level of the international civil service. From 1969 to 1978, while assigned to the UN Economic Commission for Asia and the Pacific (ESCAP) Secretariat in Bangkok, Thailand, he performed a variety of administrative and management functions ranging from facilities management, travel and contracting, conference servicing to being an Emergency Office during times of crises. He transferred to UN Headquarters in New York, USA on 16 August 1978. There, he served for some 12 years in the Secretariat of the General Assembly's Advisory Committee on Administrative Questions, rising to be its Deputy Executive Secretary. In 1991, Bock Cheng was re-assigned to the Department of Public Information, where he was appointed the department's Executive Officer. In 1995 and then in 1998 he was first selected to be Deputy Director, and then appointed the Director of the Peacekeeping Financing Division, reporting directly to the UN Controller. He served in this capacity until his retirement on 31 December 2001.

Index

Note: Page numbers in **boldface** refer to photos and text in the photo captions.

A

Aboul Gheit, Ahmed, 299
ACP. *See* African-Caribbean and Pacific
  countries
Adams, James, 186n7
Advisory Committee on Administrative
  and Budgetary Questions (ACABQ),
  300, 304–305
Afghanistan, 173, 175, 273, 293
    International Women's Day, 281
    peace operations, **21**, 237, 241–243
    SAF and, 241–243
    SCR 1325 and, 280–282
    Soviet Union and, 16–18
Africa, 20
    ACP trade and, 63–64
    African Union, 42
    capital punishment and, 81
    Ebola outbreak, 75, 271, 274
    education in, 195–202
    G20 and, 43
    HRC and, 73, 81, 173, 175
    ICAO and, 115
    IMO programs, 141
    infoDev and, 190
    NEPAD and, 42
    peace operations in, 237, 247, 251, 261
    piracy and, 142
    refugees in, **20**
    Rwanda and, 11, 281

    UNCITRAL and, 154
    UNEP and, 161
    UNSC and, 12
    WHO and, 217
    World Bank and, 195n1, 196, 196n3,
      196n4, 200
    WTOE and, 205
African-Caribbean and Pacific (ACP)
  countries, 63–64
ageing, of population, 219, 286–288
agriculture, 190–194
    environment and. *See* environment
    EU and, 63
    IAEA and, 108, 109
    infoDev and, 190
    WHO and, 210
    WTO and, 62, 76
Ahtissari, Martti, 35
AIDS/HIV, 271
AIIB. *See* Asian Infrastructure Investment
  Bank
Aljuneid, Raziff, 5, 299
Alliance of Small Island States (AOSIS),
  81
al-Qaida, 292, 293
Annan, Kofi, 28, **31**, **32**, 280, 297, 305
Ansu, Y., 195n1, 197, 201
AOSIS. *See* Alliance of Small Island States
Argentina, 97
Asian Financial Crisis, 135

Asian Infrastructure Investmant Bank
(AIIB), 33
Association of Southeast Asian Nations
(ASEAN), 30, 42, 261
ASMC and, 231
Cambodia and, 17–18
G20 and, 42
global statistics and, 258
ILO and, 126
Indonesia and, 135
Myanmar and, 282
Regional Forum, xxv
Timor-Leste and, 261
UNEP and, 163
UNESCO and, 171
Uruguay Round and, 67
WHO and, 218
WIPO and, 226
Aung San Suu Kyi, 282
Australia, **3**, 61, 63, 84, 97n3, 154, 178, 192
aviation, 113
Aw Hui Min, Miak, 165
Azevêdo, Roberto, 87

B

B4E. *See* Business for the Environment
Summit
Baker, James, 185
Ban Ki-moon, 282
Baneth, Jean, 184
Bangladesh, **28**, 70, 273–276, 304
BBC. *See* Broadband Commission
Bin Laden, Osama, 293
Black and White buildings, 168
Blue Helmets missions, 306, 307
Bogsch, Arpad, **24**, 222, 225
Boutros-Ghali, B., **9**, 29
Brazil, 12, 13, 39, 63, 66, 97, 159
Bretton Woods organisation, 33, 181, 183
BRICS Bank, 33
Broadband Commission (BBC), 149
Budget Division, UN, 265–267

Bunche, Ralph, 278
Burkill Hall, 168
Bush, George H.W., 19, 29, 39
Business for the Environment Summit
(B4E), 163

C

Calmy-Rey, Micheline, 43
Cambodia, 17–18, 30, 53, 261
Casar, Gina, 276
Champions of the Earth awards, 163
Chan, Jeffrey W.T., 157
Chan, Margaret, **22**, 217
Chan Heng Chee, **8**, 20
Chan Lee Mun, 199
Chang Li Lin, 10
Charter, of UN
Bunche and, 278
decolonisation and, 33
essentials of, ix–xii
FOSS and, 36
peace and, 13, 30, 46, 106, 278, 290
Secretary-General and, 29
Singapore and, ix, 52, 277
social progress and, 263
UNSC veto, 25
See also specific organisations
Chelliah, Mary Elizabeth, **14**, 101, 103t
Chen Tze Penn, 139
Cheung, Paul, **27**, 260
Chew Beng Yong, 264
Chew, John C. C., 302n1
Chew Tai Soo, 6–7, **10**, 14, 38, 80, 81, 101,
103t
Chia, Alphonsus, **10**
Chia Der Jiun, 137
Chiang Kai Shek, 16
Children's Fund (UNICEF), x, 28, 55, 90,
203
China, 24
Cambodia and, 17, 18, 20
G20 and, 39, 40

GNP of, 12
IMF and, 132
migrants from, 277
Taiwan and, 16
UNSC and, 10, 11, 12, 32
World Bank and, 182
Chin Siew Fei, 107, 112
Chitalkar, Poorvi, 19
Chol Yaak Akoi, 178
Chong, Julian, 99
CHR. See Commission of Human Rights
Chua, Albert, **12**, 38, 50
Civil Aviation Authority of Singapore
    (CAAS), 113–118
Clark, Helen, 272, 274, 276
climate change, 54, 76, 80, 143, 177,
    229–232
Clinton, Hillary, 35
Clinton, William, 11, 12
Cold War
    Charter and, 30
    end of, 15–21, 30, 31, 175
    Korea and, 16
    Security Council and, 15, 261, 308
    Third World and, 72
Commission of Human Rights (CHR), 73
Commission on International Trade Law
    (UNCITRAL), 152–158
Compensation Commission (UNCC), 268,
    269
Conference on Environment and
    Development (UNCED), **5**, 53, 61, 159,
    160
Conference on Sustainable Development,
    47
Conference on Trade and Development
    (UNCTAD), 90, 266
Contonou Agreement, 63
Convention on the Law of the Sea
    (UNCLOS), 13, 46, 53, 61, 79, 138, 139,
    204
Copenhagen Summit, 285

Cox, Pamela, 186n7
Cuba, 299, 300
cyber security, 275

D
Dallaire, General Romeo, 11
Daniel, Patrick, 184
Daniel, Rosa, 170
Darwinian theory, 46
D'Costa, Valerie, 193
decolonisation, 30, 33
De La Paix group, 97
Deng Xiaoping, 182
Department of Peacekeeping Operations
    (DPKO), 306, 307
Department of Public Information (DPI),
    305
Devan, Janamitra, 188
developing countries
    agriculture and. See agriculture
    climate change and, 82
    Cold War and, 72
    De La Paix group and, 97
    definition of, 184
    DS system, 97
    environment and, 163. See also
        environment
    EU and, 63, 97
    IAEA and, 76, 110, 111
    ICAO and, 117
    IMF and, 134, 137
    IMO and, 140
    infoDev and, 184, 190
    ITCP and, 140
    NGOs and, 74
    North-South divide, 76n5
    public health, 62
    refugees. See refugee projects
    sanitation and, 54–56
    SCP and, x, 77, 92
    Singapore and, 46, 213, 221, 222, 258
    TCTP and, 141

developing countries
    trade and, 153
    urban development in, 186
    WIPO and, 224, 226
    World Bank and, 183
    WTO and, 70, 97, 101
    See also specific countries, topics
Development Fund for Women
    (UNIFEM), 279
Development Programme (UNDP), **28**,
    90, 116, 147, 204, 271–276
Deverajan, Shanta, 197
Dhanabalan, S., 17
diplomatic protocol, 3–8, 22–34, 81
Disaster Risk Reduction (DRR), 93
diseases. *See* healthcare
dispute settlement procedures, 61, 64, 86,
    87, 95–104, 156
Doha Round, 62–65
DPI. *See* Department of Public
    Information
DPKO. *See* Department of Peacekeeping
    Operations
DRR. *See* Disaster Risk Reduction
DSU. *See* dispute settlement procedures
Dunkel, Arthur, 66

E
Earth Charter, 36
Earth Summit. *See* Conference on
    Environment and Development
East Timor. *See* Timor-Leste
Ebola outbreak, 75, 271
Ebtekar, Massoumeh, 163
ECA. *See* Economic Commision for Africa
ECAFE. *See* Economic Commission for
    Asia and the Far East
Economic and Social Commission for
    Asia and the Pacific (UNESCAP), 204,
    282, 285
Economic and Social Council (ECOSOC),
    36, 257, 285

Economic Commission for Africa (ECA),
    266
Economic Commission for Asia and the
    Far East (ECAFE), 303
ECOSOC. *See* Economic and Social
    Council
education
    Africa and, 195–202
    ECOSOC and, 285
    refugees and, 178
    Singapore and, 195–202, 209, 272,
        286, 289
    UNDP and, 272
    UNESCO and, **30**, 149, 166–172, 285,
        286
    WISE, 179
    women and, 281
    World Bank and, 182, 196n4, 197
Educational, Scientific and Cultural
    Organization (UNESCO), **30**, 149,
    166–172, 285, 286
Ee, Cecil K. Y., 270
El-Ashry, Mohamed, 163
Eliasson, Jan, 55
Enterprise Resource Planning (ERP)
    system, 274
environment
    B4E and, 163
    biofuels and, 191
    climate change and, 54, 76, 80, 143,
        177, 229–234
    Earth Summit, 53, 61, 159, 160
    globalisation and, xxv, 20
    Green Climate Fund, 82
    ICAO and, 114
    marine, 139, 141, 143, 144
    MDGs and, 55, 107
    MEAs, 162
    MEWR and, 165
    NEA and, 232
    nuclear power and, 109, 111
    sustainability and, 47, 164, 286

UNDP and, 271
UNEP and, 159–165
See also specific organisations, topics
Environment Programme (UNEP),
159–165
Egypt, 70, 71, 274, 275, 299
Er, Kenneth, 170
ERP. *See* Enterprise Resource Planning
system
ESCAP. *See* Economic and Social
Commission for Asia and the Pacific
Eskan, Adenan Mohammad, 241
European Union (EU), 33, 36, 63, 97
Ezekwesili, Obiageli, 197

F
financial crises, 39, 75, 267
financial operations, at UN, 37, 265–270,
300, 304-305
Foo Kok Jwee, 94
Food Crisis, 73
Forum of Small States (FOSS), **10**, 14,
35–38, 45, 53, 81
Framework Convention on Climate
Change (UNFCCC), 79
France, 10, 11, 31, 32, 182
Frechette, Louis, 298
Fredriksen, Birger, 197
Frick, Aurelia, 41

G
G20, **11**, 33, 39–44, 53, 263
Gafoor, Burhan, 84
Gardner, Booth, 69
GATT/WTO. *See* World Trade
Organization
GCF. *See* Green Climate Fund
GDP. *See* gross domestic product
Geldof, Bob, 205
General Assembly (UNGA), 5, 24, 26, 30, 304
Generalized System of Preferences (GSP),
184

Geneva Convention, 120
genocide, 11, 31, 49, 120, 122
geospatial data, 255–260
GIC. *See* Government of Singapore
Investment Corporation
Global Centre for Public Service
Excellence, 272
Global Governance Group, **11**, 39–44, 53,
263
Global Outbreak and Alert Response
Network (GOARN), 219
Global Poverty Project (GPP), 55
global warming, 54, 76, 80, 143, 177,
229–234
globalization, 9, 30, 41, 255–260. *See also*
specific topics
GOARN. *See* Global Outbreak and Alert
Response Network
GoF. *See* Group of Friends
Goh Chok Tong, **4**, 28
Goh Kee Tai, 207
Goh Keng Swee, 183
Goh Koh Pui, 182n2
Gorbachev, Mikhail, 16
Government of Singapore Investment
Corporation (GIC), 187n9
Govindasamy, Peter, 66–67
GPP. *See* Global Poverty Project
Great Convergence, The (Mahbubani),
9–10
Green Climate Fund (GCF), 82
gross domestic product (GDP), Singapore,
52, 80, 85, 113, 181, 184, 196
Group of Friends (GoF), 47, 54
GSP. *See* Generalized System of Preferences
Gulf War, 19, 238–239
Gurry, Francis, 226

H
Hague Conference on Private International
Law (HCCH), 153
Haiti, 271

Halimah Yacob, **19**, 130
Halonen, Tarja, 126
Hamid, Shirin, **28**, 276
Hammarskjöld, Dag, 78, 263
Hazri Hassan, 164
HCCH. *See* Hague Conference on Private
  International Law
healthcare, **23**, 75, 77, 109, 207–212, 281,
  286. *See also specific topics*
Heng Sou Kaw, 248
Heyzer, Noeleen, **29**, 283
High Commissioner for Refugees
  (UNHCR), 173–180
HIV/AIDS, 271
Ho, David, 220
Ho, Gerard, 299
Ho Peng Kee, 225
Ho, Peter, 99
Ho Siong Hin, 127
Hoang, Carina, 178
Hong Kong, 97
housing, 287
HRC. *See* Human Rights Council
Hu Jintao, 40
human rights, 3, 19, 20, 25, 31, 49, 73,
  75, 278, 282. *See also specific countries,
  topics*
Human Rights Council (HRC), 73
Human Settlements Programme
  (UN-Habitat), 285
humanitarian assistance, 173–180, 203.
  See also refugee projects; *specific topics*
Hurricane Haiyan, 271
Hussein, Arif, 67

I
IAEA. *See* International Atomic Energy
  Agency
ICAO. *See* International Civil Aviation
  Organization
ICC. *See* International Criminal Court

ICOMOS. *See* International Council on
  Monuments and Sites
ICT. *See* information and communications
  technology
ICTY. *See* International Criminal Tribunal
  for the former Yugoslavia
IDA. *See* Infocomm Development
  Authority of Singapore
IFC. *See* International Finance
  Corporation
ILO. *See* International Labour
  Organization
IMF. *See* International Monetary Fund
IMF-Singapore Regional Training Institute
  (STI), 135
IMO. *See* International Maritime
  Organization
India, 63, 97
Indian Ocean tsunami, 288
Indonesia, 9, **23**, 135, 238–241, 247, 278
Industrial Development Organization
  (UNIDO), 90, 266
Infocomm Development Authority of
  Singapore (IDA), 146, 194
infoDev program, 190–194
information and communications
  technology (ICT), 272, 273–275
Institute for Technical Education (ITE),
  199
Institute for the Unification of Private Law
  (UNIDROIT), 153
Integrated Mission in Timor-Leste
  (UNMIT), 248
intellectual property, 221–228
Intellectual Property Office (IPOS), 224
International Atomic Energy Agency
  (IAEA), 76, 107–112
International Civil Aviation Organization
  (ICAO), 113–118, 233
International Civil Service Commission,
  267

International Council on Monuments and Sites (ICOMOS), 168–169
International Criminal Court (ICC), 11, 123
International Criminal Tribunal for the former Yugoslavia (ICTY), 119
International Finance Corporation (IFC), 181n1, 186n7, 187, 187n9
International Labour Organization (ILO), **19**, 90, 125, 285, 287
International Maritime Organization (IMO), 138–144
International Monetary Fund (IMF), 132, 136, 181, 259
International Telecommunication Union (ITU), 145–151
International Trade Centre (ITC), 266
International Women's Day, 281
International Year of Peace, 262
Internet, 148–149, 256, 259
IPOS. *See* Intellectual Property Office
Iran-Iraq War, 16
Iraq, 16, 18–20, **25**, 175, 298
Iraq Oil-for-Food Programme, 298
Islamic State of Iraq and the Levant (ISIL), 175
ITC. *See* International Trade Centre
ITE. *See* Institute for Technical Education
Ithnin, Rossman, 66
ITU. *See* International Telecommunication Union

J
Jamaica, 97
Jayakrishnan, G., 198
Jayakumar, S., **6**, 8, 28, 79
Jesus, Jose Luis, 36

K
Kabbah, Ahmad Tejan, 291
Kamil Idris, 225
Kantor, Mickey, 69

Karzai, Hamid, 281
Kausikan, Bilahari, **9**, 34, 38, 300
Kay, Thelma, **30**, 289
Kenya, 123, 191
Kesavapany, K., xi, **15**, 71, 225
Kim, Jim Yong, 191
Koh, Joanna, 10
Koh, Tommy, **3**, 3–8, **5**, 10, 13, 79, 101, 103t, 155, 159, 160, 163, 197, 204
Koh Tin Fook, 199
Konaré, Alpha Oumar, 291
Koong Pai Ching, 171
Korean War, 16
Kuwait, 18–20, **25**
Kwok Fook Seng, 88

L
Lamperia, Louis Philipe, 68
Lamy, Pascal, 87
Law Song Seng, 199, 201
Lee, Christine, 294
Lee, Vernon, **23**, 212
Lee Hsien Loong, 184, 185, 223
Lee Kuan Yew, **2**, 26
Lee Sieu Kin, 99
Lee Sing Kong, 199
Leong Keng Thai, 150
Lewis, Stephen, 11
Liang, Margaret, **14**, 64, 66, 102, 104t
Liberia, 290, 292
Lie, Trygve, 16
Liew, Mary, 127
Lim, Janet, **20**, 180
Lim Kim San, 181
Lim Swee Say, 160
Lo Yong Poo, 241
Lome Convention, 63

M
Mahbubani, Kishore, **7**, 14, 291, 299
Malaysia, 9, 182

Malone, David, 19
Mandela, Nelson, 279
Marine Electronic Highway (MEH), 141
Martin, Paul, 39
MAS. *See* Monetary Authority of
    Singapore
Mattar, Ahmad, 160
Maycock, Besley, 36, 37
Mazower, Mark, 27
MCCY. *See* Ministry of Culture,
    Community and Youth
MDGs. *See* Millennium Development
    Goals
Médecins Sans Frontières (MSF), 73n1
MEH. *See* Marine Electronic Highway
Menon, Vanu Gopala, 10, **11**, 44, 225
Meteorological Service Singapore,
    229–234
Mexico, 97
MFN. *See* most favoured nation principle
MICA. *See* Ministry of Information,
    Communications and the Arts
Michael Fay incident, 70
Millennium Development Goals (MDGs),
    47, 89, 107, 271, 275
Ministry of Culture, Community and
    Youth (MCCY), 170
Ministry of Information, Communications
    and the Arts (MICA), 167
Ministry of Manpower (MOM), 126
Minn Naing Oo, 101, 104t
MNCs. *See* multinational corporations
Modi, Narendra, 55
MOM. *See* Ministry of Manpower
Monetary Authority of Singapore (MAS),
    183
Montreal Protocol, 162
Moore, Michael, 87
most favoured nation (MFN) principle,
    63, 65
Mselle, Conrad, 300
MSF. *See* Médecins Sans Frontières

multilateralism, 3–5, 27, 61–65, 78–85,
    162, 306
multinational corporations (MNCs), 184
Murphy, Craig, 272
Myanmar, 282–283

N
Nair, Dileep, **31**, 301
Nathan, S. R., 162
National Environment Agency (NEA), 232
National Heritage Board (NHB), 168
National Parks Board (NParks), 168
NATO. *See* North Atlantic Treaty
    Organization
natural disasters, 178, 271, 288
natural resources, xxii, 52, 91, 160, 163
Neo, Mark, 54
NEPAD. *See* New Partnership for Africa's
    Development
New Partnership for Africa's Development
    (NEPAD), 42
Ng Bee Kim, 66
NGOs. *See* non-governmental
    organisations
NHB. *See* National Heritage Board
Nicaragua, 97
non-governmental organisations (NGOs),
    63, 67, 73, 73n1
Non-Proliferation Treaty, 262
North Atlantic Treaty Organization
    (NATO), xxv, 32, 121
North Korea, 16, 107
North-South divide, 76n5
NParks. *See* National Parks Board
Nuclear Security Summits, 107–111
Nye, Joseph, 16

O
OCHA. *See* Office for the Coordination
    of Humanitarian Affairs
OECD. *See* Organization for Economic
    Co-operation and Development

Office for the Coordination of Humanitarian Affairs (OCHA), 203
Office of Internal Oversight Services (OIOS), 296–300
Office of Legal Affairs (OLA), 49
Oil-for-Food scandal, 269, 298
OIOS. *See* Office of Internal Oversight Services
OLA. *See* Office of Legal Affairs
Ong, Peter, 186
Operation Nightingale, 19, 238–239
Organisation for Economic Co-operation and Development (OECD), 40, 91

P
Page, John, 197
Panels of Experts (POEs), 293
Pang Ah San, 239
Panpac Education, 195
Paschke, Karl, 296, 300
peacekeeping missions, 235–251
    financing and, 307–308
    PKOs, 10
    refugees and. *See* refugee projects
    SAF and, 237–246, 248
    Security Council and, 10, 306, 307
    SPF and, 250, 251t
    US and, 308
    See also specific countries, topics
Pension Fund, 268
Permanent Representative (PR), 9, 23, 24, 27, 54, 61, 72, 81, 159
Philippines, 64, 271
Pillay, J. Y., 182
Pinker, Steven, 13
piracy, 142, 222
planning, programming and budgeting system (PPBS), 265
POEs. *See* Panels of Experts
Poon Hong Yuen, 170
population movements, 177
Post-2015 Development Agenda, 56

poverty, **28**, 55, 190–194, 271, 282
PPBS. *See* planning, programming and budgeting system
PrepComm IV meetings, 36

Q
Quasi-Biennial Oscillation, 230

R
R2P. *See* Responsibility to Protect
Radio Regulations, 148
Rafidah Aziz, 70
Rahim Ishak, x, **2**
Rajaratnam, S., **2**, **3**, 52, 56
Raya (muppet), 55
refugee projects, 270
    number of, 175
    post-Cold War period, 20
    refugee status, 174, 177
    Rwanda and, 11
    Southeast Asia, 173
    UNHCR, 173–180
    UNRWA, 173
    women and, 281
    See also specific countries, topics
Responsibility to Protect (R2P), 49, 54
Ridley Hall, 168
Rio+20 Conference, 47
Rossier, William, 70
Ruggiero, Renato, **15**, 68
Rule of Law, 54, 78–80
Rwanda, 11, 290

S
Sadasivan, Balaji, xi, **22**, 214–215, 286
SAF. *See* Singapore Armed Forces
Safety of Life at Sea (SOLAS), 233
salary scales, at UN, 267
Samar, Sima, 281
Samoa, 56
Sanctions System, 290–295
sanitation, 47, 48, 51–58

SARS. *See* Severe Acute Respiratory
    Syndrome
Saudi Arabia, 19, 31, 239
SCP. *See* Singapore Cooperation
    Programme
SEAYEN. *See* South East Asia Youth
    Environment Network
Second Development Partnership Forum,
    283
Secretariat, of UN
    bureaucracy in, 292
    financial administration, 265–270,
        332, 334
    functions of, 203, 291, 292, 296
    peacekeeping and, 307–308
    POEs and, 293
    Singaporeans and, 302n1
    statistical services, 255–260, 305, 307
    See also specific persons, topics
Secretary-General, of UN, vii–viii, 16
    functions of, 28–29, 203
    P5 and, 28–29
    Secretariat and, 305
    Singaporeans and, 28, 180, 204, 264,
        282, 283, 301
    See also specific persons
Security Council (UNSC), 33
    Cold War and, 15, 261, 308
    conflicts and, 262
    international legitimacy and, 30
    Iraq and, 298
    NATO and, 32
    OIOS and, 298
    OLA and, 49
    P5 group, 10–12, 25, 28, 29, 32, 49
    peacekeeping and, 279, 306, 307
    Permanent Three, 31
    PKOs and, 10
    post-Cold War, 31
    reforms of, 11, 12, 37, 48, 53
    sanctions system and, 290–295, 298
    Secretariat and, 298–299

    Secretary-General and, 28
    Singapore and, **6**, **7**, 9–14
    UNCC and, 268, 269
    veto and, 25
    WMDs and, 262
    women and, 279
See Chak Mun, **14**, 65, 99, 101, 104t
Seet-Cheng, Mary, 144
Sevan, Benon, 298
Severe Acute Respiratory Syndrome
    (SARS) pandemic, 115, 214–215
Shanmugam, K., 35
Shanmugaratnam, Tharman, 132, 133,
    134, 185, 197
shipping, 138–144
SIDS. *See* Small Island Developing States
Sierra Leone, 290, 292
Singapore Armed Forces (SAF), 19, **25**,
    237–246
Singapore Aviation Academy, **17**
Singapore Botanic Gardens, 166–172
Singapore Cooperation Programme (SCP),
    56, 90
Singapore Foreign Service, 9
Singapore Hub, 186
Singapore Issues, 63
Singapore Police Force (SPF), **26**,
    247–251
Singapore Telephone Board (STB), 146
Singapore Treaty on the Law of Trade-
    marks, 79, 226
Singapore–United Nations Story, 277–284
Singh, Amarjeet, **18**, 124
Sirleaf, Ellen Johnson, 281
SIT. *See* Sterile Insect Technique
Small Island Developing States (SIDS), 54,
    56, 93
small states, 45–50
Sng May Yen, **26**, 248
social development, 285–289
SOLAS. *See* Safety of Life at Sea
Somalia, 11, 175, 273, 275, 306

South Africa, 16, 55, 160, 192, 237, 247, 251t

South East Asia Youth Environment Network (SEAYEN), 163

South Korea, 12, 16, 157, 182, 222

Soviet Union
    Afghanistan and, 17, 46
    Cambodia and, 17, 18
    Cold War and, 15, 16. *See also* Cold War
    collapse of, 31
    developing countries and, 72, 221
    Gorbachev and, 16
    Security Council and, 16, 25, 30

Special Mission in Afghanistan (UNSMA), 241–242

specialised agencies, xi, 28

SPF. *See* Singapore Police Force

Sri Lanka, 74

Staff Union, UN, 297, 298, 299

Statistical Commission, UN, 255, 256

Statistical Division, UN, 255–260

STB. *See* Singapore Telephone Board

STI. *See* IMF-Singapore Regional Training Institute

Stiglitz, Joseph, 283

Straits of Malacca and Singapore (SOMS), 138–142

Sustainable Cities, 54

Sustainable Development Goals (SDGs), 47, 53, 56, 81, 150, 160, 164, 288

Sutherland, Peter, 66, 67

Swan Lake Gazebo, 168

Syria, 175, 176, 178, 180, 215

System of National Accounts, 256

T

Taiwan, 11, 16, 222

Taliban, 280, 281, 292, 293

Tamil Tigers, 74

Tan, Karen, **13**, 57

Tan, Leo, 199

Tan, Peter, 5

Tan, Richard, 239

Tan Boon Teik, 155

Tan Buck Song, 249

Tan Jee Peng, 202

Tan Sri Hashim, 25

Tan Yee Woan, 66

Tan York Chor, 77

TAS. *See* Telecommunication Authority of Singapore

Tay, Steven, 248

Taylor, Charles, 291

Taylor, Nigel, 170

Telecentre. *See* Telecommunication Training Centre

Telecommunication Authority of Singapore (TAS), 145, 146, 147

Telecommunication Training Centre (Telecentre), 146, 147

Teo, Joseph, 67

terrorism, vii, 62, 92, 109, 114, 262, 280, 292

Thailand, 64, 180, 303, 304, 309

Than Shwe, 282

Thant, U., **2**

Thunnel, Lars, 186n7

Timor-Leste, 238–241, 247, 248, 261, 262

Tiwari Sivakant, 101, 104t

Toepfer, Klaus, 163

Toh, Andrew, xii, **21**, 168, 170, 206

tourism, 113, 115, 162, 287

trade negotiations, 61–65. *See also specific countries, topics*

Transitional Assistance Group (UNTAG), 237, 247

Transport Operation Ethiopia (WTOE), 205

Tunisia, 37, 196, 271, 275

U

Uber app, 86

UN Office in Geneva (UNOG), 265–267

UNCC. *See* Compensation Commission

UNCED. *See* Conference on Environment and Development

UNCITRAL. *See* Commission on International Trade Law

UNCLOS. *See* Convention on the Law of the Sea

UNCTAD. *See* Conference on Trade and Development

UNDP. *See* Development Programme

UNESCAP. *See* Economic and Social Commission for Asia and the Pacific

UNESCO. *See* Educational, Scientific and Cultural Organization

UNFCCC. *See* Framework Convention on Climate Change

UNGA. *See* General Assembly

UN-HABITAT. *See* Human Settlements Programme

UNHCR. *See* High Commissioner for Refugees

UNICEF. *See* Children's Fund

UNIDO. *See* Industrial Development Organization

UNIDROIT. *See* Institute for the Unification of Private Law

UNIFEM. *See* Development Fund for Women

United Kingdom, 11

United Nations Transitional Assistance Group (UNTAG), 237, 247

United Nations–Singapore Story, 277–284

United States, 11, 12, 30, 76n5, 308

UNMIT. *See* Integrated Mission in Timor-Leste

UNSC. *See* Security Council

UNSMA. *See* Special Mission in Afghanistan

UNTAG. *See* United Nations Transitional Group

urbanisation, 47, 177, 186, 287

Uruguay, 37, 43n1, 97, 97n3

Uruguay Round, 61, 62, 70, 86, 95, 96, 97

V

Vieira de Mello, Sérgio, 277

Vietnam, 17–18, 178, 304

W

War Crimes Court, 49, 119–124

Washington Consensus, 183

water management, 26, 299

WB. *See* World Bank

WBG. *See* World Bank Group

weather datas, 229–234

Wee, Jean, 172

Wee, Judy, 287

welfare, social, 285–289. *See also specific programs, topics*

WFP. *See* World Food Programme

WHO. *See* World Health Organization

Winsemius, Albert, 52, 223

WIPO. *See* World Intellectual Property Organization

WMO. *See* World Meteorological Organization

women, **20, 29**, 280

  CEDAW, 287

  International Women's Day, 281

  Security Council and, 279

  SPF and, 248

  UNDP and, 271–272, 276

  UNIFEM, 279, 280, 281

Wong, Lawrence, 170

Wong Lin Ken, x, **2**

World Bank Group (WBG), 181–190

World Bank (WB), 136, 181–194

World Food Programme (WFP), 203, 205

World Health Organization (WHO), 90, 285, 286

  Africa and, 217

  agriculture and, 210

  ASEAN and, 218

  Collaborating Centres, 214

  Ebola crisis and, 75, 76

Fellowship Programme, 213–219
health and, **23**, 204, 207–212
World Heritage Centre, 168
World Heritage Convention, 169
World Intellectual Property Organization
(WIPO), 79, 204, 221–228
World Meteorological Organization
(WMO), 229, 231, 233
World Radio-communication Conferences
(WRC), 148
World Statistics Day, 255
World Summit for Social Development, 285
World Summit on Information Society
(WSIS), 148
World Toilet Day, 47, 51–58
World Trade Organization (WTO), **14**, **15**,
16, 66–71
dispute settlement, 61, 64, 86, 87,
95–104
Doha Round, 85, 86
facilitative trade rules, 86
General Council, 68
logo for, 71
MFN principle, 63, 65

NGOs and, 67
Uruguay Round, 66, 86, 95
See also specific persons, topics
World Weather Watch, 230
WRC. *See* World Radio-communication
Conferences
WSIS. *See* World Summit on Information
Society
WTO. *See* World Trade Organization
WTOE. *See* Transport Operation
Ethiopia

Y
Yeo, George, **11**, 63, 64, 185
Yeo Kim Eng, 303n3
Yeo, Lionel, 199
Yeo Bock Cheng, **32**, 309
Yeo Cheow Tong, 70
Yong Siew Min, 99
Yu, Geoffrey, **24**, 227
Yugoslavia, **18**, 119, 306

Z
Zoellick, Robert B., 181, 183n5, 185, 187

Published by the United Nations Department of Public Information   DPI/2470 rev.4 – 15-00040 –July 2015

Strong UN.
Better World.

70

The United Nations System

UN Principal Organs

General Assembly

Subsidiary Organs

Main and other sessional committees
Disarmament Commission
Human Rights Council
International Law Commission
Standing committees and ad hoc bodies

Funds and Programmes[1]

UNDP United Nations Development Programme
- **UNCDF** United Nations Capital Development Fund
- **UNV** United Nations Volunteers

UNEP[2] United Nations Environment Programme
UNFPA United Nations Population Fund
UN-HABITAT[8] United Nations Human Settlements Programme
UNICEF United Nations Children's Fund
WFP World Food Programme (UN/FAO)

Research and Training

UNIDIR[2] United Nations Institute for Disarmament Research
UNITAR United Nations Institute for Training and Research
UNSSC United Nations System Staff College
UNU United Nations University

Other Entities

ITC International Trade Centre (UN/WTO)
UNCTAD[1,8] United Nations Conference on Trade and Development
UNHCR[1] Office of the United Nations High Commissioner for Refugees
UNOPS United Nations Office for Project Services
UNRWA[1] United Nations Relief and Works Agency for Palestine Refugees in the Near East
UN-Women[1] United Nations Entity for Gender Equality and the Empowerment of Women

Related Organizations

CTBTO Preparatory Commission Preparatory Commission for the Comprehensive Nuclear-Test-Ban Treaty Organization
IAEA[1,3] International Atomic Energy Agency
ICC International Criminal Court
ISA International Seabed Authority
ITLOS International Tribunal for the Law of the Sea
OPCW[3] Organization for the Prohibition of Chemical Weapons
WTO[1,4] World Trade Organization

Security Council

Subsidiary Organs

Counter-terrorism committees
International Criminal Tribunal for Rwanda (ICTR)
International Criminal Tribunal for the former Yugoslavia (ICTY)
Mechanism for International Criminal Tribunals (MICT)
Military Staff Committee
Peacekeeping operations and political missions
Sanctions committees (ad hoc)
Standing committees and ad hoc bodies

Advisory Subsidiary Body

Peacebuilding Commission

HLPF High-level Political Forum on sustainable development

Economic and Social Council

Functional Commissions[8]

Crime Prevention and Criminal Justice
Narcotic Drugs
Population and Development
Science and Technology for Development
Social Development
Statistics
Status of Women
United Nations Forum on Forests

Regional Commissions[8]

ECA Economic Commission for Africa
ECE Economic Commission for Europe
ECLAC Economic Commission for Latin America and the Caribbean
ESCAP Economic and Social Commission for Asia and the Pacific
ESCWA Economic and Social Commission for Western Asia

Other Bodies

Committee for Development Policy
Committee of Experts on Public Administration
Committee on Non-Governmental Organizations
Permanent Forum on Indigenous Issues
UNAIDS Joint United Nations Programme on HIV/AIDS
UNGEGN United Nations Group of Experts on Geographical Names

Research and Training

UNICRI United Nations Interregional Crime and Justice Research Institute
UNRISD United Nations Research Institute for Social Development

Specialized Agencies[1,5]

FAO Food and Agriculture Organization of the United Nations
ICAO International Civil Aviation Organization
IFAD International Fund for Agricultural Development
ILO International Labour Organization
IMF International Monetary Fund
IMO International Maritime Organization
ITU International Telecommunication Union
UNESCO United Nations Educational, Scientific and Cultural Organization
UNIDO United Nations Industrial Development Organization
UNWTO World Tourism Organization
UPU Universal Postal Union
WHO World Health Organization
WIPO World Intellectual Property Organization
WMO World Meteorological Organization
World Bank Group[7]
- **IBRD** International Bank for Reconstruction and Development
- **IDA** International Development Association
- **IFC** International Finance Corporation

Secretariat

Departments and Offices

EOSG Executive Office of the Secretary-General
DESA Department of Economic and Social Affairs
DFS Department of Field Support
DGACM Department for General Assembly and Conference Management
DM Department of Management
DPA Department of Political Affairs
DPI Department of Public Information
DPKO Department of Peacekeeping Operations
DSS Department of Safety and Security
OCHA Office for the Coordination of Humanitarian Affairs
OHCHR Office of the United Nations High Commissioner for Human Rights
OIOS Office of Internal Oversight Services
OLA Office of Legal Affairs
OSAA Office of the Special Adviser on Africa
PBSO Peacebuilding Support Office
SRSG/CAAC Office of the Special Representative of the Secretary-General for Children and Armed Conflict
SRSG/SVC Office of the Special Representative of the Secretary-General on Sexual Violence in Conflict
UNISDR United Nations Office for Disaster Risk Reduction
UNODA United Nations Office for Disarmament Affairs
UNODC[2] United Nations Office on Drugs and Crime
UNOG United Nations Office at Geneva
UN-OHRLLS Office of the High Representative for the Least Developed Countries, Landlocked Developing Countries and Small Island Developing States
UNON United Nations Office at Nairobi
UNOP[2] United Nations Office for Partnerships
UNOV United Nations Office at Vienna

International Court of Justice

Trusteeship Council[6]

Notes:

1 All members of the United Nations System Chief Executives Board for Coordination (CEB).
2 UN Office for Partnerships (UNOP) is the UN's local point vis-à-vis the United Nations Foundation, Inc.
3 IAEA and OPCW report to the Security Council and the GA.
4 WTO has no reporting obligation to the GA, but contributes on an ad hoc basis to GA and Economic and Social Council (ECOSOC) work on, inter alia, finance and development issues.
5 Specialized agencies are autonomous organizations whose work is coordinated through ECOSOC (intergovernmental level) and CEB (inter-secretariat level).
6 The Trusteeship Council suspended operation on 1 November 1994, as on 1 October 1994 Palau, the last United Nations Trust Territory, became independent.
7 International Centre for Settlement of Investment Disputes (ICSID) and Multilateral Investment Guarantee Agency (MIGA) are not specialized agencies but are part of the World Bank Group in accordance with Articles 57 and 63 of the Charter.
8 The secretariats of these organs are part of the UN Secretariat.

This Chart is a reflection of the functional organization of the United Nations System and for informational purposes only. It does not include all offices or entities of the United Nations System.

The United Nations System Chart is reproduced with permission of the United Nations (downloaded from the United Nations website in July 2015).

www.ingramcontent.com/pod-product-compliance
Lightning Source LLC
Chambersburg PA
CBHW081735270326
41932CB00020B/3274